D0113907

NOT ON SPEAKING TERMS

NOT ON SPEAKING TERMS

Clinical Strategies to Resolve Family and Friendship Cutoffs

ELENA LESSER BRUUN

SUZANNE MICHAEL

W. W. Norton & Company
New York • London

For my children, David and Noah
ELB

For my parents, Carola and Walter
SM

CONTENTS

PREFACE

It is late fall, the nights are getting colder. Two elderly women, strangers, are sitting on a park bench catching a few rays of sun.

Woman One: *It's getting cold; I wish could move south, but I can't.*
Woman Two: *Why not?*
Woman One: *I can't because I'm still hoping my daughter will come back. If I move, she won't know where to find me.*
Woman Two: *How long has it been?*
Woman One: *Thirty years.*

Personal communication, Carola Michael, December 2012

GENESIS OF THE IDEA

Scratch the surface of almost any family and you will find a significant cutoff. For those who have not had the pleasure, trust us that there are few more gut-wrenching experiences than being summarily dismissed by a close relative or friend. Examples abound in fiction, film, and the press. Nearly everyone we spoke with in our personal and professional circles, in chance encounters, or in the interviews we held with therapists had a story to tell. They or someone they knew had been at one time or another at the receiving end or had initiated a cutoff. In some instances, whether they initiated it or not, a sudden, cold, or angry cutoff literally made them sick. So we had plenty of anecdotal data and our instinctive sense that cutoffs were often excruciating. But 20 years ago when the idea for this book began to germinate, we found nothing in the literature to suggest that cutoffs are important for therapists to understand, with the singular exception of Murray Bowen (1978/1994). He saw their significance and incorporated the concept into his theory.

The idea for this book came to Elena as she realized the import of cutoff stories from clients and friends. Lacking personal experience, or so she thought, and no clinical training on the subject, she was unsure what to do. Elena remembers it this way:

> When I first thought about cutoffs, none came to mind, either in my family of origin or in my current nuclear family. I knew of one in the extended family, but it seemed a strange aberration at the time. No one close ever stopped speaking. We weren't immune; it was just that I was unaware of the nature and intensity of cutoffs, that they could be subtle, below the radar. I just figured that as a family we had another way of doing business. We yelled, carried on, and occasionally slammed doors, but we never stopped talking, never! This wasn't better or even good; it was just different. Later on, after the book was already in progress, the cutoff problem hit home, and I learned first-hand how painful a family or friendship cutoff can be, for those involved and for those who helplessly watch. The exploration of cutoffs became a personal imperative.

Elena enlisted Suzanne, originally a clinical social worker, who had been a colleague and close friend since their days at Kings County Hospital in the 1970s. Suzanne, who went on to become a PhD sociologist, had the perfect background and skill set to be her co-author and collaborator.

Of interest is that Elena's and Suzanne's early friendship was interrupted by a several-year cutoff. The writing of this book together is testament to the possibilities of reconnection and the rewards of repair.

DATA GATHERING

With minimal effort, we found over seventy cutoffs in literature, history, and the lives of contemporary public figures. The client cutoffs we found were almost without exception with family members. We also gathered personal stories from over forty people—ourselves, family members, friends, and strangers. We then issued a quick paper-and-pencil survey to twenty-three therapists participating in a training program. Finally, we engaged in interviews of an hour or longer with twenty-five therapists about cutoffs in their caseloads. Our sample included psychiatrists, marriage and family therapists, PhD psychologists, clinical social workers, pastoral counselors, and a family lawyer. We noted each interviewee's reactions, opinions, and strategies used to help clients repair or make peace. A few therapists gave us multiple cases. To some extent, it was snowball sampling. For example, a friend suggested we speak to a friend of hers who had experienced a major cutoff. That friend referred us to her therapist, who had told her she worked with other clients struggling with cutoffs. And so on. Though not random, we believe our sample is sufficiently representative of a typical therapist's client population in an urban setting.

It was easy to collect stories. People were eager to share. By the end of our data collection, we had too many cases and could not use them all. We stopped the process when we had identified basic themes, categories, and types of cutoffs and were hearing similar versions. We stopped at the point of saturation.

Although everyone we approached or solicited ultimately provided an instance from their own lives or instances in their families or friendship network, sometimes even the clinicians had to be prodded beyond an initial knee-jerk reaction like "I don't think I have any cases or examples . . . cutoffs must be pretty rare." Once they focused, though, examples flowed, and the data confirmed our initial hunch: that cutoffs are a generally unrecognized substantial problem, often not well understood and lacking a considered approach or set of treatment options. Specifically:

- Little is known about cutoffs beyond that they occur.
- Little is known about how to assess their severity.
- Little is known about whether, when, or how to attempt repair.
- Little is known about prognosis for reconciliation.
- Little is known about underlying issues, reasons, true causes.
- Little is known about how therapists can help cutoff parties reconcile.

There have been a number of popular books on cutoffs between friends or family members, such as Sichel's *Healing from Family Rifts* (2004); LeBey's *Family Estrangements: How They Begin, How to Mend Them, How to Cope with Them* (2001); Davis's *I Thought We Would Never Speak Again* (2002); Yager's *When Friendship Hurts* (2002); and Netzer's *Cutoffs: How Family Members Who Sever Relationships Can Reconnect* (1995). However, given the magnitude of the problem, the pain it causes, and the psychological complexity involved in either resolving a cutoff or healing from an irreparable one, it is surprising that relatively little (with the exceptions of Dattilio & Nichols, 2011; Titleman, 2003; Taylor, 2002; and Heitler, 1993) has been written for *clinicians* to help them understand the origins of, the often-intricate dynamics involved in particular cutoffs, and the best ways to undertake the delicate work of helping clients consider or work toward reconciliation. Our aim in writing *Not on Speaking Terms* is to help close this gap.

STRUCTURE OF THE BOOK

Each chapter addresses a particular cause for cutoffs or a reason people cut off or are the recipient of a cutoff. We chose not to focus on relationship type such as father-child, mother-child, siblings, former spouses, colleagues, or friends. We simply felt that while relationship type is important, all kinds of relationships suffer cutoffs, and though some types tend to predominate in one theme category over another (e.g., siblings or friends tend to cut off over jealousy), the reasons themselves ultimately provide the initial entry point for the therapist's work.

Major themes explored chapter by chapter are abandonment, jealousy, betrayal, matters of principle, and mental illness or substance abuse. And yet, often there are no clean lines separating causes. Instead, there are frequently multiple causes that overlap. We have situated a case or issue in the chapter that we believe reflects the best fit for our discussion. However, we also refer to the issue and case in other chapters as relevant and appropriate. In some instances, chapter placement was just a coin toss.

We tried as much as possible to use the client's perceptions of the reasons, since we want to begin where the client is and not jump ahead to our own perceptions of unconscious reasons. But it was impossible to eliminate our own perceptions entirely. Complicating matters further, participants involved in a cutoff may experience it differently by virtue of their perspective as the initiator, recipient, or therapist/witness. For example, parents with a gay or lesbian child may cut the child off, believing that the child has betrayed them. Such children feel nothing of the kind. They feel that they are just being true to themselves and instead might feel abandoned by their parents when they most need them.

We generally assigned cases to chapters based on the perception of the initiator; however, there are exceptions. For example, in some instances, the chapter assignment was based on the perspective of the person who sought therapy. In a few cases, chapter assignment was the direct result of our knowing more about one person than another in the cutoff—and thus could provide richer material from his or her perspective. Had we taken the other perspective, we might have assigned the case to a different chapter.

CLINICIANS AND CLIENTS

The majority of clinicians interviewed live in the United States, practice in urban areas, and reflect ethnic and religious diversity.

Their client populations and the cutoff cases were global, including individuals born in the United States and migrants from five of the seven continents. The geographic and economic diversity of clients was impressive, though most but not all were college educated and at least middle class, reflective of the clients seen in our clinical practices.

QUICK OVERVIEW OF FINDINGS

Our interviewees, respondents, clients, and perusal of relevant literature yielded the following:

- Cutoffs are common experiences—prevalent, but embarrassing, and thus an elephant in the room.
- It is easy to discuss other people's cutoffs, less easy to discuss one's own.

- Addiction to alcohol or drugs was a factor in about a quarter of the clinical cases in the book.
- Initially there may be a sense of relief or an attempt to not care, but cutoffs are extremely damaging. As one clinician put it: "People tell themselves the other person is expendable. But it goes against their humanness. Cutoffs induce involuntary suppression of feelings. There is an artificial hardening of one's heart. The cutoff would not have happened otherwise."
- Symptoms included depression, devastation, dismay, shock, denial, rage, sadness, isolation, loss of appetite, weight gain, worsening of irritable bowel syndrome (IBS), insomnia and other physical/psychosomatic problems, use of marijuana or heavier drugs, as well as work problems.
- Loss of community or family connections was often the impetus for seeking therapy.
- Cutoffs, even decades old, are not always clients' presenting problem(s). However, they often surface later on.
- Clinicians recognize cutoffs as a problem, but many do not seem sufficiently aware of the serious consequences a major cutoff may have, nor do they see promoting attempts at reconciliation as a necessary part of their role.
- Most clinicians believe, at least in the ideal, that cutoff parties should try to reconcile. Exceptions to this rule would be ongoing abuse (verbal, physical, sexual, or emotional) and the sense that the client would be further damaged by attempting reconciliation. Substance abuse, severe mental illness, and long-term toxicity for the client were also considered contraindications. In addition, one therapist said that the amount of energy needed to reconnect in these cases might not be worth it.
- Therapists who use an assessment instrument such as a genogram, which many do, do not always ask about cutoffs.
- When they hear about a cutoff from a client, some therapists take a stab at encouraging reconciliation, but they more often limit their effort to helping the client mourn the loss where appropriate, "accept," and "move on."
- Clinicians expressed concern about imposing their agenda if they were to inquire about cutoffs, encourage discussion of them, or probe clients' feelings about reconciliation.

- Many cautioned that cutoffs are delicate, complex clinical problems. Many cautioned going slowly. One said, "It feels like a dangerous area to explore both for the client and for me."
- Clients involved in a cutoff are often highly reactive. This tendency makes it hard for them to avoid cutoffs and hard for them to repair without assistance.
- Very few clinicians encourage clients to bring cutoff family members or friends into therapy, or actually see cutoff parties together in the room.
- Despite their hesitancy, therapists report success more often than not in working with a cutoff client who attempts repair. Their clients succeeded in a variety of ways, from achieving a satisfactory level of reconnection, reduction in depressive symptoms, reduction in self-blame for the lost relationship, reduction in physical symptoms, fewer nightmares, less reactivity, greater empathy for the other person, and lower anxiety in general.

ACKNOWLEDGMENTS

First of all, we want to thank our families and friends for tolerating our retreat during portions of the writing of the book. We are not sure how much you missed us, but we know we've missed you. We hope to make up for our absences now and that you won't find it necessary to cut us off!

It has been a long haul, and a number of people have been instrumental in our being able to complete what we've all along called "the cutoff project." We start with Barbara Merling and Patricia Horn, both PhD psychologists and good friends who signed on and worked with us in the beginning but whose lives and schedules made it too difficult to stay. They gave us ideas and moral support for which we are eternally grateful. We also thank each of the following extremely busy academics and clinicians. Some read early drafts; all gave us their invaluable time, input, and support: Naomi Andrews, Anita Bardin, Carolyn (Carrie) Fried Sutton, JoAnn Magdoff, Harriet Oster, and Judith and Daniel Walkowitz. Then there are the exceptional clinicians who gave hours of their time to our interviews, providing us with case material and insights we could not have gotten elsewhere. They deserve mention by name, but we all agreed it would be better for them to remain anonymous for the sake of their clients' privacy.

Clients' names and cutoff situations have been disguised as much as possible without destroying the essence of the stories. In some instances we combined similar stories. We hope the resulting case examples and composites are no more than barely recognizable to their therapists, even less to clients themselves who may come upon the book. To set off the cases, we have set all case examples in italics.

We are forever indebted to Deborah Malmud, PhD, vice president and director of Norton Professional Books, and to her team (including Kathryn Moyer, Kevin Olsen, Ben Yarling, Sara Peterson, and Sophie Hagen). Deborah gave us the chance of a lifetime to write and publish this book; made incisive, often "critical" comments; and made sure we finished! Most important, she is not just our editor. In moments of panic, she was also our therapist. Responding to Deborah's "suggestion" that Elena completely rewrite a chapter using more of her own voice, Elena claimed she wasn't sure how. Deborah settled the matter with a cogent comment: "Why don't you read your first book . . . you did it there!"

Our last acknowledgment is for Elena's husband, Nils Bruun. He was a full-fledged team member, putting aside his own projects to read and comment on drafts and catch errors with his eagle eye. He was cheerleader, one-man computer help desk, personal chef, and all-around "guy Friday"—a shining example for other good men to follow.

We hope *Not on Speaking Terms* makes a meaningful contribution to the small but growing literature on the subject of relationship cutoffs. We hope clinicians will appreciate the collegial spirit with which we speak to them and take our criticisms, direct or implied, with a grain of salt. We hope it will motivate and convince them to take more responsibility for unearthing cutoffs, encourage them to help their clients work toward reconnection with lost loved ones, and provide them with the strategies they need.

INTRODUCTION

It is generally recognized that humans are social animals who cannot survive alone. Yet, it is also true that many people have difficulty preserving even their most precious relationships. Some attribute this difficulty to the primitive "fight or flight response" to perceived threat in particular the propensity to flee, served humans well in the distant past; however, it now frequently threatens the very relationships on which people depend for their well-being.

Are human relationships really built to last? Perhaps relationship rifts, though painful, are as natural as the mother-child bond or as inevitable as the seismic shift in an earthquake. In the animal world there is affinity and loyalty, but also what appears to be tremendous cruelty, abandonment, breaking apart. All of us whether as individuals or as groups have the capacity to bond, and also to develop antipathies, disengage, stop speaking. It is not only true love that fails to run smooth.

Western literature and life are replete with examples of family conflict, feuds, and severing of ties. The Bible is rife with sibling rivalry and excruciating cutoffs (Cain and Abel, Jacob and Esau, Joseph and his brothers). Shakespeare's Capulet and Montague families pried Romeo and Juliet apart, as did the real families of Johnse Hatfield and RoseAnna McCoy, lovers who in our own pioneer days defied a generations-long cutoff decree.

Most societies, and families, create rules to ensure cohesion by defining who is in, who is out. In the process, they control behavior they believe insures well-being and general welfare. Those who disobey the rules may be excluded through the mechanisms of shunning, ostracism, isolation, or excommunication. In Judaism, exile from the group may take the form of Shiva (conferring a living death on anyone who breaks "cardinal" rules). The proclivity to cut off seems to be universal.

Contemporary life is filled with conflict, war, and disengagement. Conflict may not be avoidable, but there are also instances in which hostile countries manage to live side by side in peace. There are also examples of conflict resolution by negotiated truce, however fragile (Oslo accords, North and South Korea, Bosnia and Croatia, Hutus and Tutsis). There are also heartening reconciliations by cutoff family members. In fact, some societies and some religious groups go so far as to mandate apologies, forgiveness, and reconciliation.

Given the likely universality of cutoffs and the pain they cause, our first goal in writing this book is to increase therapists' awareness of their significance. Our second goal is to help therapists understand the causes of cutoffs and how to assess them. The third goal is to encourage therapists to actively work, as appropriate, on helping clients reconcile after a cutoff. Fourth, we want to share our and other therapists' experiences and knowledge about strategies that can assist cutoff parties. And fifth, we want to foster the prevention or reduction of cutoffs.

CONTEXT

To assist an individual or family experiencing a cutoff, it is crucial for therapists to know the broader context in which the cutoff is occurring. The context can be singular or multilayered and may involve ethnicity, religion, culture, gender, social background, historical precedents, economics, geography, class, and/or culture, as well as their dynamic intersections. Complicating matters is the fact that social norms change across generations. Yesterday an adult child could count on being cut off for marrying "below" his or her class or someone of another race or religion. Today a parent may accept a child who is gay or lesbian but not transgendered.

Space precludes us from providing the full context for every case we selected, but we want to impress upon the reader the importance of recognizing the significance of the context in which his or her clients live. The following two vignettes should drive this point home.

Most cutoffs have serious causes and consequences, but in spite of that, sometimes even a serious cutoff contains irony, if not comedy:

My mother's working-class parents emigrated from Tsarist Russia at the turn of the twentieth century. By the 1920s, the family had nearly "made it" into the middle class in New York City but were not yet firmly established and still felt insecure. At this point, one of my uncles fell in love with an assembly-line worker in his clothing factory and married her over everyone's objections. A year later, when my mother got married, she invited this brother to the wedding, but not his lower-class wife. My uncle planned to attend anyway, but his wife hid his shoes, so he couldn't go. My mother was so angry she never spoke to her brother again!

Funny? Yes! But, the fact that the sister could not see past her new sister-in-law's socioeconomic status to accept her brother's choice is also sad, as is the new wife's resorting to hiding her husband's shoes, as is the uncle's betrayal of his wife by wanting to attend the sister's wedding without her. Blink once, and it is a comedy in which everyone is childish. Blink twice, and a therapist might see how high the stakes were for each of the parties.

The mother believed that the status the whole family had struggled to achieve in the new world was threatened by her brother's choice of a wife. The brother was torn between his sister and the woman he loved, his family of origin and their values and new-world democratic values that challenged the importance of class. The new wife felt rejected by both her husband and her sister-in-law's family. The cutoff represented a perfect storm in which all contextual layers combined—psychological, ethnic, social-historical, economic, cultural. Unpacking and appreciating this incredible mix of issues would have been the therapist's task, had one been enlisted to help.

Our second vignette typifies how a cutoff may have a completely different meaning from one culture to another. The ensuing gulf dividing this multicultural couple was never bridged:

Akito and April have been married for 43 years. He is a dermatologist with a thriving practice; she is his nurse and office manager. They separated 15 years ago when she could no longer take his verbal abuse at home, but they continued to work together, and collaborated well regarding their two sons. He slept in the office; she kept their apartment. Both wanted to keep the marriage, but he was still resentful because she would not agree to leave Los Angeles. Once, when Akito was particularly abrasive, April threatened divorce. His response was that if she carried out the threat, he would move back to Japan and never see his children again. Honoring what she believed was in her children's best interests, April backed off. Although she never clarified it at the time, from a Japanese standpoint, she recently learned, her husband's threat could be interpreted as respect. By cutting off from his family, Akito was in effect signaling permission for his wife to have another husband, who could move in without interference from her first husband, and as stepfather help raise the children.

Sound odd? To Westerners maybe, but a therapist would be wise to fully explore the attitudes, meanings, and cultural pressures motivating a client such as Akito to cut off. Without delving into it, a therapist might conclude that the man did not care, whereas a simple question like "What makes you say you will never see your children again?" would probably yield the surprising answer.

EXTERNAL PRESSURE

If human relationships are inherently tenuous, external forces can also pull relationships apart. And it seems the more human beings "progress," the more "advanced" they become, the more external pressure is placed on relationships. Consider contemporary marriage.

Thanks largely to advances in preventive and curative medicine, people are living into their eighties, nineties, and beyond. That was the case for only a lucky few in the past. Today many people marry later, waiting until their thirties. They are having children later, too. Given increased longevity, couples marrying in their thirties expect to stay together for at least 50 years—twice the time couples expected in earlier eras.

In addition, given changes in women's opportunities, including economic independence, the reasons to get married or stay married have changed. Most people still want to marry for belonging and intimacy, but these are less stable reasons to be or to stay married than the formerly powerful social and familial pressure, or economic necessity.

Advances in scientific knowledge, the diminishing authority of clergy, and greater freedom of speech equal more freedom in what to believe and what to do. If I can think for myself, express my needs, and pursue my own interests, why should I stay in an unhappy marriage, or even marry in the first place?

Globalization has radically transformed our social world. It is now easier to travel, and extensive travel is often part of a job, leading to bicoastal careers and homes. With the increase in dual-career marriages, more couples spend significant time apart in long-distance relationships. It is now normal to change jobs several times over a lifetime and to move innumerable times, neither of which was typical in the past. Living apart for long periods is stressful, harder for couples to negotiate inevitable tensions. Despite phone calls, Skype, and email, communication over long distances may be disrupted—incomplete—without face-to-face contact, with each party missing the nonverbal signals or voice inflections, not to mention touch and sexual intimacy.

John Gottman claims that little moments of shared experience are a key to keeping relationships vital (Gottman & Silver, 2009). When couples live apart, these moments, such as seeing a beautiful bird alight in the backyard together, are lost. Similarly, tensions not offset by repair gestures may escalate, leading to distortions or distrust of the partner's motives, and so on.

Being curious about people one has lost or been cut off from is not new. People have always searched for lost friends and family. Interest in old lovers, friends, and family genealogy vastly predates Facebook. Social media has just made it easier. However, is it possible that the same Facebook that blesses one with innumerable "friends" may at the same time decrease the depth of relationships to the point of shallowness? Does access to social media 24/7 make one less likely to fully invest in the important relationships in one's life? Does one ask oneself, "Who is really my friend? Who can I count on? Who will really be *there* in a pinch?"

INTRODUCTION

This same concern was expressed by Catherine Saint-Louis in the *New York Times* (2012). She identified social media as a mechanism used by estranged family members and other cutoff individuals to keep abreast of one another's lives. Using Facebook pages and Twitter feeds, individuals learned about these people's births, weddings, and illnesses, among other activities and occurrences, but did not actually communicate with them. Thus, while social media is championed as a means to locate people from one's past, it seems to simultaneously diminish the need to actually connect. One can read the particulars of someone's life without engaging. As such, social media may keep people from putting in the effort to repair a relationship gone sour, especially if they now have an expanded network of "friends" to latch onto.

While on the topic of social media, we cannot resist saying that in addition to fostering casual ties, it also provides opportunities for bad behavior in relationships that would be better left to wither on the vine. Lena Dunham, the young comedy writer, catapulted to fame for her TV sitcom *Girls,* provides a marvelous example of being gratuitously "unfriended":

> August 17, 2010 I got an email from Facebook notifying me that I had received a message. It was from my ex-boyfriend's mother. Its subject heading was "Goodbye from Nancy and Bill . . ." I opened the message with great curiosity and a little terror. Why was Nancy saying goodbye? Was she finally moving to Switzerland to live near her brother and his Japanese wife? Did she have a terminal illness? The message said: "Hi, Lena—Bill and I remember you with such pleasure and fondness! But it's time to sever the Facebook connection so I'm going to block you. We wish you all the BEST!"
>
> I was dumbfounded . . . I wanted to write back, "Why?" I wanted to write back "What the fuck?" I wanted to write back "Like I'd even notice if you just un-friended me, or even if you died, you crazy fucking hag." But I couldn't write anything. Because she had blocked me! (Dunham, 2012)

Are some cutoffs good or healthy, non-pathological, even necessary to protect or save oneself? Are they an alternative to exploitation, abuse, or violence? Yes, but even then, we contend that the cutoff can be declared in a civil, non-confrontational way. A cutoff does not always have to be permanent; the door need not be slammed as it was by Groucho Marx in a funny not-so-funny dismissive quip "I never forget a face, but in your case I'll be glad to make an exception!"

In *Not on Speaking Terms* we concentrate on family and close friendship rifts that were not precipitated by extreme abuse yet that still hurt and could have been or could still be repaired. A clinician's ability to pinpoint the—obvious or hidden—cause(s) of a particular cutoff is critical to helping family members or friends reconcile, or, when reconciliation is not possible, helping clients to heal without reconnection.

DEFINITION

At the inception of what we originally called the "cutoff project," we arbitrarily, and as it turns out naively, set a minimum cutoff duration of at least six months as a criterion for the inclusion of a case. Our six-month rule does apply to almost all of the clinical cases, but not all of the personal, literary, or public ones. We abandoned the rule for two reasons. First, we found cutoffs of shorter duration that were exquisitely painful as well as longer ones that were less so; second, there appeared to be a spectrum of cutoffs from incipient to complete, all of which deserved inclusion. Therefore, we shifted our criterion from length of cutoff to the meaning and pain of it. Suffice it to say that the cutoffs we heard about were pretty evenly spread from less than six months to 40 years!

To give just one example of a short cutoff we could not bear to leave out, one client's husband left for a ten-day business trip right after announcing he wanted to separate. Years of marital discord had resulted in his need for "space," but he promised "on a stack of bibles" to be accessible during his absence by email, text, or phone. When push came to shove, however, he was unreachable. To say that the wife was unprepared to handle the prospect of a separation or divorce is an understatement; her pain at being unable to reach him during those ten days was unbearable.

The definition for a cutoff that we established is:

- A purposeful painful often abrupt rupture, resulting in the loss of a close or important relationship that in most cases existed for a significant period of time. The cutoff usually occurs when one or both parties are emotionally upset over an incident(s), a decision, a changed behavior or circumstance. In some instances the impetus may be less anger than a need for self-protection.
- The cutoff parties are "not on speaking terms" (no direct oral or written communication) or their interaction is seriously limited or curtailed.

Not included in the definition are developmentally appropriate leave-takings in which both parties gradually let go, move, or drift apart. Examples abound: young adults leaving home with their parents' bittersweet blessings; friendships waning when interests, experiences, or direction in life diverge; divorced couples recasting their relationship to effectively co-parent; mentors supporting their mentee's inevitable independence. All are normal developmental phenomena. These are partings, but they are not cutoffs, because there is no trauma, anger, or intentional hurt to anyone.

In contrast, and as we shall see, a cutoff is often precipitated by a family member's or friend's inability or refusal to accept someone's need to grow or individuate or when a family member or friend holds on too tight. A cutoff may also occur when relationships become too distant—when people who were or otherwise would be close are unable or refuse to engage in a meaningful way. In other words, many cutoffs may be understood as a normal developmental process gone awry.

THEORY

A number of theories and theorists have contributed to our understanding of cutoffs. In this regard there is considerable overlap with the influences on our clinician interviewees.[1] Among our theorists,

---

1. Our interviewees reported the following influences: Minuchin's structural family therapy; family life cycle theory à la Carter & McGoldrick; psychoanalytic theory; Bowen's theory and therapy; Ellis's rational emotive therapy (the A-B-C exercise); Horney; cognitive behavior therapy; integra-

Murray Bowen is foremost, but we start with psychoanalytic theory which developed first, return to Bowen, and then touch on Ivan Böszörményi-Nagy, Salvador Minuchin, Susan Johnson, Daniel Siegel and John Gottman. In reviewing each one in relation to our topic, we briefly examine the relevant hypotheses, see what the therapy consists of, discuss the goals for therapy, and consider some similarities and differences.

Psychoanalytic Theory

Although we are unaware of material pertaining specifically to relationship cutoffs in the psychoanalytic literature, at least two concepts in the theory help us understand the tendency to cut others off or to be at the receiving end. The first is defense mechanisms, conceptualized by Sigmund Freud, then fleshed out and elaborated on by his daughter, Anna (1936). According to the theory, individuals try to avoid the ego being flooded with anxiety (from id impulses) by deploying protective defenses. Scanning the now-familiar list of defense mechanisms , it is easy to see how these efforts to protect the ego would make intimate relationships a challenge: denial, repression, displacement, projection, intellectualization, rationalization, and regression. (The only "healthy" defense identified by Freud and thus omitted from consideration for causing a cutoff is sublimation, by which the unconscious converts socially unacceptable feelings into acceptable behavior.)

In psychoanalytic terms, someone with a fragile ego is likely to run away from high-conflict, anxiety-producing situations. He or she might also use any of the defenses to end a relationship in which there is fear of being overwhelmed or abandoned. Given such an individual's use of protective defenses, it is not surprising that others would find it hard to be intimate with the person and might be inclined to cut off.

In addition to the defenses, there are personality disorders. Basically, ten personality disorders are specified in the *Diagnostic and Statistical Manual of Mental Disorders* (*DSM*-5): paranoid, schizoid, schizotypal, antisocial, borderline, histrionic, narcissistic, avoidant,

---

tive behavior therapy; Imago; Böszörményi-Nagy; Pesso-Boyden system; and attachment theory.

dependent, and obsessive-compulsive (American Psychiatric Association, 2013).

According to *DSM-5*, the main hallmarks of personality disorder relevant to our topic are:

> an enduring pattern of inner experience and behavior that deviates markedly from the expectations of the individual's culture and is manifested in at least two of the following areas: cognition, affectivity, interpersonal functioning or impulse control (Criterion A). This enduring pattern is inflexible and pervasive across a broad range of personal and social situations (Criterion B) and leads to clinically significant distress or impairment in social, occupational, or other important areas of functioning (Criterion C). The pattern is stable and of long duration, and its onset can be traced back at least to adolescence or early adulthood (Criterion D). (p. 647)

Simply put, individuals with personality disorders—about 9% of the population according to the National Comorbidity Survey Replication (Lenzenweger, 2008)—are often too insecure or immature to withstand the vicissitudes of intimate relationships.

In recent years, the immutability of personality disorders has been called into question by abundant neuropsychiatry research (Noggle & Dean, 2012). Nevertheless, Mark Sichel (2004), a psychoanalytically oriented psychotherapist whose clinical focus is family cutoffs, writes that the tendency to cut off is usually attributable to one person's unalterable narcissism:

> If we look back at some of the stories of the families who disowned children, parents, and siblings . . . in each case it was a response to an uncontrollable feeling of narcissistic rage that caused . . . the estrangement. Most often instigators . . . are individuals who demand compliance and submission, coupled with an underlying feeling that if a family member is not submissive, that person is being disrespectful. The message the instigator perceives is that the non-submissive family member is treating him or her as if they were worthless. The excommunicator basically is saying, "You've made a life choice, not because you wanted what you chose, but because you wanted to make a fool of me and humiliate me." (Sichel, 2004, p. 71)

We will revisit narcissism again in Chapter 7, but suffice it to say here that what Sichel claims seems only partly true. Widening the angle of our built-in camera lens, while some cutoffs may have their origins in relatively fixed aspects of personality (such as the rigidity and overreaction of someone with narcissistic personality disorder), there are many other reasons cutoffs come about.

Moreover, this approach could be harmful in that it could tempt the therapist to blame or take sides against the "narcissist" and thus overlook opportunities to facilitate restoration of a relationship. A cutoff may just as easily be initiated by the family member under the thumb of the narcissist. And other cutoffs, perhaps most, have their origins in a more complex, systemic, multigenerational set of relationships.

Although Sichel is a family therapist, like many of the clinicians we interviewed, it is not clear that he brings cutoff family members together in the room. However, he does discuss ways to build an individual client's self-esteem, and he provides an excellent set of communication skills and strategies for individual clients to use in approaching someone from whom they are cutoff.

Systems Theory

Family therapy pioneer Murray Bowen is often credited with being the bridge between psychoanalysis and systems theory. Midway through his career, he also "discovered" cutoffs, both their significance and deleterious effects. He is credited with inventing the term and with incorporating the concept into his family systems theory and practice. Further, he observed that cutoffs occur when a family member is "undifferentiated" or "fused"—in short, when individuality and individual differences are being stifled in a family. Bowen saw the tendency to fuse as a pathological reaction to anxiety, as is cutting off, which he saw as the individual's generally misguided attempt to escape the family and recover the self (Bowen, 1976, 1978, 1994).

In other words, when anxiety in a family system becomes too great, Bowen saw two unhealthy options—fusion and cutoff—and one healthy option, differentiation, akin to the normal developmental process of "launching." The goal in Bowen's therapy, therefore, is to lower the level of anxiety in individual family members and in the family system as a whole. A moderate amount of anxiety in a family allows members to be independent, yet at the same time be part of the family. Differentiation of self is everything:

> The one most central theoretical premise of family systems theory concerns the degree to which we all have poorly "differentiated" selfs, or the degree to which we are "undifferentiated" or the degree of our unresolved emotional attachments to families of origin. These are all different descriptive terms to refer to the same phenomenon. The one most important goal of family systems therapy is to help family members toward a better level of "differentiation of self. (Bowen, 1978/1994, p. 529)

Like Sichel, Bowen sees narcissism as a characteristic of the most undifferentiated souls and among those most likely to initiate a cut off. However, Bowen also saw that it is not just the narcissistic. Anyone in a family system may cut off:

> The greater the undifferentiation or fusion between the generations, the greater the likelihood the generations will cut off from one another. Parents cut off from their children as much as their adult children cut off from them. (Kerr & Bowen, 1988, p. 271)

Further, Bowen cautioned that while a cutoff may temporarily lower a family's emotional temperature, ultimately these same emotions reappear, transformed or reenacted in other family relationships and friendships. People who cut off from their family of origin need to trace, understand, and minimize their intense reactions. And they need to recognize that the intense reactions of other people outside the family are based on *their* prior experiences and are often not "personal."

An individual, couple, or nuclear family cut off from the preceding generation is at risk not only for repeating prior patterns but also for being lost or isolated when the inevitable stresses of life happen. In Bowen's therapy, therefore, adult children are strongly encouraged to resurrect weak family-of-origin or cutoff relationships and work on their particular family-of-origin issues. As Gilbert (2006) explains:

People reduce the tensions of family interactions by cutting off, but risk making their new relationships too important. For example, the more a man cuts off from his family of origin, the more he looks to his spouse, children, and friends to meet his needs. This makes him vulnerable to pressuring them to be certain ways for him or accommodating too much to their expectations of him out of fear of jeopardizing the relationship. New relationships are typically smooth in the beginning, but the patterns people are trying to escape eventually emerge and generate tensions.

The person who cuts off from his or her family is no more independent than the one who never leaves home. They are both reactive to a huge degree of fusion. Relationship "nomads," or serial monogamists and hermits all represent versions of intense cutoff. One who cuts off from parents is vulnerable to impulsively getting into an emotionally intense marriage that ends in the cutoff of divorce. (p. 60).

Reconnection with family of origin means an immersion in family "field work"—i.e., discovery, study, and observation of dysfunctional patterns and gradual detachment from dysfunctional "triangles." To increase one's level of differentiation, one must become less emotionally reactive. An important side note: Bowen did not entirely rule out the possibility that couples and nuclear families could lower anxiety by working on differentiation solely within their current relationships, but he believed that immediate or lasting success would be less likely if they did not also work on their families of origin.

To avoid getting caught up in their clinical families' interactional webs, Bowenian therapists receive training that consists largely of revisiting and reworking relationships in their own family of origin. Doing so is reminiscent of the psychoanalytic training analysis. However, in contrast to the training analysis in which the student's transference to the therapist is explored, in Bowenian therapy family problems are worked through directly with family members. The focus is on changing dysfunctional, ingrained family patterns, mostly by altering one's own behavior in those relationships.

Nonetheless, similar to many of his psychoanalytic colleagues, Bowen (1978/1994) adhered to the stereotypically calm, cool, collected style of classic psychoanalysis and resisted the notion that emotional expression or enactments of problems could have therapeutic value. Although he did not feel it was necessary to bring cutoff parties into the room, when he did, he subscribed to the wheel model of communication in which all communication between family members is channeled through the therapist. Any hint of anger or hostility is stopped in its tracks.

Bowen's notion of fusion was expanded on by Ivan Böszörményi-Nagy to include unholy alliances and "invisible loyalty" to family of origin (Böszörményi-Nagy & Spark, (1973/1984). As we shall see in a few of our cases, the notion of loyalty to someone or something in the past can inhibit, contort, or wreck relationships in the present. Böszörményi-Nagy was so concerned about the strength and destructive power of these hidden ties that he insisted on having not only parents and children in therapy but grandparents as well, with all three generations in the room. The wisdom and potential benefit of this intergenerational approach is undeniable. However, the impracticality of the demand was expressed by a trainee: "I didn't see enough cases in my training program with Nagy. It was too hard for us to get the grandparents in, or sufficiently involved" (Wendy Danzig Glass, personal communication, 1993).

Böszörményi-Nagy's concern was essentially ethical. He felt that belonging to a family carries obligations within and across generations: parents to children, spouses and siblings to each other, and, at the end of the day, children to parents. If these obligations are not met, or if loyalty expectations are extreme, resentments build and relationships crumble. Of necessity, loyalties must shift over time. A spouse, for instance, owes primary allegiance to spouse, and then to children, but cannot forget his or her parents. Addressing, shifting, and balancing the strength of these invisible loyalties is the task of each generation (Böszörményi-Nagy & Spark, 1973/1994).

The fusion and cutoff poles of Bowen are strikingly similar to Salvador Minuchin's (1974) concepts of enmeshment and disengagement. Moreover, as the following illustration shows, each theorist identifies a healthy choice in between:

Fusion --------------------Differentiation-----------------------Cutoff
Enmeshment ------------ Clear boundaries------------Disengagement

Despite their similarity in conceptualizing the pitfalls of nuclear families, unlike Bowen and Böszörményi-Nagy, Minuchin was not interested in looking back, in working on relationships with prior generations. Perhaps it was the urgency or constant crises for Minuchin's mostly poor, struggling families in inner-city Philadelphia that demanded his attention here and now (Anita Bardin, personal communication, March 2013). Regardless, Minuchin focused on the nuclear family and on helping families find that "clear boundary" middle ground between enmeshment and disengagement.

Minuchin's approach to cutoffs was crafted and strategic. He often first met with subsystems, a classic structural family approach, focusing on how they fit or did not fit into the family gestalt. Then he proceeded in steps—putting pieces slowly together as if the family was a puzzle to be solved. In fact, Minuchin would not put whole families or cutoff parties in the same room until he believed the individuals and subsystems were properly aligned, in sync, and, prepared for the work. We will see a few examples of this approach in the chapters that follow.

Attachment Theory

Susan Johnson is the main proponent of attachment-based *emotionally focused therapy* (EFT) (Johnson & Whiffen, 2003). She follows in the steps of Bowlby (1969/1999, 1973), Ainsworth and her colleagues (1970, 1978), and others who studied infant- and toddler-parent attachment. She further observed that most adults choose partners based in some way on their early family experience. These clinician-researchers found that infants who experience insecure or threatening kinds of attachment become anxious or fearful and exhibit avoidant or dismissive behavior toward their parents or caregivers. As adults, they then avoid close relationships, dismiss their importance, or desperately look for security in marriage or other adult partnerships.

Bowen and Minuchin stress the importance of differentiation and independence; emotionally focused therapy highlights the need to connect, bond, and belong. Johnson strongly values secure attachment not only in childhood but also as something to strive for in adulthood. These theories do not essentially conflict; rather, their emphases are different. At the same time, Johnson does not work much on family-of-origin issues beyond helping couples recognize that their adult attachment styles are probably a carryover. For her, the current "source of pain is in the room"—in the couple's relationship—and that is her focus.

Two common maladaptive patterns Johnson sees in adult couple relationships have been classified as "pursuer-distancer" and "dominant-submissive." Although Johnson does not specifically say so, it follows that couples locked into either pattern and left to their own devices eventually either implode or cut off.

EFT brings distressed couples whose attachment is frayed from hurts they inflicted on each other into a more secure, trusting state. Unlike Bowen's and Minuchin's approaches, Johnson's first step is to create a strong alliance with the couple through which they are enabled to explore dynamics and maladaptive patterns in their relationship. Most important, Johnson helps them unearth and express their hurt feelings. She then guides the couple toward empathic understanding and healing. Thus, unlike Bowen (and most behavior therapists), Johnson actively encourages titrated, controlled emotional expression. As one colleague wrote:

> When both are able to express their deepest feelings, attachment needs and yearnings, and these are understood and accepted by their partner, it is possible to co-create a "Positive Cycle." In my practice, cutoffs are often triggered by experienced trauma (small *t*), sometimes when needed connection has been broken repeatedly in the same way, with no apparent understanding by the partner. When the therapist helps the couple to express these feelings and they are in turn understood and accepted, a new bond is forged. Sometimes, as we are seeing increasingly, when trauma is due to war or the aftermath of exile (large *T*), the historical context experienced both in the world and internally, need to be addressed. (JoAnn Magdoff, PhD, personal communication, June 2013)

Like Minuchin's structural family therapy, this stripped-down, laser-focused therapy is a departure, perhaps even a far cry, from earlier family therapists, who like Bowen tended to think multi-generationally and in larger family systems. For Johnson, there is no need for parent-child multigenerational work, because for many the most important adult relationship is marriage, and everything the therapist has to know can be observed in the couple. We would add that EFT's release of pain in the moment can be successfully applied in situations other than marital distress, to assist individuals after any type of relationship distress or cutoff.

Next, we want to mention the work of Daniel Siegel (2010a, 2010b), a psychiatrist, interpersonal neurobiologist, and clinician at the University of California Los Angeles (UCLA). He is studying and substantiating the beneficial effects of meditation and mindfulness on a physiological level. He is specifically interested in people's ability to recover from and grow after insecure, unhealthy early childhood attachments have left them unable to handle the types of relationship difficulty that often lead to cutoffs. He stresses the value of other healing relationships, most notably the "attunement" of clinician and patient.

The key finding here is that brain development is a two-way street. We've known for a long time that behavior is heavily determined by genetics, but what has only recently come to light is that the brain is more malleable than originally believed. Its development is an ongoing process that can be influenced, molded, and changed through interactions with others. The old notion that people are entirely encapsulated in their own heads also turns out to be wrong.

On the contrary, it seems individuals are wired together by invisible threads, and both positive and negative relationship experiences affect the brain and its development. Positive ones will enhance emotional and intellectual capability; negative ones may have the opposite effect and depress its capacity. Whether because of slowly formed, insecure attachment to parenting figures or trauma at almost any point, some people either did not develop or have lost the ability to be open to experience, to respond appropriately (not to mention creatively), or even simply to adapt to new circumstances.

Daniel Goleman, author of *Emotional Intelligence* (2005), calls the panic reaction to perceived threat getting "hijacked." And the thrust of Siegel's work is to help clinicians and their clients learn to regulate and ultimately control emotions that will only be self-destructive in the end. Since hijacking is an issue that comes close to explaining how cutoffs erupt "out of nowhere," we will return to this concept throughout the book.

Finally, Gottman and his colleagues' studies of marital interaction (Carstensen, Gottman, & Levenson, 1992; Gottman & Krokott, 1989; Gottman & Silver, 2009) yielded a number of related findings about factors that predict divorce and what couples can do to avoid it. First, couples should, as much as possible, minimize making each other anxious or angry by succumbing to "the four horsemen of the apocalypse" (i.e., criticism, defensiveness, contempt, and stonewalling). Second, based on the fact that men heat up physiologically faster than women do and tend to tolerate less conflict, Gottman recommends a "soft start-up" when wives want their husband's attention (Gottman et al., 1998; Gottman & Silver, 2009). Third, husbands who want to stay married should let themselves be influenced by their wives. Last, since conflict is still inevitable, Gottman stresses the power of making and responding to "repair attempts" after a fight. While Gottman's work is with couples specifically, as is the case with EFT, the principles are undoubtedly applicable to other close relationships.

To summarize our theoretical underpinnings, theorists generally agree that cutoffs are precipitated by intolerable anxiety, conflict, or feelings of threat to the self. Cutoffs result from an emotional reaction that amounts to a rush to judgment. Decisions are made in fear or anger without much deliberation. A flight response is often initially protective, but it is one for which people pay later, with the loss of an important relationship and the opportunity to work it out. Finally, we observed that the theories about psychological mechanisms underlying cutoffs are not really so different. The differences are in the therapies, the levels of intervention, and the methodologies employed.

ORGANIZATION OF THE BOOK

Chapter 1: Assessment

In the majority of situations, we hear about cutoffs from an individual client. It is relatively rare that two parties or a family seek help to mend a cutoff where both parties have had prior discussion and already agreed to try. We therefore use the individual client as the contextual perspective for the book.

A cutoff is not always or often the presenting problem: we therefore discuss the use of genograms and other assessment tools to identify cutoffs in the immediate or extended family or friendship network. We then present a series of questions as a template to assess the cutoff, including the seriousness of the cutoff and the potential for reconnection. We provide a cutoff spectrum to pinpoint the degree of disconnection. Then, we identify the stimulus for the cutoff, such as abandonment, jealousy, betrayal, or matters of principle, as well as the role of mental illness and communication skills in triggering and perpetuating cutoffs. These stimuli or themes are explored in depth in the chapters that form the core of the book.

Chapter 2: Strategies

This chapter provides a compendium of strategies that can be used to explore and resolve cutoffs or help make a decision to move on. They come from our own work and that of the therapists we interviewed. Many strategies reappear in the chapters that follow within the context of a specific case. We present them not as a recipe book but rather as a reference source for effective practices the clinician can suggest, recommend, or employ. The myriad options include finding ways to reach out; using a go-between or third party outside of therapy; using family events and occasions; considering whether or when to discuss circumstances precipitating the cutoff; making apologies, making amends; bringing the cutoff parties into the room; and deciding how to work with them to rebuild the relationship. The clinician's own understanding and control of his or her own countertransference issues are also stressed here and throughout the book.

Chapter 3: Abandonment

This chapter is divided into three sections. The first focuses on cutoffs that take place when someone who is critically important was "not there" physically or emotionally over an extended period of time—the client feels neglected, or literally abandoned. This can be a child's feeling about an adult or parent. The section also includes cutoffs based on a feeling that the other person was not there at a critical moment or did not meet certain reasonable—or unreasonable—expectations. The second section is devoted to giving up a child, "surrendering" him or her to foster care or adoption. Whether the caregiver decides on this course of action by choice or necessity, the child cannot easily distinguish between the two, feels abandoned, and may then reject the parent's attempt to reunite. The chapter concludes with cutoffs owing to illness and death and a discussion of how clinicians might handle these seemingly irreparable circumstances.

Chapter 4: Jealousy and Envy

In reviewing our data from clinicians, the personal stories we heard, and the key pieces of public material we gathered, we easily identified fifteen kinds of jealousy and envy powerful enough to cause rifts in an important relationship: romantic jealousy; money; objects, property, land; beauty; family; youth; friends; talent/creativity; accomplishments; health (including mental health); meaning, purpose, passion; power; happiness, satisfaction, goal attainment, striving; courage; and public recognition. The source for many of these painful emotions can be traced to what the person learned was important from parenting figures, including favoritism of one child over another. We highlight the importance of identifying the sources of jealousy and envy for reconciliation and offer specific strategies for handling each case.

Chapter 5: Betrayal

We begin this chapter by explaining the difference between jealousy, envy, and betrayal. Whereas jealousy and envy are about desiring or wanting something one cannot have or is not supposed to have—about uncomfortable feelings—betrayal involves acting on those desires or impulses to the detriment of the other person. However, jealousy is not the only reason people betray. It can be retaliation for having been betrayed in the past, by a particular person or in general. We identify ten types of betrayal: divulging or withholding secrets; breaking promises; lying or undermining; theft; enmeshment; incest extra-familial infidelity; verbal cruelty and public humiliation; and rape, physical assault, and murder.

Chapter 6: Principle

A cutoff can occur when an individual believes someone else has not acknowledged a "truth" or has failed to subscribe to a value or belief that structures the other's life. Religious beliefs are often the foundation for cutoffs based on principles, but there are others, including social norms or the interpretation of these norms. This chapter examines a range of principles that have been violated and the cutoffs that followed, including religious, scientific, ideological, and political principles. Principles regarding identity and affiliation that cause exclusion of the individual from not just the family but also the group are explored. In addition, we look at cutoffs that occur when someone is perceived to have crossed a boundary from ethical to unethical behavior or has failed to act responsibly. In each case, we present illustrative cases, along with the strategies that were employed.

Chapter 7: Mental Health

Here we turn our attention to the role of mental illness as a factor in producing relationship cutoffs. We speculate that a pattern of repeatedly cutting off or being cut off is a red flag clinicians should ponder in assessing a client's situation and ability to tolerate self–examination or reconnection. A pattern of cutting off or being cut off or of trouble sustaining adult relationships often echoes traumatic childhood ruptures, suggesting that the person has a more significant mental health issue than first meets the eye.

We return to a number of cases discussed in other chapters, to focus on specific diagnoses that relate to the client's situation and capacities: generalized anxiety disorder, major depressive disorder, antisocial personality disorder, bipolar disorder, borderline personality disorder, schizotypal personality disorder, schizophrenia, narcissistic personality disorder, paranoid personality disorder, and substance abuse.

In our experience and that of our clinical interviewees, where parties have tried but no resolution or reconciliation is forthcoming, there is often a problem with mental illness. But we hasten to add that this should be a default consideration, not the first go-to.

Chapter 8: Conclusion

In the final chapter we speculate as to why clinicians have generally been slow to focus on the issue of relationship cutoffs and what can be done about it.

We offer ways clinicians can help clients prevent or avoid unnecessary cutoffs and present ideas for the training of clinicians, to prepare them to better handle these extremely challenging ruptured relationship cases. Broadening the context, we discuss the need for preventive educational policies, from allotting curricular time to practice communication skills and conflict resolution in order to minimize the number of relationship cutoffs in the population at large. Hopefully, we are making a contribution to the repertoire of strategies a young clinician needs for the realities of practice outside the classroom.

Chapter 1

ASSESSMENT

Look before you leap
for as you sow
ye are like to reap
Samuel Butler

All clinical encounters begin with an assessment, implicit or explicit, formal or informal. The client assesses us; we listen closely, ask questions, gather an impression, try to grasp why a client has come. We gradually formulate the problem and begin to think how we can help. It is the same with cutoffs.

In this chapter, we provide and seek answers to a series of questions about the client, the cutoff, and its impact. We then discuss goals and expectations for the therapeutic work. We follow with a typology to assess the nature of disconnection.

THE CLIENT

Our client can be either the initiator or the recipient of the cutoff. The client may not even be directly involved but heavily affected by a cutoff elsewhere in his or her family or friendship network. Whether one has been cut off, has cut off, or is simply an affected bystander, all parties surrounding the cutoff may suffer.

In the majority of situations, we first hear about a cutoff from an individual client. Occasionally, two parties or a family seek help to mend a cutoff where both or all parties have had prior discussion and already agreed to attempt reconciliation.

IDENTIFYING THE CUTOFF

A cutoff can be identified in several ways. It may be the only problem prompting a client to seek therapy. Or, it may be one of several issues a new client presents. However, as mentioned in the Preface, a cutoff is not usually the presenting problem, nor even on the client's mind when he or she enters therapy. Instead, cutoffs generally come to light during an initial assessment or during the course of therapy.

Recognizing the significance of cutoffs in so many of our clients' lives, we believe it is important to ask about them as part of an initial assessment. Further, as therapists trained in systems theory, we strongly encourage all clinicians, regardless of the potential uncovering of a cutoff, to construct a three-generation genogram early in their work with individuals, couples, and families.

As most family therapists know, *genograms,* as developed by Bowen and fleshed out by McGoldrick, Gerson, and Carter (Carter & McGoldrick, 1999; McGoldrick, Gerson, & Petry, 2008), are a snapshot and overview of the client's family, including cutoffs, within and across generations. Genograms are a helpful tool for identifying family patterns as well as opening up significant territory that might otherwise stay hidden. Even if the therapist does not encourage focusing on the past, there are nuggets of valuable information to troll.

In creating a genogram, among other things, clinicians can home in on and probe the client's perception of how closely he or she and other people in the family feel connected, to assess issues of fusion and estrangement. We also recommend both the Differentiation of Self and the Family Fusion Scales to assess the degree to which individuals as well as spouses are emotionally fused or cutoff (Kerr & Bowen, 1988).

SIGNIFICANCE OF THE CUTOFF

The identification of a cutoff is, however, just the first step. Next, we weigh its significance in the client's emotional life and how it fits with other issues on the client's mind. We need to know how the client experiences the cutoff and what he or she may want to do about it. Even an emphatic "I never want to see X again," may change in time. So, before leaving the topic, it is a good idea to—gently—introduce the possibility that feelings can moderate, that the cutoff may be important to revisit later on.

If and when a client expresses an interest in reconnection, we use a set of questions to help us and the client assess the client's readiness. We ask the client to tell the story of the cutoff in his or her own words. As we listen, we gather information about the cutoff and about the client. What are his or her emotional strengths? What are his or her cognitive capacities and style? What does his or her social world look like and his or her interactions with others? Is there any indication of a severe psychological problem such as a mood disorder, a personality disorder, or psychosis?

By listening closely, we can assess the type and severity of the cutoff, as well as the degree to which the client may desire reconciliation. In addition, we assess the client's capacity to do the work it takes. If insufficient information is forthcoming, we need to be more proactive.

EXPLORATION OF THE CUTOFF

The following set of questions can help in this process:

1. *Is this cutoff new and fresh or old?*
2. *Are we dealing with the one who cut off, the recipient, or an affected third party?*
3. *Who is cut off from whom?* Is it siblings, parent and child, friends, cousins, lovers, colleagues, mentor-mentee, former spouses? Each of these relationship dyads have characteristic issues that may lead to a cutoff; for example, siblings are likely to cut off because of jealousy; children may cut off from parents or parents from children as a result of abuse or abandonment. Even if not actively exploring the reasons in the first session in which the cutoff surfaces, the clinician needs to consciously think about these potential and characteristic triggers.
4. *Is this a primary or secondary cutoff?* Was the client involved in the original—primary—cutoff, or is the client one or more degrees down

the line? For instance, are the client and his mother cut off, or is the client now cut off from his daughter? Or, has the client's father cut his brother off, and the client is now struggling to decide if and how he should interact with this "cutoff" uncle?

5. *How close was the relationship?* A relationship that was close but reached an impasse may well be worth trying to save. If the parties were never very close but are closely bound by blood or external forces as, say, siblings are, a real relationship may have to be built from scratch. The work is more difficult in these cases, but still possible.

On the other hand, if the cutoff represents an attempt of someone in a "too close," fused, enmeshed relationship to separate, or in the case of enmeshed families to build some walls where boundaries were crossed, the work may need to focus more, at least initially, on differentiation of self than on the cutoff.

6. *What is the nature of the client's other relationships?* Here we assess whether the client relationship with the cutoff party is typical of the way the client's relates. Is the client usually able to establish clear boundaries, or does the client tend to lose himself or herself in a relationship? What is the client's capacity for autonomy, for intimacy? Is the cutoff part of a pattern in the client's life?

7. *How important was the relationship?* The quality of the relationship throughout its history matters. Has the client weighed the costs and benefits of reconnection, including the potential for further hurt and damage?

8. *How urgent is the matter for the client?* Even if the cutoff was not the primary or a presenting reason for the client to seek therapy, we sometimes find that when a cutoff emerges in therapy, something clicks and the client is suddenly eager to address the cutoff. At other times, the cutoff recedes as the work focuses on building the client's self-esteem. On the other hand, once the client increases or restores the sense of self, he or she is often ready to tackle the cutoff.

9. *If the cutoff is not the presenting problem, is there a connection between the cutoff, and other reasons the client sought help?* In the process of assessing the client's capacities and other social relations, the clinician—or sometimes the client—discovers a link between the presenting problem and the cutoff. When the clinician makes the connection between the cutoff and other issues facing the client, the client's motivation is sparked to working on the previously elusive or

challenging underlying issues. Assessment and detective work pay off when it comes time to strategize with the client.

10. *How does the client tell the story of the cutoff?* Here we listen with our whole clinical apparatus. In relating what is usually a painful event in the client's life, what emotions come forth? Is there any dissonance between the narrative and the expression, "intellectualization," or lack of emotion in the client's demeanor or voice? How does the client frame or explain the factors or identify the cause(s) of the cutoff? Does the client self-reflect about his or her possible contribution to the cutoff? If the client does not or cannot do so, it does not augur well for reconciliation.

11. *What is the client's level of emotional health, and how has he or she been emotionally affected by the cutoff?* As noted earlier, we cannot work on a cutoff without understanding the client's emotional or psychological status. As we look for strengths, we also register indications of serious mental health issues. This is a critical part of unpacking the cutoff, understanding its impact, and selecting appropriate strategies to help the client decide whether to mend the relationship or move on.

Separate from any preexisting emotional states or mental health issues, emotional reactions to a cutoff can be acute and severe, even for the person who initiated it. Common sequelae are rage, fear, anxiety, and depressive symptoms such as insomnia; changes in appetite; preoccupation with the event, loss of interest in otherwise engaging activities; blaming the other person; lack of empathy for what he or she may be experiencing; blaming oneself, recrimination, or guilt. We therefore need to assess the extent to which these symptoms are attributable to the cutoff and to what extent they preceded it or might even have, in some way, contributed to it.

As we listen, we also consider the timing and intensity of reactions. Here the Elisabeth Kübler-Ross (1969) stages are helpful. While her work elucidated stages of emotional adjustment to terminal illness, she later expressed the belief that the stages also explain reactions to other traumatic situations, such as the relationship cutoffs we are exploring here. It is well known now that the five stages (denial, anger, bargaining, depression, and acceptance) are not always sequential and sometimes overlap. Some people experience only one or two stages, while others appear to go through a traumatic event unscathed. According to Bonanno (2009), this "nonre-

5

action" might well reflect resilience, someone's ability to adjust to a traumatic event asymptomatically.

Given, however, that we are talking about a client population and that most clients come to us distressed about "something," it is more likely that a cutoff, even if not pressing or on the client's mind, has had a profound effect, compounding other mental health problems. So with a cutoff client, we should be thinking in terms of stages of adjustment, but in a fluid way, being careful not to impose them as the "necessary" scaffold or "normal" set of reactions.

12. *How has the individual responded physically?* Individuals vary in their degree of access to and consciousness about their emotional reactions to life's vicissitudes. And yet, there is a dynamic interaction between emotions and physiology (Larsen et al., 2010); a simple example is the flushing and a racing heart people experience when they are afraid. Long term, physiological manifestations can appear that do not have an underlying etiology but are the embodiment of psychological problems—somatization. While the type of somatization varies across cultures, there is agreement that it is a defined syndrome and is included as a disorder in *DSM*-5. It is therefore important for the clinician to explore the client's health status over a period of time, especially in cases where the client's physicians have not found a cause for physical symptoms. Borrowing psychiatrist Alice Miller's (2006) phrase, "The body never lies." Here's an example:

> *Cindy was struggling financially, with her mortgage and her son's college tuition. After years of verbal abuse from her parents, she asked them for a loan to refinance her house. They refused. Cindy had helped her parents through a number of health and legal problems, while her brother was "missing in action." She was so angry at the parents' refusal, she cut them off. She went on with her life without much difficulty until a few years later, when her brother, who all along sided with their parents, cut Cindy off. This time Cindy was thrown off balance. She developed many of the symptoms mentioned above, coupled with a mysterious stomach ailment that kept her in constant pain. She became a virtual recluse, unresponsive to phone calls from extended family and friends. Cindy's husband brought her to a therapist, who made the connection between her medical problems and her now total cutoff from family of origin.*

13. *When the cutoff first occurred, what was the perceived level of trauma?* Since most of the cutoffs we discuss in the book stem from frustration, hurt, and anger, the immediate response of the person cut off is quite dramatic. Clients describe feeling "nauseated," "crushed," "stabbed in the heart," and, especially if the cutoff was unexpected, "numb" or "in shock." These "gut" reactions usually wear off in a few days to weeks, but they become worrisome if they persist.

The person who cuts off may also experience shock, feel a sense of loss, and question himself or herself. The person may feel guilty at his or her behavior, wonder whether the action was justified, or harp on his or her reasons.

In any event, there is no point expecting the client to be reasonable or to look at his or her own behavior until the highly emotional period has dissipated. Meanwhile, the client needs to express the full range of emotions. Such emotions, even outbursts, become part of the clinician's assessment. And the clinician's ability to ride the waves is part of establishing a safe environment wherein the client feels that someone really hears his or her frustration and pain. Sue Johnson calls it "fostering the therapeutic alliance" (Johnson & Whiffen, 2003).

14. *What is the current level of emotional pain or trauma?* While strong reactions are normal at first, if the cutoff is old and the pain or trauma goes unmitigated, clinicians have to explore and rule out other psychological issues. If the cutoff is recent, the clinician also needs to assess whether the client might be at risk for harming himself or herself or acting out against the other—or against someone else, such as happens when a couple's argument goes out of control against a third party.

15. *Has anyone attempted to reconnect? If so, how, and what was the reaction?* The exploration of previous attempts to reconnect, as well as existing barriers or impediments, is part of the history of a cutoff. This history helps the clinician determine how to proceed and what other avenues the client could pursue. Dependent on the client's experience of the attempt, his or her emotional readiness or capacity (see #16), the clinician might help the client reassess expectations for the relationship or develop a new strategy for reconnection.

16. *How well has the client handled the cutoff?* This is similar to information sought in #15; however, there the focus is on actions, and

here it is on emotions. This is an assessment of the emotional strengths of the client, including his or her coping skills, and how any underlying mental health issue may affect his or her ability to move to next steps.

17. *How strong is the client's support system?* Obviously, if the client has a rich network of friends, relatives, and a spouse or partner, one can probably assume that he or she has social skills and the capacity for successful relationships. In these cases, the negative effect of a given cutoff may be buffered. If the client has few friends or a weak support system, this lack may mean the client has difficulty with relationships in general. In these cases, the cutoff may be experienced more intensely and may have a greater negative effect on the client's well-being.

18. *Is cutting off a pattern for the person either as initiator or recipient?* Is the cutoff a unique event in the client's life, or are cutoffs a regular part of this person's social experience? (See #19 regarding family history of cutoffs). If there is a pattern, who cut off from whom? Is the client more frequently the person who cuts off or is cut off?

When a client has a history of multiple cutoffs, clinician and client must explore the client's contribution. What are the client's needs and expectations of other people, of himself or herself? How does he or she deal with frustration or disappointment? How well does he or she express needs or feelings; or hear the needs and feelings of others? Does the person use resources or reach out to others, or is he or she passive, waiting for decisions or relationships to "happen"? The answers help make sense of the cutoffs, and the process hopefully engages the client in a quest to expand his or her proactive capacity.

As always, but especially in probing the client's contribution, the alliance formed with the client will be tested. It is wise to preface this probe with a statement like "We need to find the common thread in these cutoffs, what triggers you, sets you off, and how you might handle things differently. In no way am I—are we—looking to judge or blame you, but we need to understand in order to avoid these problems in the future. Are you okay with this?"

19. *Is it a family pattern? What other cutoffs have happened in this person's life, as participant or witness? Is this a secondary cutoff?* As clinicians we are always looking for patterns. Patterns may signal learned behaviors that limit a person's range or flexibility of responses to life

events and relationships. All families have defined patterns—some keep the door open to alternative possibilities and others do not. If the client is habituated to a certain way of being in the world, then alternative perspectives, problem-solving strategies, or actions may initially be outside his or her comprehension or repertoire. Genograms, as we have discussed, facilitate the recovery of these hidden repetitive relationship issues.

Secondary cutoffs may be a family pattern but may also be the consequence of a particular cutoff. An example of the latter is a cutoff of former spouses whose mutual antipathy and failure to communicate cascades down through the family system. This kind of split not only severs the spousal relationship but also destroys the relationship between each spouse and his or her in-laws. Following the adult child's lead, the in-laws decide or are expected to cut off from the daughter- or son-in-law. Children may be drawn in too, or one parent may succeed in alienating the children from the other one. In *We're Still Family* (2005), Ahrons shows that divorce does not have to be this way.

Many years later we may see children of these cutoff couples in therapy, long after the secondary damage is done. These clients often have significant attachment issues—having lifelong difficulty forming or sustaining intimate relationships or never marrying at all.

Noncustodial parents often enter therapy to find a way to reconnect with their children or to find a way for their children to reestablish connections with their grandparents.

20. *How motivated does the client seem about discussing the cutoff?* If the cutoff is not the presenting problem, the client may be uninterested, unmotivated, or unable to discuss it, even after it emerges during the assessment. Other matters may seem more urgent, or the client may fear that exploring the cutoff would open a Pandora's box. Connections between the client's current issues and the cutoff may be apparent or at least create a working hypothesis for us as therapists. But we need to be cautious and sensitive to where the client is in the process.

As the client delves into the presenting problem(s), we slowly introduce questions about the dynamics of his or her relationships. However, prematurely pushing the client to discuss the cutoff may backfire. Clients who are not ready may continue to attend sessions but be emotionally disengaged as a means of protection. And further, if cutting off is the only coping strategy the client has used to handle difficult feelings, he or she might cut off from therapy altogether.

21. *How interested does the client seem in a possible reconnection?* One way to further assess motivation is to ask how the client will feel if there is never any reconciliation. Down the road, would the client come to regret what might have been, for himself or herself or for other family members affected by the cutoff? Here it is important to keep the reason for the cutoff front and center, as it may have been something intolerable such as parental sexual abuse. We then have to gauge the level of closeness or intimacy that the client can tolerate. At times, while we might believe the impact of a continued cutoff would be negative, the formerly enmeshed or undifferentiated client or one with attachment issues may resist or reject the thought of reconnection. We listen not only to what the client wants, but also to what lies behind that choice.

22. *If the client seems ready and willing to explore the cutoff, what is the client's actual capacity to do the work?* Here the clinician needs to ask a series of questions. Is this client really sturdy enough to unpack the material? Is he or she able to contemplate both reconnection and the opposite letting go if attempts fail? If the clinician finds himself or herself saying "no," more preparation is needed for the client, to build his or her self-knowledge, self-esteem, or communication skill. Without adequate preparation, chances for success of any attempt at reconnection are reduced. It will also be harder for the client to recover from a failed attempt. Finally, preparatory work on the client's past helps the client reestablish the relationship from a position of strength rather than weakness.

23. *Are both cutoff parties in the room, or just the client?* The client may be ready to deal with the cutoff person, but can he or she do so without the help of the therapist, outside the therapist's office? Some clients are able to do so without prior coaching or role play; others need practice. Still others require the support or presence of the therapist, wanting the other party to join them in a session.

Generally speaking, we think that the complex, intense nature of estranged relationships warrants a "neutral" person to mediate, and luckily a few clinicians embrace this challenging work. In these triadic sessions we can facilitate the parties' speaking their minds. And, often most important, we can help them properly interpret and distinguish what is actually felt and spoken from what they thought they heard or "knew" was meant.

THE NATURE OF DISCONNECTION

Part of the assessment process is establishing the degree to which parties are currently disconnected. Cutoffs are often dynamic, changing over time. What started as emotional cooling or detachment may end in a total cutoff. To better understand the sequencing of cutoffs, possible points of intervention, and the potential for reconciliation, we have developed a continuum. As we listen to clients' descriptions of their relationships, this typology helps us analyze not only current cutoffs but also potential or incipient ones. Following are the points along the cutoff continuum:

Emotional Disconnection
This describes a relationship in which two parties once had trust and openly shared emotions but where this is no longer the case. The parties are in contact, but the intimacy is gone and the relationship has a stilted quality.

Incipient Cutoff
Individuals experience a sense of foreboding about the relationship. One individual may be more critical of the other's views or actions. He or she may threaten to cut off if some expectation is not met. There may be less contact over time. Red flags signal that problems in the relationship need to be addressed.

Partial Cutoff
Family members or friends who once sought each other's company are now emotionally disconnected or even hostile and do not initiate contact. However, when circumstances do bring them together, they are able to speak and be civil. Typical partial cutoffs can be seen with divorced parents attending a child's teacher's conference, a parent's eightieth birthday party where cutoff siblings gather to celebrate, or former friends meeting at a mutual friend's house. One of the clini-

cians we interviewed shared the story of a divorced couple who for years maintained a partial cutoff: They never spoke except that the former wife kept her ex-husband as her dentist!

Indirect Cutoff

Indirect cutoffs are those in which communication between cutoff individuals continues through a third party. Frequently, a member of the family becomes the conduit. In a child-custody case one clinician shared, separated parents spoke only through their ten-year-old daughter or their divorce mediator.

Third parties who form a bridge for cutoff individuals may themselves be drawn into the "battle." Questions of trust and loyalty emerge, as well as the potential for betrayal. In indirect cutoff cases, it is important to explore and comment on the role of and possible impact on the third party, including that one or both cutoff individuals may wind up cutting off the third party when a perceived boundary is overstepped or an expectation is not met. Finally, in some cases, to preserve his or her own emotional boundaries, the third party may actually cut off either or both individuals he or she was originally trying to help.

Temporary Cutoff

While we concentrate on the negative aspects of cutoffs, there is at least one positive benefit. Several clinicians say they suggest brief relationship respites to some clients as an emotional "time out." The breathing space allows a client to calm down, step outside the situation, "count to ten." It may also force the other person to think things through as well. Another benefit of a short-term or temporary cutoff is that it may enable the person in the "underdog" position to gain better control of self and of the relationship. "All cutoffs are painful," one therapist said, "but a temporary one can also be empowering."

The individual initiating the break must inform the other person of its purpose and temporary nature. Withdrawing without explanation leaves the other one in limbo, and the cutoff is less likely to be beneficial. An agreed-upon temporary cutoff may actually prevent a relationship from reaching the brink or the point of no return. Invoked in a civil manner, it can work wonders, especially if the time period is set in advance.

Conditional Cutoff

A conditional cutoff is one in which there is no communication, but the door is left ajar for future reconnection if—and only if—conditions change. A client imposing such a condition has to understand that the other person may never want or be able to meet the condition, and thus the cutoff may become permanent. In these cases, as mentioned previously, the clinician has to help the client assess the importance of the condition, as well as the costs and benefits of a permanent cutoff.

A client given the condition must explore feelings about it, whether it is reasonable or possible to meet the condition, as well as the pain of possibly losing the relationship. In the chapters on betrayal and principle, we will see how difficult some conditions are to swallow, but happily many conditional cutoffs do get resolved.

Preemptive Cutoff

Sometimes an individual initiates a cutoff out of fear or conviction that the other person is about to cut off; this is common in romantic relationships. One party is sure he or she will be "dumped" and to save face "bails out" first. The problem is that the prediction may be off base, and he or she may lose someone worth keeping. Or it may be right that the other person is unhappy but wrong that the relationship cannot be saved by addressing the problems. Preemptive cutoffs occur when one individual feels anxious or vulnerable. As with some temporary cutoffs, the hope is to regain control by leaving first. Let us call the preemptive cutoff a defense mechanism.

Forced or Instigated Cutoff

These cutoffs are initiated by third parties. Forced cutoffs are usually mandated by the legal system, as in orders of protection or closed adoptions. Forced or instigated cutoffs also include "parental alienation" by which an estranged (or enraged) former spouse prohibits a child from seeing the other parent in violation of the other parent's legal rights. These cases are usually secondary cutoffs but also belong here, as the following brief case illustrates:

> Leah's parents divorced when she was thirteen. Shortly after that, the mother cut off from the father completely, moved away with Leah, and told Leah her father had died. Eight years later, Leah recognized her

father on the street. Emotionally fragile to begin with, the sight of her father precipitated Leah's sudden psychotic break

In cases of domestic violence, the parental cutoff may become quite complicated. A parent, most often the mother, might file an order of protection for herself and the children, yet the children still want to maintain some connection with the other parent.

Forced cutoffs also occur when a cult requires new members to sever ties to their family of origin and prior social network. The cutoff is thrust upon the mystified recipients without their agreement, and without their understanding why. Usually, but not always, the cult disregards the best interests of the new member.

Complete Cutoff

Complete cutoffs are those in which there is absolutely no communication or interaction. With the parties given no opportunity to experience one another even in a neutral situation, complete cutoffs often become permanent. They are typically the hardest cutoffs to undo.

The media have a field day reporting on complete cutoffs of famous people: Angelina Jolie and her father Jon Voight, Bernie Madoff and his son, Casey Anthony and her father; Steve Jobs and his biological father—these are just a few examples that have filled the tabloids and mainstream newspapers in the past few years. Cutoffs are also the dramatic focus of novels, such as Leo Tolstoy's *Anna Karenina* and John Steinbeck's *East of Eden*.

Complete cutoffs tend to color and resonate throughout the lives of the individuals involved, even if they are not consciously attended to, as well as affect the lives of families and social networks. Our clinician interviewees agreed that a complete cutoff should, therefore, be only the last resort for an embittered relationship. Too often, they said, individuals in the heat of battle wreck the relationship, seeing destruction as the only way to lower their emotional temperature or regain control.

CLINICIAN SELF-REFLECTION

Our focus thus far has been on the clinician's assessment of the client, the cutoff, its impact, and other contextual issues that need to be attended to in the therapeutic process. Now we briefly look inward, at ourselves, because there is a need for self-reflection and self-assessment.

As exciting and satisfying as our work can be it, it is also difficult. At times the issues our clients bring are ones we face in our own lives—if not directly, at least tangentially. We all have less-than-positive reactions to some clients, their issues, or their behavior. We may disagree with a client's politics, worldview, or decisions. A client may stir up our own unresolved conflicts or force us to reexamine how we see the world. We constantly wrestle with these issues in order to be there for the client as he or she engages in the work.

Despite years of training and experience, however, we all still deal with insidious transference and counter-transference issues. These are the feelings, reactions, assumptions, and biases that unduly influence *our* thoughts and behavior even as we try to concentrate on, and immerse ourselves in, the client's world and try not to judge. Self-awareness and reflection are keys to avoiding transference pitfalls.

If and when transference does interfere with meeting the client's needs, we must step back, rein ourselves in, and ask if it is our discomfort or their behavior that is bothering us. If it is "them," we might share our reactions in a calm supportive way, to exemplify why others may react to him or her as they do. If it is us, our own discomfort with cutoffs, perhaps we should step further back and discuss it with a colleague, supervisor, or therapist.

As we proceed, we need to be attentive to how our own experiences with cutoffs affect our empathy for a client dealing with one. To facilitate this reflective process, we have generated the following questions for clinicians to ask themselves, as well as discuss with others:

- What are my experiences with cutoffs? Have I ever cut someone off? Has someone cut me off? How did I feel, how do I feel now, what did I do, and might I do something different now?
- Have I ever resolved a cutoff in my own life?
- Am I being vigilant that my past experience with cutoffs or my anxiety is not impeding my work with the client—that it is the client who is setting the agenda for therapy?
- Do I believe that in most cases it is crucial to resolve a cutoff?

Or do I think work on the self is sufficient, that a cutoff is not so important? Am I acting on either of these "biases" and not truly listening to how the client feels about the potential for action and change?

- For those clients who lost parents early in life through death or desertion and subsequently experienced major cutoff(s) in adulthood—am I prepared to be, at least for awhile, a surrogate parent? For clients with attachment issues, am I ready to deal with their anxieties—to be on call? A client in the midst of a major cutoff may need phone access nearly 24/7 to deal with feelings of grief, rage, and loneliness, to experience the sense of security they missed as children. Can I provide that, or is it too much?

- Do I move too quickly for clients because of my own agenda, because of my anxiety, or because I think I see the big picture? Do I accept that some clients need to take baby steps? Can I allow my client to experience a "rebirth" in his or her own time, not on my schedule?

- Do I encourage risk taking, change, or holding back? Have I helped my client say "no" as he or she needs to? Or have I taken that power away? Do I take some risks in my own life?

- How do I respond to issues of power, status, and money? Am I able to draw a boundary between the feelings that these issues engender in me and how the client perceives and responds to these hot-button topics? Do I find myself judging the client— and how is that affecting our relationship?

- How comfortable am I with the release of intense emotion, such as anger or despair? Do I quickly deflect or in some way suppress the client's expression? Whose comfort is it I am attending to, mine or the client's?

- To what degree am I comfortable with confronting or being confronted by a client? Do I generally avoid confrontation and attempt to maintain the status quo? Who were my role models for dealing with conflict or risk taking to bring about change?

- What are my religious beliefs? What are the principles by which I live my life and practice my profession? Am I basing my reactions strictly on my own value system, or am I truly listening to my client's perspective and values? Can I tolerate, even respect, a client's perspective that is very different from or even hostile to mine?

- What do I need to learn or unlearn or monitor myself about with this particular client, in this particular situation, and with respect to cutoffs in general?

We ask a lot of ourselves—but it is important to both be clear about our limitations and know when our limits have been reached. Am I comfortable working with a client who is actively discriminatory? Can I work with a parent who sexually abused his or her daughter but now wants to reconcile? Do I have space in my life to be available to a client who needs repeated reassurance and nurturance as the first step toward being able to change his or her perspective on life? If we cannot, it is important to recognize the situation and stretch ourselves to become even more empathic. Some would argue that a difficult client is sent to us for a reason, but at times the best course may be to refer the client to someone else.

The need for clinician self-reflection is certainly not specific to cutoffs, but resisting it will significantly impede one's ability to help clients handle the cutoffs in their lives. As you assess yourself and work with clients' cutoffs, we encourage discussion of the above issues with peers or a supervisor in order to be acting fully in the clients' best interest.

The next chapter looks at specific interventions we and our clinician interviewees have found helpful to clients.

Chapter 2

STRATEGIES

The best way to destroy an enemy is to make him
a friend.

Abraham Lincoln

The previous chapter focused on assessment of cutoffs. In this chapter we offer a set of strategies that we or our interviewees found helpful to clients. As clinicians, we constantly assess and reassess our actions. It is the nature of the beast. Also, as we discover our client's capacities and enter his or her world, we confirm or change our ideas about which issues to focus on, including the direction—either back to reconnection or forward to healing without it. We leave to you, the reader, the task of weaving assessment and strategies together, varying them according to client needs, along with your unique presence and use of self.

SAFETY

Therapists, like clients, get hijacked and overreact when a client thrusts a morally challenging or seemingly insoluble problem into their clinical lap. We thus start the chapter with something that seems obvious but that tends to get lost: helping the client feel safe. Even if the clinician does not identify with attachment theory per se, his or her social world and clinical work are nevertheless informed by it. A safe environment and a close bond with the clinician are especially important for clients who have experienced a major cutoff early in life. Very simply, they need to express a full range of feelings without fear of judgment or rejection.

Clients with early cutoff histories have intense feelings of frustration, sadness, and rage. They often feel injured and powerless. It is therefore crucial to communicate both verbally and nonverbally that the therapist is open to hearing what they have to say and is able to weather their emotions, whatever they may be. At times the therapist may actively press for the client's feelings when they lie unexpressed beneath the surface.

For example, when someone close dies, it is not uncommon to be angry, try though one may to suppress that feeling. Intellectually, adults know that the person did not leave or die on purpose (unless it was suicide). Yet, for some, feelings of abandonment and anger fester. Death may not be understood by children, and they may blame the person who died or themselves for their hostile feelings. A child may be called upon to take on adult responsibilities. Years later, he or she comprehends that the death was unintentional yet continue to experience hurt and anger that may be as raw as "abandonment" as a result of substance abuse, family desertion, or mental illness.

It is often helpful to normalize the client's feelings. Doing so gives the client permission to fully experience previously vague or uncomfortable feelings. By attending to and pointing out discrepancies between verbal and nonverbal behavior, the therapist also helps the client to name the feelings. Usually there is ambivalence—love and hate, or anger—that, when finally acknowledged and accepted, constitutes the first step toward healing. For clients who were not permitted to express themselves to family members or who felt judged when they did—the therapist's openness, empathy, and steadfastness provide a corrective emotional experience. Their "inner," rather than their "social," self is given space to breathe, and in the process the client achieves integration of the two.

All along the way, clinicians need to track their own level of anxiety in order not to inadvertently short-circuit the client's. They also need to monitor if and how emerging feelings, especially anger and depression, may be affecting the client's other relationships or if the client is turning them back on himself or herself. Further, his or her triggers should be explored—how he or she responds to the emotions of others and how he or she expects others to respond.

At times we suggest that clients do "homework," usually writing exercises to help them track their emotions. We ask them to keep a journal noting all emotions that surface during the day, as well as the thoughts or situations preceding the emotions. Further, we ask clients to record what they did when they felt a particular emotion. What did they experience when someone else expressed an emotion—either directly toward them or toward someone else in a work, social, or family situation? We have found that journaling enhances the client's self-awareness. It allows emotions to be labeled and to be fully experienced even if not fully expressed, simultaneous to helping the clients gain control over the behavioral expression of volatile emotions.

If anger is a recurrent problem, we work on how to manage it better or suggest that the client seek additional help. The web has an array of anger management resources, books, and courses. Within the clinical session we use some of the steps outlined by the Mayo Clinic (n.d.):

- Breathe deeply, take time out.
- Collect your thoughts—think before you act or speak.
- Use "I" statements versus "you" statements.
- Express frustration without being hurtful.
- Be as specific as possible.
- Identify possible solutions.
- Use humor but not sarcasm to break tension.

In addition, we suggest relaxation techniques, yoga, and meditation to improve and promote general well-being. There are a host of approaches to be culled from the literature, many a blend of Eastern and Western traditions. We will suggest a few resources when we return to this topic in Chapter 8. We also strongly encourage clients to exercise regularly, which we now know greatly improves both physiological and emotional well-being (Weir, 2011).

At times, when a client is emotionally fragile, dealing with intense feelings or without a support network, we offer additional sessions and make ourselves available by phone, as needed. Our accessibility affirms the client's experience and confirms that he or she is not alone, not existing solely in our 50-minute time slot. For some this will be akin to reparenting. For clients who have a strong urge to beg, berate, or scream at the cutoff person, we buy them time to calm down with a distracting instruction to call someone else or us instead. In the next session we discuss the impulse and delaying tactic with the client, which usually relieves the underlying pressure.

CLIENT SELF-REFLECTION

Since the likelihood of changing the other person cannot be guaranteed, we focus on emotional and behavioral changes the client can make (Sichel, 2004). These may include developing or refining the client's capacity for self-reflection, increasing problem solving skills, achieving a better understanding of his or her own needs and limits, and enhancing his or her ego functions. The goal is the client's sense of "effectance" (White, 1959).

A genogram is helpful not only for assessment but also as a way to ease into a discussion of the client's family, including cutoffs. We look for patterns in terms of expectations, behaviors, and emotional connections. Even if these probes do not directly relate to the cutoff, discussing them stimulates the client's thoughts about how he or she interacts with others and how others have reacted to him or her. Examining how parents or other primary caregivers treated the person—socialized him or her to specific types of behaviors and responses, helps the client see how early experiences shaped his or her subsequent behavior and current problems.

With our support the client now has an opportunity to move out of habitual patterns and adopt new ways of interacting with others. Obviously, for clinicians drawn to the more "modern" theories that minimize the importance of the past and intergenerational work, the genogram is perhaps less useful.

In any case, where the client has few solid relationships with family members or others, this sort of exploration usually clarifies what stands in the way. In essence, we ask the client to look in the mirror and see his or her role in, and possible contribution to, the overall success or failure of his or her relationships, and not just in the actual cutoff:

- What mistakes did the client make in past relationships?
- Have expectations been too high, or assumptions incorrect?
- Did the client recognize that someone could hurt him or her, yet stayed in, or even pursued a relationship?
- Has the client tried to understand the perspective of others?
- Has the client been too self-absorbed or unavailable for serious relationships?
- Has the client depended too much on the other person to shape his or her life or make decisions?

Asking these kinds of questions helps identify the client's typical behavior, how the client perceives others, and how he or she relates in the world.

Individuals with a poor relationship history may not realize they have come to see us about cutoffs, passively referring to their latest loss as "just one of those things." But at times, it is the primacy and uniqueness of a lost relationship that precipitates the individual's call for help. If the cutoff is part of a pattern in the client's family or in his or her own life, the work will focus in on issues of attachment and early relationships with parents or other caregivers.

Clients with low self-esteem may have sabotaged prior relationships. In these cases, we help them identify and label strengths, coping strategies, and resources that were not recognized, acknowledged, or supported in the past. We then discuss how these can be amplified and employed to even better use going forward.

This work segues into helping the client define acceptable behavior on his or her part as well as on the part of others—for example, violation of ethics or principles, abusive behaviors. The client's elasticity of patience and his or her levels of tolerance are also explored. Clinicians told us they often encourage clients to expand their social circle and to engage or reengage in community or professional activities that provide opportunities to meet new like-minded people. Ideally their choices help them achieve some social status and recognition, such as serving on a community board of directors, volunteering at a homeless shelter, or becoming a church deacon.

If the client is mentally ill and has few or no solid relationships apart from us, we coax him or her to explore available community resources. Isolated clients often have multiple needs. In that case, we connect them with a community agency that either provides or will help them acquire a range of services, such as housing, transitional employment, financial assistance, and educational opportunities.

Helping clients identify and maintain certain limits and boundaries is another critical aspect of our work. Regardless of the cutoff outcome, if a client does not have sufficient boundaries, he or she will always have difficulty protecting his or her interests, avoiding being taken advantage of, and ultimately staying in an otherwise healthy relationship.

We also want to know whether the client puts up too many barriers to forming relationships. We therefore engage in a dialogue about what tends to transpire with his or her relationships, both those that have worked well and those that have not. We ask the client to speculate why some succeeded and why others, including the cutoff, failed. What lessons can be drawn from the comparison? In retrospect, what might have been done differently to prevent the cutoff?

If there was parental child abuse, it is critical to clarify what was and was not in the client's control. If mental illness was or is present in any past or current relationship, we explain the limitations of volition. Clinicians know that clients often feel responsible way beyond what is realistic in a relationship with someone who is mentally ill. Guilt is common—and must be addressed. The establishment of boundaries and affirmation that the client is not culpable for "deeds" of the other can do wonders for the client. The following phrase often settles the matter: "You did not cause the problem, but you can make it better or you can make it worse."

CAUSES

Now we come to the history of the relationship. How did the parties meet? What drew the client to the other person, and what did he or she enjoy about the relationship? In situations with family members, the focus is on both good and bad experiences the client had with the cutoff individual. We then explore what the client believes caused the cutoff and the reason, if any, the other person gave.

Clients often identify one reason, only to discover that the "alleged" cause was, in fact, only the top layer in a Pandora's box. Such discovery happens when we push the client to generate alternative reasons the other person might have cut off, changed in some way, behaved badly, or provoked the client. For example what was the other person dealing with that made him or her act that way, was it a change in life situation, transference from an earlier poor relationship, poor health, or even mental illness status or addiction? The list of alternatives could be endless.

In cases in which there is mental illness or substance abuse, the clinician may take on an educational role, helping the client understand the nature of the disease, the effects on the family, and the frequent lack of control the individual may experience. Comprehension of the other's capacities is not to negate their impact on the client or to excuse them, but to help place the other one's behavior in context, and thereby remove it from the realm of a personal rejection of the client. In effect, it becomes depersonalized. The enhanced reality testing shifts the client's expectation and improves his or her capacity to assess what the other individual is capable of, thus changing expectations for the future as well as helping explain the past.

If the cutoff is related to a perceived or actual violation of a client's principle, we gradually shift the focus away from the principle and toward an exploration of what may lie underneath. First with the client, and if possible later in a joint session with the cutoff party, we support the integrity of both parties' choices. For example, in a cutoff over a young client's cross-country move, one of our clients asserted that his parents were "way too controlling, making me feel guilty for asserting my individual rights, my personal freedom." The parents were holding fast to another principle, which was "Family comes first. We stay together, no matter what." Supporting the client's right while simultaneously reframing the parents' "controlling behavior" as a value with considerable merit respects both parties, which is prerequisite to starting family sessions and finding middle ground or compromise. Additionally, since both parties are right and no one is wrong, and both are supported by the clinician, they are more often willing to see the other's point of view and reconcile.

Some clients enter therapy to deal with a cutoff from a parent. This sometimes happens as a result of the parents' contentious divorce. The custodial parent is said to have badmouthed the other, provided false information, withheld positive information, or hidden or thrown away letters to or from the child, all to destroy the child's attachment to the other parent. The estranged parent may have tried to stay connected or reconnect and, having failed, placed blame on the child. Or, the estranged parent feels he or she should have done more to keep or restore the connection.

Though we have included one case that supports a claim of "parental alienation syndrome," as proposed by Richard Gardner (1985/1998), from our perspective it is unlikely that "PAS" is the sole or perhaps even primary cause of cutoffs between parents and children in divorce cases. Despite the growing literature and debate about whether it is a legitimate diagnosis, it is not recognized by and thus does not appear in *DSM-5*. However, there is an oblique code in the *DSM 5* for a "child affected by parental relationship distress" that refrains from placing blame on either parent.

As always, and especially when working with such sad histories, it is imperative to avoid the easy trap of joining the client in castigating the absent parent. Rather, the therapist needs to affirm the client's experience, to confirm the impact, as well as help the client take a deep breath and step back to consider what went on for everyone. This is not to suggest that alienating or abusive parents' actions are acceptable. Certainly not, but if we too quickly label them toxic, we risk short-circuiting a potential reconnection and an opportunity for the client to receive an apology.

We and some of the clinicians we interviewed have worked with clients who were verbally, physically, or sexually abused as children. In these cases we all strongly affirm that the client was not responsible, that responsibility lay with the adult(s) and, in some cases, with legal authorities who did not properly respond. If the child was removed from the household and never understood why, we explain it was probably because he or she needed to be protected. Of course, here we want to learn how the child experienced relocation, which may have been for protection but was experienced as betrayal or abandonment.

Once an adult client understands that as a child he or she had no control over what was decided for him or her, the client is empowered to make a choice: "to reconnect or not to reconnect" with an estranged parent, even with one who abused him or her.

At times, the therapeutic aim is to develop the client's capacity to view the past relationship from multiple vantage points, including different cultural contexts. To what degree did past socialization limit the client's worldview or expectation of others? Here we might introduce the notion of different relationship intensities. By this we mean that some relationships, while still worth the effort, are simply bound to be or are better when they are more limited in scope. In this regard, we have a good and humorous example in President Obama's remark on CNN that he "likes" former President Clinton "in small doses"!

Traditional cognitive therapy techniques (CBT) may also be helpful at this point, including teaching the client to generate alternative explanations and shifting (if not restructuring) perceptions of the situation and the other person (Dattilio & Nichols, 2011). New research in CBT suggests the value of separating the problem from the client's reactions to the problem and using mindfulness and acceptance strategies in addition to more classical CBT (see Arch et al., 2012; National Association of Cognitive-Behavioral Therapists, n.d.)

We also work on the client's ability to handle disagreement and conflict. Can the client live with a lack of agreement? An unaccusatory "why or why not?" is the question. Why must the other person agree on this or that point? If at this juncture the therapist supports the legitimacy of the client's view (that is the strategy here), it often almost miraculously gives the client clarity about his or her own views and allows him or her to stay friends with people whose views are not entirely "simpatico."

At the same time, we work on problems of tolerating ambiguity or uncertainty in which the client feels he or she must either know what is going to happen or will precipitate a cutoff. This inevitably circles us back to the client's early experience, to unsafe times when basic needs were not reliably met. Problems with ambiguity may also signal borderline characteristics or a borderline personality disorder. In these cases especially, clinicians' attention to ambiguity is important not only to help the client understand and perhaps fix the cutoff but also for the client's potential to have other solid relationships in the future.

Finally, we look for red flags that may have been present but that the client did not recognize. While this retrospective endeavor may be difficult, even embarrassing, the effort is worthwhile for the client to understand that the cutoff did not appear out of the blue. Further, this process increases the client's observational power and stimulates the development of a broader repertoire of responses to defuse or prevent cutoffs.

IMPACT

The impact of a cutoff may be more far reaching than is initially obvious to client or clinician. It may lead to other cutoffs and stunt an individual's social or psychological development. As we said in the Preface, often unbeknownst even to the client, the cutoff may have made him or her literally sick. Therefore, before the client can truly decide about reconciliation, our role is to help him or her consider the short- and long-term impact of the cutoff on his or her life.

At times, given the cause and nature of the cutoff, we must affirm the client's reactions and normalize them. This, as we pointed out earlier in another context, is especially critical in cases of abuse, and it may also be true in cases of betrayal. To help the client process the experience, we need to "bear witness" to what they have gone through. We have to understand how the client's life has been altered—what he or she suffered or lost as a result of the cutoff. To what extent did it leave the client anxious, or unable to trust? Does the client feel guilty and therefore withdraw from other relationships? Does the client feel diminished, thus unworthy to seek new relationships? Did the client cut off to regain a sense of self, where previously he or she was too submissive? Or did the client fear that a cutoff by the other person was imminent? Better to cut off, then be cut off? Our examination includes not the just the "residual" emotions, but also how they became embedded and transformed into behaviors and expectations.

NEXT STEPS

Next we suggest that the client analyze short- and long-term costs and benefits of restoring the relationship with the cutoff person. On what scale can they be weighed? Here we help the client begin to take charge. He or she decides which option is in his or her own best interest. This consideration comes first, but does the client also want, or need, to be concerned about the impact of the cutoff on other family members, on the next generation, or its resonance in the community? Can he or she balance care of self with a legitimate need to "protect" others? Or, in other circumstances, can a client see that "once again" he or she is being expected to be the "better person," when no one else ever took the high ground?

Before taking even baby steps to reach out, the client needs to be clear as to the reasons for reconciliation. Is it simply because the client misses the person? Has the original "issue" paled over time compared to the loss of the relationship? Is the reconciliation for the sake of someone else, such as a parent whose dying wish is for the children to reconcile? Is the reconciliation to regain an inheritance? Or is the attempt actually a desire to prove its impossibility?

We help the client closely examine the residual wounds—the anger, pain, sadness of the cutoff—and ask whether these can be overcome, or are they too painful and thus necessitate a lasting barrier to reconciliation? Surely if it seems over time that the client is only going to be hurt again, if the hurt is too likely to be ongoing, we advise the client to proceed with caution or draw the line.

What does the client want or expect from the renewed relationship? Is it the same degree of closeness as before, or a different level but still a sense of connection? Regardless of the past degree of intimacy, the client needs to recognize that the former relationship may not be replicated, ever, but especially not at the beginning of reconnection. Is the client able to accept the fact that the other person has limitations or may not be able to change? The need to at least be respected is often the sine qua non for both parties, if the renewed · relationship is to have a chance.

Clearly, the client needs to determine if he or she is willing to accommodate change. What could the client do differently or better? If the client has imposed "requirements" or conditions, is he or she ready to negotiate until both parties feel satisfied? Is the client ready to consider meeting a condition that he or she may have previously rejected? Can the client predict the outcome if he or she decides not to bend or comply?

We often have to remind a client that the other person may not be equally motivated to end a cutoff or even be ready to explore the possibility. Despite the client's best effort, an overture toward reconciliation might not even be acknowledged.

So far our discussion has been geared to the client who wants to reach out. What about the client who rejects the idea of initiating or responding to an offer from the other party? In both situations the task is to identify the barrier. It could be fear of further rejection. It could be, as mentioned earlier, that the insult or incident was too horrific—that there is no action or material exchange that could begin to compensate, and thus no possible restitution. Or, despite wanting to end the cutoff, the client may still be too fragile and afraid he or she will be unable to hold his or her own in the relationship, and will feel worse for the effort.

At this juncture we reexamine our own biases about the importance of reconciliation. As we stated in the preface, for us and for most clinicians the ideal is to move the client toward reconciliation except in cases of abuse or likelihood of future damage. One clinician even stated, "A formal rejection or cutoff of an important person in one's life is in effect splitting off a part of yourself . . . to be whole, there needs to be continuity between past and present." Nonetheless, a few of our clinicians minimized the importance of reconciliation and opined that it was probably best to leave the question of reconciliation up to time and happenstance.

Regardless of their stance, all clinicians agreed that helping the client heal and regain a positive sense of self are paramount. And all agreed on how important it is to move slowly, to discourage choice or action until the client truly processes his or her emotions and examines the cutoff from multiple perspectives. We would add that while it may be terribly difficult for the client to accept or reestablish contact, keeping the door open is critical. Can the client imagine a future without any form of reconnection? Will he or she one day look back and see a missed opportunity? This is especially important if the estrangement is with someone who is ill or elderly. We like to share stories (without identifiers) of other people who experienced a similar cutoff or decision point. These stories help the client see multiple options and different ways to respond to a cutoff.

However, at the end of the day, it is the client's decision as to the next steps. We are only there to listen, support, encourage, advise, and when needed, figuratively hold their hand.

COLD FEET

Even when the client clearly desires reconciliation and seems prepared, he or she may suddenly get cold feet. We encounter resistance and the process stalls. The client realizes or "knows" that the other person will not agree to speak or meet. Perhaps the client is not quite ready. Perhaps the client is prescient and his or her assessment of the possibilities is more accurate than ours. If so, the completion of preparatory work has to involve acceptance of a low probability of success. Or, perhaps the resistance is simply last-minute fear of change, of moving off the position the client took at the time of the cutoff, a position from which he or she may derive secondary gains. If so, we can only help pinpoint the locus of reluctance and emphasize that one cannot truly know the outcome until the risk is taken and the other person accepts or spurns the client's reaching out.

We cannot leave this section without a reminder to check our own biases and possible agenda in favor of reconciliation to see if we have pushed the client too fast or too hard. If the client is unable or unwilling, the work focuses on, or returns to, other issues the client has identified. He or she may be more prepared to pursue rapprochement at a later time.

If, however, the client's resistance arises strictly from fear of taking the first step alone, we raise the possibility of a go-between (see below, or offer to help with the first approach or first meeting (also see below).

INITIATING CONTACT

Once a client is really ready, the work focuses on the best way to reach out, steps after the initial outreach, and the possibility of either success or failure of the attempt to reconnect.

At this phase of the work, it is essential that we be alert to the client's potential to sabotage his or her own efforts. This is different from "cold feet." People with a history of major disappointment or cutoffs often engage in self-fulfilling prophecies. To combat this tendency, we direct attention to the possibility. At every step we reexamine the client's expectations and the possible benefits if the reconciliation does not happen exactly as anticipated or as painstakingly planned. By having the client verbalize his or her expectations, fears, and anxieties, we assist him or her in setting more realistic goals for the initial contact.

We help the client generate possible positive or negative reactions from the cutoff individual and discuss how the client might react to each. Returning to our prior work with the client, we focus on the client's Achilles' heel and the triggers that may cause the client to give a flippant response or to lose his or her cool. Above all, we encourage the client to move slowly and buy time to think.

Another useful strategy at this juncture is having the client imagine the rejection and decide how he or she might handle it in the moment. The client can also plan how to soothe the hurt if the rejection is total, and move forward.

There is no recipe to guarantee success. However, in our conversations with clinicians, a consensus emerged. All agreed it was critical that subsequent to any approach, the other party needs private time to consider what is being asked or offered. Email and letters were most frequently mentioned as the best methods. At the same time there was some difference of opinion about a letter versus an email. Some clinicians felt a letter would be too formal; others were concerned that an email would be too informal, blocked, or lost in an avalanche of incoming email or spam.

All agreed that a phone call should be avoided. They observed that suddenly hearing the voice of someone from whom one has been cut off can be a shock, causing anger or confusion. Without the anticipatory work the client has engaged in, the estranged individual is on the spot, expected to give an immediate response. Clients report that the phone was slammed down. Others have shared that before they can say much, they are dismissed with a "don't ever call me again." In contrast, an email or letter gives the person a chance to collect his or her thoughts and time to consider how he or she really wants to respond.

But what should be said in the email or letter? Less tends to be more. The initial letter is not to rehash the past, to explain, or to ask for an explanation. Instead, the communication should simply put forth the client's wish to reconnect. Possible ways to express it are as follows:

"It is so long since we have been in touch, and I miss you in my life."
"We went separate ways a few years ago, but I often think about you and would like a chance to reconnect."
"X happened to me and it feels strange not to share it with you.

So even though there has been silence between us, I want to let you know."

"Since X died, I realize life is too short. I miss you and would welcome a chance to speak and possibly reconnect."

The emphasis is on reconnection, not on questions or accusations. The other person is only being asked to consider speaking—no commitment, just opening the door part way.

In some cases, even if one is not "friended" or is without a direct link, social media engines provide access to some information about the estranged person. The client may decide to use a posted event as a "hook": "I saw the adorable photos of your daughter's twins on Facebook. I would love to hear about them and also share recent photos of my grandchild. It has been too long. Can we meet for coffee?"

If the situation warrants it—as with significant illness—the client might suggest meeting "not necessarily or only for ourselves, but for the sake of X and the family as a whole."

Ritual occasions and celebrations, such as the wedding of a mutual friend or relative, are other opportunities to test the waters. The function acts as a protective umbrella during which casual conversations can take place and the parties can sense if they are ready to meet one on one. Social functions provide distractions and opportunities to gracefully drift off or drop the conversation, if need be.

Further, a cultural or religious event might be used to actually facilitate reconnection. For instance, before the Jewish New Year celebration, Rosh Hashanah, members of the faith are expected to mend fences, leaving grudges of the past year behind. Reconciliation is thus built into the social fabric of the community. Subscription to this practice can provide an almost automatic reentry into the fold without the need to resolve underlying issues—to let bygones be bygones and start anew.

Regardless of the strategy, clients must know that their first overture may be rebuffed, that they may have to try again, and perhaps again. Each time the estranged person rejects the overture, the client has to process the rejection and entertain the possibility of waiting some time before again reaching out. Depending on the particular cutoff situation, we have suggested the client write a note restating his or her wish to reconnect, but noting that if this is not the time, the door is open.

In cases of family estrangements, including those involving cults, an effective strategy is to have the client write a note or notes over time to the cutoff individual in the cult simply stating that the door is always open and they are always welcome to return home: "I will always care about you and love you."

If the estranged person responds positively, the way the client handles the next step is critical. The work is now focused on keeping the door open, helping the client control his or her expectations. In some situations it is best to begin with a series of emails or letters to update the other person about what has transpired in his or her absence. In others, a series of short phone calls can serve the same purpose. Seeing each other too quickly may raise anxiety, causing the other person to cut off again, necessitating restarting the process from scratch.

If multiple attempts fail or a seemingly definitive rejection occurs, an intermediary can be helpful.

INTERMEDIARIES

A client may be too afraid to initiate contact because the cutoff was so dramatic or so painful that an out-of-the-blue letter from the client would likely cause immediate rejection. In some cases, a third party can work miracles. However, the decisions as to whether to use a third party and whom to ask must be made carefully, or the intervention can actually perpetuate or seal the cutoff for good.

The third party must be as neutral as possible. He or she may have been affected indirectly by the cutoff, but it cannot be anyone who was triangulated into the cutoff relationship or who is perceived by the client or the other party as having taken sides. In this regard, most children, even as adults, are not the ones to serve as intermediaries, though later they may help restore contact between the parents by their testimony of the impact of the cutoff.

Further, it is important to assess if a potential go-between could benefit or lose by his or her involvement in the situation, especially if rapprochement fails. Will he or she gain or lose status in the family system or social network? Can he or she withstand pressure—subtle or explicit—to take sides? In addition, it is important to gauge if the go-between will be able to step aside after brokering the initial contact or meeting and not get enmeshed in the actual work of reconciliation.

PREPARING FOR THE FIRST MEETING

Clinicians talked about the importance of preparation for the first meeting, including attention to the client's communication style and his or her observational skills. Clients often use declarative statements or ones that contain embedded meanings or assumptions. They may mishear or misinterpret what the other person said or assume an intent that is incorrect, resulting in new misunderstandings. To improve communication, clinicians can help clients develop the skill of asking clarifying questions. Role play and the Gestalt's "empty chair" exercise are effective means to develop clients' skills, "checking out" what has been said and intended. In the safety of the therapist's office, the client can observe when and how he or she makes assumptions, leaps to conclusions, or tends to interrupt. The client enhances his or her capacity to self-observe and observe others, resulting in more effective assessments prior to action.

In addition, therapists work with clients to enhance or expand their ability to advocate for themselves. The clinician may choose to give the client homework assignments to practice self-advocacy. For instance, the therapist might suggest that the client ask to move to a different table at a restaurant, or tell someone who interrupts them that he or she had not finished speaking.

In addition, the clinician may suggest that the client look at websites or books on assertiveness training. The client can engage friends or family in an exercise from the '60s called "the line." A hypothetical case is developed, such as returning a pair of shoes 31 days after they were purchased. Four people form a line, with each one offering an increased level of resistance to the client's request. The first person is relatively friendly and accommodating, while the last is demeaning and hostile. The client has to convince each one that the shoe return should be accepted. At the end of each step down the line, people on the line and any other observers provide feedback on what worked and what did not, and offer suggestions to improve performance on the next try. The client repeats each step until he or she gets it right. This game can also be enacted with the therapist playing all four parts with increasing levels of difficulty.

Part of preparing clients is alerting them to the possibility, however slight, that the other party may get cold feet and not show up. This is not a wasted opportunity, because it gives the therapist—and client—a chance to see if the client takes the no-show personally or weathers it well. Will the prospect of a no-show or an actual no-show hijack the client, or will he or she be able to step back and ponder the reasons it could have happened other than the person thwarting him or her once again?

In any case, before the client schedules the first meeting, he or she may need a support person or support system in place. Who, besides the therapist, can be a phone call away if the meeting does not go well? Is there enough backup to support the client through disappointment or new waves of anger? Can the identified support people tolerate a period of ups and downs as the client tries to reengage the cutoff person—or, equally important, celebrate with the client if things go well?

SETTING UP THE FIRST MEETING

In most cases the first meeting should take place in a neutral location like a quiet café or restaurant. Having other people around dilutes the intensity and allows the parties to focus out, observe others, and have useful distractions if the conversation falters. Having coffee, breakfast, or a casual lunch is probably better than dinner. Each is usually shorter, less formal, and easier to exit should either party become too uncomfortable and want to leave.

Along with deciding the location, it is important to frame the conversation, ideally in advance. The following statement is usually sufficient: "Let's just spend some time together, talk about other things, and not discuss what happened, at least not right away." Such an agreement allows the parties to gradually take each other's emotional temperature. Based on that reading, each can decide how much to reveal, share, or say.

THE FIRST MEETING

Interestingly, our clinicians differed on how best to start, with two schools of thought. First, "Don't discuss the issues that caused the rift, just move on from there, start fresh. Especially when the cutoff is long-standing, this approach is probably preferable. Over time, perspectives can change about the cutoff, and one or both individuals may have adopted new priorities about what is truly important. Some clients support this view saying that it was not necessary or even helpful to look back at the schism.

Some of our clinicians believe that clients should not skip past the hurt feelings. Rather, they should address them with the other party before moving to rebuild. Both parties need to be assuaged with apologies and kind words to genuinely facilitate reconnection and pave the way to a renewed richer and deeper relationship.

Just as we began this chapter discussing the need to establish a safe environment, we believe the first meeting between the cutoff parties needs to do the same. Therefore, we advise clients not to broach or discuss underlying issues at the first face-to-face meeting. The cutoff has been difficult and painful for each party, although not necessarily at equal levels. In most cases the client will not yet know how the other person feels or thinks about the cutoff. The client has spent time working on the issues associated with the cutoff, but the other person may not have done similar preparatory work. The estranged person may thus not be ready or able to discuss the issues without heating up. If the client jumps in too quickly, and starts off the first meeting with something on the order of "I understand that you were jealous of me, and I've forgiven you," it may actually backfire, put the other person on the defensive, and short-circuit the rapprochement.

In general, the first meeting should probably stay clear of the tensions that led to the rift. Let the parties catch up on events and activities in their lives and reminisce about the good times shared prior to the cutoff. If things go well, we then suggest planning a joint activity, something that they will enjoy now or that they previously enjoyed together. This experience hopefully creates a positive new foundation to build on for future meetings.

Yes, after the drama and intensity of the cutoff, the first meeting as described here may seem superficial. However, the underlying agenda is only to establish that the client wants the other person back in his or her life and to engage with the person to explore that potential.

CLINICAL SUPPORT

At times, given the intensity of the emotions around the cutoff, the history of the relationship, or the potential impact of the cutoff on one or both individuals, the clinician's office becomes the location of choice for rapprochement. In this context, the clinician acts as a facilitator or mediator who can help all parties express themselves fully and effectively and lessen the chance of volatility.

Even today, some people are leery about therapists and the therapeutic process. Therefore, requesting that an estranged individual attend a therapy session may raise anxiety or resistance. The non-client may assume the client has the advantage, with the therapist having intimate knowledge of the client. The non-client might wonder if client and clinician will gang up on him or her. If the invitation clearly states that the session is an opportunity to explore the possibility of reconnection, not to fix blame or focus on reasons for the cutoff, the non-client's concern may be reduced. Further, the invitation can suggest that the estranged individual bring someone with him or her to sit in the room as an ally. This strategy may defuse the individual's sense that the session will be lopsided in favor of the client. However, it needs to be clear that this additional person is not expected to be an active participant.

For inviting the estranged individual, we sometimes offer the following to clients as a template to use or adapt:

> As you may know, I am in therapy to deal with my issues. I have worked through them to a point where I realize how much I miss you being in my life. I would like to reconnect but feel I need some help to do so. I therefore would very much like it if you would come to one or more sessions with me. My therapist will help us explore if and how we can move beyond our estrangement. Will you agree to join me? I very much hope so.

It is important that the client communicates that he or she is the client and that coming to the session does not reflect anything about the other person's mental health. Still, people get anxious about what they are signing on for, so it's best to suggest a limited number of sessions: "Let's meet once and see how it goes, though we may need two or three sessions to work things out."

If the client is unable to do the outreach because of anxiety or emotional fragility, the therapist might reach out to the estranged individual on the client's behalf:

I am X's therapist. We have been working together and he has tackled many issues. One outstanding issue is the loss of you in his life. He would like to meet with you, share how important you are to him and how much he would like to reconnect. He realizes that what took place between you was difficult and painful, but he hopes that you would agree to a meeting with him in my office. I will be there to support both of you as you explore the possibilities. It would mean so much to X if you would agree to come.

In situations of family estrangement, we may suggest that someone else in the family come to the initial meeting with the client. It can be someone who has an ongoing relationship with both the client and the estranged family member, or it can be someone else the client feels can help facilitate the reconnection, even if he or she has previously taken a side in the cutoff.

Finally, in certain cases, a client may be willing to have the estranged person meet with the therapist alone first to tell his or her side of the story. This can work when there is solid trust between client and therapist, and when this is the only way the estranged person is willing to consider reconnection.

FIRST APPOINTMENT

When initial meetings between estranged individuals take place in a clinician's office, the first thing that needs to be explicitly stated is that the clinician is not there to take sides or judge but rather to facilitate the communication, observe, and at times reflect back what is taking place. For openers, the clinician must explicitly state that the estranged person is brave to have come. It speaks to his or her interest in making things better, even though the outcome is, for the time being, unknown. Further, it is also important to state that the person's presence is not understood to mean that he or she agrees about the nature or cause of the cutoff, or about ending it.

We want to be aware of the comfort level of the estranged person and whether he or she feels that his or her interests are also being considered. We ask the person at the outset to let us know if he or she is uncomfortable in any way. The same is done with our client, because this situation is similarly tense for him or her. This is critical if we want to prevent an abrupt departure of either party.

If, however, the estranged person leaves early or refuses to return, it is imperative that the client or the therapist reach out again. Ask what happened that caused the retreat, and find out whether anything can be done to enable the individual to return to the session or continue a dialogue with the client outside a session.

In an ideal situation where a one-way mirror is available, we have found it helpful to meet with each of the individuals first, while the other individual observes from behind the mirror. Exploring what each individual wants out of the meeting and his or her interest in either reconnection or closure without the physical presence of the other person can free up the expression of feelings and allow the observing person to take in what is said without having to respond immediately.

The assumption of the conjoint session is that each has agreed to come and each wants something to happen—even if it is just testing out one or the other possibility. The clinician therefore initially asks questions, and the flow of conversation is back and forth with the clinician, à la Bowen. That is, the individuals do not directly address one another but can hear what the other is saying.

Next, we ask each individual to speak directly to the other and reminisce—to summon up good memories of the relationship, stories from the past they can share and enjoy. The clinician then asks what was lost by being apart. Attention here is focused less on what happened than its resonance in each person's life. As in couple therapy, the clinician asks each individual what he or she heard the other say and his or her reactions. The question is delicate because we cannot ask either person to agree or disagree with what the other person said, or commit to the same desire or perspective. As relevant, the prompts might be any of the following:

"Did you know that X felt so bad about the cutoff?"
"Did you know that X wanted to reconnect all these years but was afraid to approach you?"
"What is it like for you to hear that X wants you back in his or her life?"
"What have you missed about being apart?"
"What do you think happened to split you apart?
"Why do you think he or she was so hurt or angry about what happened?"
"What might you be willing to do to help repair the rift?"

The strategy is to have each party respond separately to the clinician and not the other party in the room. The clinician needs to listen to the content of the responses and to the underlying emotions that are engendered. The clinician may detect a contradiction between what is being said and the emotion expressed by voice or body. It is important to point out these mixed signals, as they reflect natural ambivalence each party is bound to feel about the other and about reconnection. Reflecting back the contradictions between content and affect can also help each party realize that he or she is giving mixed signals and become more aware of the ambivalence.

If the communication thus far in the session conveys a mutual willingness to move on, the therapist can encourage more free flow. The only essential ground rule is that no one is allowed to judge the actions of the other—just to describe them and the ways in which those actions were hurtful. We explain that judgment will only trigger a defensive response and start a destructive cycle in which nothing good happens. We also remind the parties of the basic "I" statement rule. Compare the first couple of comments with the second set, and consider what may result:

"You hurt me so much when you did xyz."
"You were so self-involved, you didn't care what I thought or felt."

versus

"I felt hurt when such and such happened."
"It really upset me that I didn't feel heard."

As the exchange begins, the clinician listens carefully to the choice of words each person uses, as different communication styles (kinetic, auditory, or visual) may be an underlying issue separate from a specific reason for the cutoff. For example, someone who uses kinetic language might not understand if the other person responds with visual language: "I was really *moved* by what Y did, but you seemed not to care." While the second individual responds with, "Yes, I *saw* what happened and it also upset me." The clinician needs to point out these different speech patterns and how they may be misinterpreted.

The actual exchange can be prompted by the clinician asking:

"So, what did you learn that you did not know?"
"What surprised you about what you heard X say?"

Depending on the pace of the first session, the work then turns to mediating a dialogue between the two individuals, giving each individual a chance to share his reactions to what the other said to the clinician about the cutoff and the hurt or anger it engendered.

The goal is not to have the parties agree about the event or issue, although that might occur. Rather, the goal is for the individuals to reach an understanding about the impact of the event or issue on each of them. The parties may apologize for having caused hurt without mentioning specifics or may reach an agreement to drop the past and start over. Or, they may agree to disagree, after acknowledging that their actions obviously caused hurt or anger. They might apologize for the hurt, and ask, "How can we move on?"

In many cases, the acknowledgment of impact is all the other individual needs and wants. In most cases, what happened in the past cannot be undone. The question thus becomes how the person who caused the "hurt" can demonstrate that he or she realizes the impact of his or her behavior or decision, and how it may have resonated beyond their relationship—e.g., early parental abandonment, abuse, or betrayal affecting the person's ability to engage and to sustain other relationships.

We indicate that we know an acknowledgment cannot undo the damage itself but that it can enable the affected individual to experience validation of his or her humanity and feelings.

Frequently some type of action or reparation is asked for or expected. It may be material or symbolic. Exploring what is possible or not possible is important within the session in order not to introduce a new set of issues or misunderstandings. If money was involved in the original dispute, it may be gone and that problem therefore impossible to correct. There may be only one family heirloom that two children care about. We will discuss these issues more in specific cases in the chapters that follow. Suffice it to say here that it is essential to explore ways to compensate the aggrieved party.

Whatever is decided by the individuals, it will be important to review each individual's understanding of what, how, and when the reparation(s) will be provided and then schedule some follow-up to be sure that what was agreed on was actually implemented. We have found, however, that the reparations matter less than the sincerity, acknowledgment, and emotional accessibility that foster a renewed connection. We thus encourage clinicians to focus as much or more on the emotional versus the material aspect of the reparations process.

Much of this conjoint work involves identifying interactional patterns that resulted in misunderstandings and stymied problem solving. It also means unearthing unexpressed vulnerable feelings and the emotional content beneath statements. Here our role is to help each individual clearly express feelings and needs in a way that enables the other person to truly hear them. We encourage slowing down to clarify meaning and feeling behind statements. This slow, seemingly drawn out back and forth fosters deeper more effective communication, even if the parties never actually agree. It is about enhanced "attunement" (Siegel, 2010a) that can help individuals move away from objectifying the other toward experiencing him or her as a person, akin to Martin Buber's "I-Thou" relationship (Buber, 1923/1958).

THE THERAPIST'S EDUCATION ROLE

As we mentioned in the Preface, cutoffs are not an inevitable consequence of developmental life cycle changes. Still, we think therapists should do what they can to minimize anxiety and normalize much of what their clients' experience when there is a gradual drift apart during a life stage transition.

In most cases, clients experience their cutoff as unique and feel "I'm the only person on the planet with this problem." In fact, their experience is often part of the push and tug of relationships, a somewhat extreme version of a normal stage in the life cycle.

In the West and other egocentric cultures, adolescence is a period of separation and individuation. The adolescent establishes his or her own identity, which may or may not coincide with that of his parents or caregivers. In some families, especially where family members are enmeshed, it is critical to remind members that what seems like abandonment, even betrayal, may only be exaggerated steps— albeit perhaps poor choices—toward leaving home. Normalizing the process, even if one cannot condone specific choices, is the point.

Similarly, in cases of mentorship, formal or informal, it is important to remind a client mentor that his or her role involves letting go, stepping aside, and not impeding the developmental shift as the mentee is ready to fly solo. Attention to developmental issues, and to the pride a mentor can take in the success of the mentee, helps reduce the sense of abandonment, jealousy, even betrayal, that some mentors experience.

Finally, we need to discuss with our clients the impact of time. Individuals do change, yet for many the image of the estranged person is frozen at the time of the last interaction. We therefore have to remind our clients that just as much as they may have changed, so might the person from whom they are estranged. Further, for each party, priorities shift, gaining or receding in importance. Many times siblings rediscover one another in later life when a parent or spouse dies. Even if a client is not ready to attempt reconnection, hearing the therapist explain how relationships can evolve and change over a lifetime plants the seed for reconsideration at a later time.

APOLOGIES

Making an apology is an art, and often necessary to achieving rapprochement. Much has been written about apologies. The best work we've found, written by the psychiatrist and educator Aaron Lazare (2004), dissects apologies as well as places them in a social and cultural context. Other popular books on apology and forgiveness include Chapman and Thomas's *The Five Languages of Apology* (2006),

Kado's *Effective Apology: Mending Fences, Building Bridges, and Restoring Trust* (2009), and Engle's *Power of Apology: A Healing Strategy to Transform All Your Relationships* (2001). There are also many websites about apologies and apologizing. One site offers products such as wristbands that say "I am sorry" on one side and "I forgive you" on the other (IMsorry.com). This same site offers the opportunity not only to mend a relationship but also to help with a charity. It sells cards to be sent to the estranged individual, with a percent of the proceeds going to a charity that feeds children around the world. This sounds a bit gimmicky as a form of absolution. But for some it may make a significant difference—a form of public reparation. What is critical regardless of the medium is the nature and intent of any apology rendered.

"Apologies" are rampant in our society after sexual infidelities, financial fraud, and political misdeeds. However, saying "I am sorry" does not necessarily mean it is experienced as an apology. Too often, as Lazare points out, the words are empty of real feeling, insincere, and at worst, fraudulent. They are mouthed to accomplish some goal in the social landscape, but they are only "pseudo-apologies" that do more harm than good.

Apologies require self-reflection and recognition of the hurt or sense of betrayal inflicted on the other individual. An apology needs to acknowledge the other's experience and make clear that the apologist takes some responsibility for what transpired. It need not convey that he or she is entirely at fault but should indicate that whatever was done had an unintended negative effect. This harkens back to our discussion about the importance of taking the other person's perspective. Good apologies read like these:

"I am truly sorry my actions hurt you. It was not my intention. I hope you realize how much I care and want you back in my life. In the future I will try not to do . . ."

"I don't know or understand exactly what happened between us, but maybe we can move on. I thus apologize for whatever I did to hurt you. I have missed your presence in my life ever since. Please accept my apology."

Embedded in an apology is a sense of remorse and some indication that the "offender" will do what it takes to prevent a repeat offense. The remorse might explicitly contain a wish to move the clock back so that "none of this would have happened." However, in reality, the clock only moves forward. Therefore, part of the apology should be a question: "How we can we move on from here?" "What can I do to let you know I am sincere in my desire to either repay you or take some other action to show you can trust me again?"

A sense of shame may need to be part of an apology. It signals that the offender knows he or she violated some social or community value. An absence of shame may suggest to the one to whom the apology is issued that the individual "lacks awareness of the inter-connectedness of human beings" (Lazare, 2004, p. 115). The absence of shame or remorse also suggests that self-interest is the predominant motivation for the apology.

To counteract this possibility, in cases of serious abuse (often resulting in cutoffs), part of Cloe Madanes's (1995) powerful social action approach requires a mortifying public apology to the victim and the family. At a gathering of the clan, the victimizer apologizes *on his knees* to those present, who decide as a group whether or not the apology is sincere. The apology is accepted or restitution of the relationship granted only when there is consensus that the "victim-izer" shows sufficient remorse. Only then, Madanes writes, can the victim, and victimizer who also suffers, begin to recover:

> Most therapists feel that they can understand the pain of the victim. But I believe that in order to truly understand spiritual pain, one must understand the pain of the victimizer. To be a therapist in the true sense of the word, we must be able not only to help the victim heal, but also to pull the offender out of his spiritual despair. (p. 100)

In families where ethnic or religious intermarriage or same-sex partnerships are not accepted, the person involved may assert his or her right to choose a life partner regardless of the family's attitude. In these cases, the apology can only indicate that he or she under-stands the parents' psychic pain and is truly sorry about it. These apologies require not only the statement but also ongoing work to help all parties accept different points of view and establish clear boundaries. There also needs to be explicit attention to what each party loses if the cutoff continues.

Sometimes just saying, "I was wrong" or "I did not mean to hurt you" is sufficient. Other times, however, an explanation is necessary. What is said in these circumstances and how it is said are important. It must be the truth and include a sense of personal responsibility (Belkin, 2010). It must come from within the individual, and not shirk the truth or excuse behavior. Not to do so undercuts the very act of apologizing. Benjamin Franklin put it well: "Never ruin an apology with an excuse." Witness the difference in the two statements below:

> "I am really sorry. I am not an awful person. I just had one too many. Please try to understand."
> "I am so sorry that I hurt you. My behavior was awful and really does not reflect who I want to be. I promise not to do it again."

The recipient of the apology needs to be clear about his or her expectations. What is the minimum they need from the other person? As Chapman and Thomas write, "forgiveness is not a feeling but a decision . . . to continue to grow the relationship by removing a barrier" (2006, p. 139). Can you pardon the offense, violation, or betrayal? Acceptance does not mean that you immediately trust the person again but that you are willing to try, despite the transgression.

We spoke earlier about the importance of moving slowly, not trying to hurry though the process of reconciliation. Someone first hearing an apology and being asked for forgiveness in the same breath may not respond well. He or she may need a bit of time to digest it and decide how to respond. A personal communication Elena never forgot says it perfectly. "Sometimes you save time by losing it" (Clarence Karrier, professor of education, University of Rochester, personal communication, 1973).

Finally, both sides of the cutoff dyad must understand that neither the apology nor its acceptance mean the incident is forgotten. Forgiveness only means commitment to an effort to accept what happened and to renewing contact—"in spite of what he or she has done" (Chapman & Thomas, 2006, p. 150).

Situations vary, but if we help clients learn to both apologize well and accept sincere apologies from others, we can more easily help restore relationships after a cutoff.

MOVING ON WITHOUT RECONCILIATION

At times reconciliation, or even reconnection, is not possible. The reasons vary; the client may be unable to locate the other person, the person may be too ill or may have died, the client feels that the trauma inflicted was just too great, or the conditions set by the other person are unacceptable. Or, the reverse: the estranged person refuses to respond to the client's outreach, feels that what was done in the past cannot be "undone," or feels he or she cannot meet the client's set of conditions. It may also be that reconnection was improbable all along, but as clinicians, for our own reasons, we pushed it, perhaps more for our own sense of accomplishment than for the parties themselves.

For some clients, certainty that the cutoff will not be resolved brings relief; for others, the sense of loss intensifies. Regardless, it is important that client and therapist not see the lack of reconnection as a failure of the therapy. Instead, we believe the clarity of non-reconnection provides an important learning opportunity. As relevant, we can help the client complete his or her process of mourning and acceptance of the finality of the cutoff. Along with the finality, however, is the perhaps bittersweet sense of satisfaction that he or she at least tried to resolve the cutoff and now is "free" to move forward, no longer wondering "if only . . ." or what might have been. Thus, the experience can actually strengthen the client's sense of efficacy, because he or she gave their all. That is what matters in the end. Most frequently, the work now shifts to increasing the client's independence and ways to engage with others in a more effective manner.

Unexpressed Anger

If the client wanted to engage but that was not possible, or if an invitation was rejected, it might help for the client to express the feelings that he or she has harbored. Once again, the therapist provides a safe place for the client to cry, scream, or rage. And the clinician has to tolerate the intensity, which may be difficult even though not directed at him or her. Opening the floodgates only to retreat will signal to the client that these impulses are inappropriate or over-

47

whelming to others and could set off a chain of self-deprecation that may cloud or ruin the rest of treatment.

In addition to encouraging full expression in the office, we suggest the client write a letter to the cutoff person expressing rage and disappointment. It can be softened or revised the next day or week, or never sent. In fact, some clients may find that the act of writing the letter and then shredding it brings relief and closure.

Compassion and Forgiveness

To forgive is not necessarily to forget. If there is no way to undo what happened, healing must include some kind of forgiveness, of self and the other person. There may not be a good explanation for what happened, but the client must somehow let go. If the anger and stress are not relieved, as mentioned in Chapter 1, they can lead to a range of physiological problems, including eating and sleep disorders, gastric distress, intestinal problems, high blood pressure, or heart problems (Harvard Health Publications, 2012; Karren et al., 2010; Suarez, 2004). Forgiveness may not cure these sequelae, but it enables the client to release psychic energy that can then be harnessed to move forward and live more productively.

The clinician can help the client play out what, ideally, he or she needed to hear from the other person. Writing it down and then saying it out loud can be a release. The therapist can repeat it back, taking the role of the other. Meditation and yoga are helpful. Exercise, especially the kind that increases heart rate is beneficial. Even a long walk may offer a sense of release, a new insight, or an enhanced sense of calm.

Along with forgiveness—sometimes prior to, sometimes subsequent—comes compassion. Our aim here is for the client to accept who he or she is despite the rejection and then to extend that acceptance to the other person. This does not mean the client is being asked to understand or like the person, but rather to acknowledge that everyone has weaknesses and limitations and that the other person's limitations both contributed to the cutoff and prevented reconciliation. A shift from resentment to compassion frees the client to be more open to himself or herself as well as to the other people with whom he or she will interact in the future.

Mourning the Loss

After a cutoff, clients are often more in touch with their anger and hurt than with feelings of sadness and loss. Anger, however, continues the connection and does not help with the task of moving on. Our work as clinicians, therefore, is to explore the client's loss. What will he or she miss about the other person or about the experiences they shared in the past?

When someone close to us dies, we eventually remove most of their personal effects but save a few mementos. We have therefore suggested that clients feel free to return belongings, give them to someone else, or donate them to a charity. If the estranged person has died, visiting the cemetery and saying he or she is forgiven may bring peace. Even if not the desired outcome, saying goodbye can provide closure and allow the client to move on with his or her life. Asking other people about the deceased may also provide the client with a fuller perspective, potentially adding weight to positive memories to be stored. This we have found particularly helpful in situations of abuse or abandonment, as well as a history of substance abuse or mental illness.

Growth

In addition to closure, the therapist can help the client grow from the cutoff. What has the client learned from the relationship and the cutoff? How can these lessons become integrated in the client's life such that he or she can establish and maintain more satisfying relationships going forward?

When an individual believes that he or she has been betrayed or abandoned, it is very important that the post-cutoff work focus on how the client can rebuild his or her life without the other individual. We have worked with clients helping them recall or identify latent interests and talents that can give them new pleasure, as well as opportunities to meet like-minded people. Joining and volunteering in religious or secular communities, especially helping others, can provide a sense of social and spiritual renewal.

The remaining support system is critical. If the cutoff was with a close family member or member of a tight social group, the client may now be at sea, without the anchor of friends or family. In these and other circumstances, Sichel (2004) highly recommends "second-chance families" composed of friends one chooses, new families, who are there to celebrate one's successes and provide support when one faces difficulties. In his book Sichel describes the second-chance family he built for himself after his parents cut him off.

A clinician we interviewed who works almost exclusively with LGBT clients told us her clients often speak of the families they created after they were estranged from parents or siblings who did not accept them. Thus, after a cutoff, with or without the possibility of reconciliation, we can help our clients seek out people to establish an alternative life-affirming network—help them establish a new family.

In the following chapters, we describe the ways we and other clinicians use the above strategies to help clients cope with a cutoff, reconcile, or move forward with their lives after a final cutoff. We begin our thematic journey with cutoffs stemming from abandonment.

Chapter 3

ABANDONMENT

Sometimes I feel like a motherless child
Sometimes I feel like a motherless child
Sometimes I feel like a motherless child
A long ways from home
A long way from home

                                        Traditional Song

Abandonment may mean a literal leaving or defined as the absence of caring behavior when such behavior is called for. Someone is called upon but does not take responsibility for something that can rightly be expected. The Catholic Church calls it the "sin of omission," a critical failure to act. Abandonment can also be defined as a failure to recognize that something took place (Bernheimer, 2005), such as when the extended family and community do not acknowledge the tragedy and ongoing impact of a stillborn child (Cacciatore, Schnebly, & Froen, 2009).

Just the word *abandonment* evokes primitive fear. As Eric Fromm (1941/1994) so eloquently reminded us, the world is frightening, and we are born into it helpless. For an infant, being alone is unbearable. Over time, the terror is muted by loving parents, relatives, life partners, children, and deep friendships. Through these attachments individuals learn to tolerate times that re-evoke the panic of infancy, "crying it out" in the crib, moments that feel like forever.

The end of an important relationship is often compared to severing a limb, an emotional loss as traumatic as the bodily one. Unlike jealousy and betrayal, which breed hot angry emotions, abandonment is cold. After a cutoff, the recipient feels frightened, helpless, lost, frozen out.

Abandonment can range from mild emotional withdrawal to a full-blown cutoff. It often consists of a chain of events beginning with one person's perceived or literal cutoff, prompting the other to retaliate by cutting off the same person or someone else. Actions and reactions proceed in escalating fashion.

A typical feature of the cycle is that individuals who experience abandonment early in life may later short-circuit the process, preemptively cutting off someone they only suspect will cut them off, thus becoming abandoners themselves. We will see this cycle played out as theme and variation in a number of the cases described in this chapter.

As discussed in the Introduction, we can also view abandonment through an historical lens across generations in a family. Some cutoffs recapitulate an original leave taking, as when a biological parent hunts for a biological child he or she "surrendered," only to be rejected by the child. Others are secondary experiences, as when a breakup between two adults echoes an earlier abandonment by a parent. In these secondary cutoffs, the adult who was abandoned in youth stands on shaky ground, and the therapist may need to help the person rebuild his or her self-esteem before reconnection is attempted or moving on is possible.

We divide our abandonment cases into three groups: unavailability; adoption/foster care/desertion; and illness/death. The order is meaningful in that the cases range from subtler kinds of abandonment to sudden disappearance; from present but unaccounted for and uncertain or temporary abandonment, to absent and permanently gone. We describe and comment on the strategies used by the clinicians (including us) who worked the cases, or suggest how a given case might be handled if a clinician were involved. Where a case resolved without a clinician, we present the means by which it was accomplished.

UNAVAILABILITY

Let us first distinguish emotional unavailability from neglect. The former is primarily involved with feelings, whereas the latter is the failure to perform basic physical functions; they are two ends of an undesirable continuum. For example, at the unavailable end is the parent who runs for political office and has no time for or "forgets" his or her children, or the mother who is out of work, preoccupied with how she'll support their children. Not being there at a crucial time is a failure to respond to a real or perceived crisis. Neglect is more extreme in that it represents a failure of basic caretaking, such as providing food, clothing, and shelter.

⤷⤶

Emotional Detachment

Erik is the only child of Norm and Bettina, whose stormy marriage ended when Erik was five. Bettina returned to Denmark, her birthplace, with Erik. Norm stayed in New York, which Erik visited in the summer. Norm remarried two years later and he and Alice had Jared. The attention Jared received from Norm was hard on Erik, but after college Erik tried living with Norm and Alice. But he also soon joined a Neo-Sullivan community of like-minded therapists and clients.

Before long, Erik moved out and stopped speaking to his father and stepmother. Seven years later, Norm bumped into Erik at an antique car show. In response to "How're you doin'?" Erik shot back, "Look, I can't be around you." "Why?" "Because you were a terrible father!" "How was I terrible"? "You weren't there. Even when you were home, you weren't there."

Norm blames a lot on the Neo-Sullivanians he believes promoted the cutoff. Throughout the twelve-year silence, Norm made efforts through Jared but to no avail. Then out of the blue, Erik called "to at least see if anything is there now." They have met a few times, kept it simple, and never speak about the cutoff.

Norm employed three strategies that can be used in many other situations. First, though it was not his nature, Norm held his temper. "Be patient," Norm advises. "Never give up." Second, keep trying to connect, and when you do, listen, don't be reactive. Third, by persisting, Norm conveyed seriousness of intent to compensate for his former unavailability. It is heartening to see that in some cases of parental abandonment, it may never be too late.

Not There at a Critical Time

Not being there for a family member or friend in a crisis is a more sudden jolt than chronic unavailability, but just as damaging.

Laurie and Jane were friends for fifteen years when Laurie developed a serious disk problem in her back and was bedridden. Laurie researched the options and quickly decided to have back surgery regardless of the significant risks. Jane raised concerns that she was not considering alternative options such as physical therapy or acupuncture. However Jane clearly stated she would support Laurie through whatever route she took. Laurie did not register Jane's support separate from her concerns about the surgery. Laurie only heard that Jane disagreed (i.e., might abandon her) and preemptively cut Jane off.

After a year, Jane called Laurie. Fortunately, Laurie's back surgery had been a success, she was doing well, and the friendship resumed as if nothing had happened. Then one day while she was shifting furniture around in her house, Laurie felt acute pain in her back and legs. This time Laurie was told that a second back surgery would be more risky than the first, so she opted for PT and acupuncture—which miraculously worked. Today, despite living on opposite coasts, the two friends are closer than ever.

This cutoff resolved without therapy, perhaps because the parties are therapists themselves. They *meta-communicated,* which is to say, that they communicated about their communication problem. Finally, each understood the other's perspective and Laurie was convinced that Jane really cared. This is painstaking work, but they succeeded in resetting their priorities, put the misunderstanding into their overall relationship context, and recovered their almost lost friendship.

The following story illustrates how attention to red flags can spare someone the pain of a cutoff. It is also an example of how the context of a cutoff influences how devastating a cut off will be.

Their consciousness having been raised in women's movement groups that proliferated in the 1970s, Ellen and Maya had much in common. Friends at work and gym buddies, they also snuck out to shop at lunchtime. Both married in their thirties and by their early forties were divorced, single mothers with teenage kids. Barely coping was the order of the day, and they kept each afloat by laughing a lot and fantasizing ways out of their predicaments.

They supported each other with an annual mammogram routine. They went together and celebrated after. Twenty years into the friendship, Ellen was advised to schedule a six-month follow-up to reexamine a "tiny blip. I'm sure it's nothing, just want to double-check," the radiologist stated. But Ellen had breast cancer; Maya did not call to find out what happened; Ellen did not call to tell her.

Ellen told her therapist that Maya had not contacted her and how hurt she was. They concluded that Ellen had enough to deal with medically, and it did not make sense to fight for the relationship now—better to have a temporary cooling off. Additionally, although she was hurt, Ellen was not entirely unprepared. Having watched Maya in other relationships, Ellen knew she could not always count on Maya. Ellen had never before expected more than Maya could deliver, though this time she had believed Maya would come through.

The loss of Maya was buffered by the fact that Ellen had the support of her new husband, many other family members, and friends. By then—and this was important to Ellen—she and Maya no longer had mutual friends, making it unlikely that this break would lead to others. Fourth, a cutoff would have no professional consequence, as she and Maya were no longer working together. Finally, Maya's abandonment did not feel personal—just mindless.

Ten years later, Maya called; they met for dinner. They discussed where they had been in their lives when the friendship "ended." Maya explained why she was not there for Ellen. It was a bit of fear for herself, but mainly she was with a man who she allowed to control her friendships. For Ellen it was a reminder to keep expectations close to what friends can deliver and to cherish them for what they can do. Few friends are quicker, quirkier, and funnier than Maya.

Unmet Expectations

Shakespeare's *King Lear* centers on Lear's iconic cutoff with Cordelia, his favorite daughter. She loves her father but refuses to obey his command that she declare her love publicly. His devastating rebuke is

> Here I disclaim all my paternal care,
> Propinquity and property of blood,
> And as a stranger to my heart and me
> Hold thee, from this, forever. The barbarous Scythian,
> Or he that makes his generation messes
> To gorge his appetite, shall to my bosom
> Be as well neighbour'd, pitied, and relieved,
> As thou my sometime daughter. (I.i.114–122)

Whew! After disowning Cordelia, Lear leaves the realm to his two other insincere, obsequious daughters. They in turn scheme to plot his overthrow.

We include this literary example because abiding love is actually a strategy. Despite Lear's narcissism and cruelty, Cordelia remains true and rescues him. Realizing his demand was excessive and that it was a mistake to cut her off, Lear reconciles with Cordelia before they are both murdered. Lear gains humility, and we learn that fighting rejection with love, disregarding the other's irrational behavior and holding fast rather than retaliating can be a winning strategy. Here we have a child holding steady in the face of her father's temper tantrum.

The following vignette describes abandonment by a friend when he or she fails to meet expectations set in place by social mores and by the nature of a long close relationship.

⤜⤛

Rachel's parents and Pamela and Ronan were friends from college days. Pamela and Ronan became, in effect, Rachel's adopted aunt and uncle. When Rachel was nine, her father's brother died, leaving a young son. "The two families were very close until my cousin came to live with us. Then one day, Ronan told me he thought my parents were wrong to take my cousin in." A very upset Rachel told her parents. They were furious. Ronan had crossed an adult/child boundary, was insensitive to Rachel's situation, and ignored how much Rachel's parents wanted to be there for their nephew. And so, they broke off the decades-old friendship.

Years later, Rachel recognized now-divorced Pamela during intermission at a concert. The two got together and kindled a friendship despite more than 20 years difference in age. They began to spend time going to movies, having dinner, and visiting each other's country homes. They even spent a few holidays together with Pamela's now adult sons.

When Rachel's father died a few years later, Pamela, who had moved to Florida, did not call or write. Shocked, but thinking Pamela did not see the obituary, Rachel sent a copy. No response. So Rachel phoned, worried that seventy-five-year-old Pamela might be ill. Not so. Pamela was sorry, wanted to write, but "did not know what to say." Rachel still mourns her father, but also mourns the loss of her adopted aunt. "I thought we were good friends. We shared celebrations like when I took her out for her seventieth birthday and when I passed the bar exam. But I now feel abandoned. She was absent when I needed her most."

We will never know why Pamela failed to connect, except that not knowing what to say suggests an emotional paralysis. Was Pamela angry that Rachel's parents had cut her off and so unconsciously took it out on Rachel? If Pamela had a therapist, he or she might have pushed her to examine her odd passivity in this situation. He might have pointed out that when something happens to someone with whom one has a long relationship; it is incumbent upon the person to say something, somehow. Failure to do so hurts both parties.

Sometimes there truly is not much to offer—but one's presence speaks volumes. Even if all one can muster is, "I don't know what to say," one must say it. The action and statement keep doors open and provide needed support. Pamela could have prevented the cutoff. A therapist might have helped her understand why she resisted conveying condolences, helping her push past it for the sake of the friendship.

In the next case, developmental issues unbalanced a close relationship, making it difficult for one party to meet previously understood or expressed expectations. Often, a new demanding job, a baby, any significant life cycle change may mean a decrease in availability of a friend or family member. If there is unclear communication, one or the other party may feel abandoned.

The good news is that a circumstance or status change can also allow a friendship to be restored. Thus, it is important that clients understand the shifting nature of relationships, as well as the particular set of events that create a sense of abandonment. Clients who feel abandoned can articulate their feelings to the person who has moved "ahead" and suggest the possibility of recalibrating current expectations or reconnecting later on.

Ava and Allison were close friends for 5 years. Ava at thirty-eight was not in a committed relationship and had no children, while Allison, forty-eight, was divorced, had children, and was remarrying. Perhaps inevitably, strains on the friendship developed out of differences in age as well as life stage, not to mention different marital and financial statuses. Most important, Allison had less time once she remarried. Ava reached out but did not clearly state her needs or how upset she was at the changes in the relationship. There was no showdown; they just stopped calling each other.

Ten years later, they bumped into each other on the street. They met for brunch and shared where they had been. Ava had a doctoral degree and a wonderful job, so their lives and statuses were now in better balance. The friendship rekindled and deepened, and they became close friends again, collaborating on a research project and enjoying each other's company.

A stormy break is usually harder to breach. Sichel (2004) the clinician already referred to in the Introduction, was twice cut off by his father. After the shock of the first cutoff wore off, he and his wife inventoried their possible contributions to the problem and made a concerted effort to reconnect. It worked for a while, but a new infraction ignited his father's rage, and as of 2009, the second cutoff was ongoing:

The last conversation I had with my father, in 2001, was about the fact that I had not called my sister in a timely manner to congratulate her on the engagement of her son. The conversation deteriorated . . . culminating in his telling me I would never again be welcome in his home. The tardiness of my congratulatory phone call was the excuse for the estrangement . . . my father was really saying that I had shattered our family's myth . . . of a close and tight-knit family in which everyone was in complete agreement about everything, that is, in complete agreement with my father. (p. 57)

This is a perfect example of a parent whose expectations are extreme and who cannot allow a child to differentiate, to deviate, or to lead his or her own life. After the second cutoff, Sichel wrote *Healing from Family Rifts* (2004) to help himself and others rebuild self-esteem, reengage, or move on after an excruciating, apparently permanent cutoff.

In contrast, the next story showcases how a simple apology can heal a rift caused by unmet expectations. As discussed in the Strategies chapter, an apology is not always accepted when first offered, but here, one "I'm sorry" worked. Evelyn had a long history with Veronica, and Veronica was one of very few relatives left in their generation. Evelyn very much wanted to be back in contact.

Evelyn and Veronica, only children, are cousins from San Francisco, 2 years apart. They lived in the same apartment building and grew up together. Veronica, the elder, was dominant. Evelyn admired Veronica and needed her approval. Veronica was often critical of Evelyn and not afraid to express this criticism. During their teenage years, Evelyn's family moved to Oregon, and the cousins saw each other infrequently. Also, Veronica was a bit wild, and Evelyn was scared of the gang she ran with. In her late thirties, Veronica moved back to San Francisco.

The two cousins "hung out" in their forties. Veronica, who was married without children, would call Evelyn almost daily, wanting conversation and to go to movies, as both were avid film buffs. Evelyn tried to meet Veronica's expectations, but she was single, was working

full time, and had a teenage daughter. She was not always on time or
prompt returning calls.

  One day, Evelyn called and after saying "Hi, how are you," got an
earful about how unreliable she was, how Veronica was fed up. Eve-
lyn slammed down the phone vowing she would not contact Veronica
again. She did not really mean forever, but she could not picture break-
ing the ice.

Two years later, Veronica called to apologize "for whatever I said,
because I really can't remember." Evelyn did not ask to discuss the
precipitating phone rant, because Veronica's apology was enough.
She immediately said, "Sure, but . . . I want you to accept that I can't
fulfill your expectations, because of stresses in my own life. Also, if
you're ever angry at me again, please tell me rather than blow up."
Veronica agreed, and the cousins reunited. Though they spend less
time together, Evelyn says, "I still love Veronica and will be there if
she ever needs me."

In this case, the apology was enough, obviating the need to rehash
the cutoff. Also, Evelyn was able to state her own limitations and
expectations, and Veronica reset her expectations for their relationship going forward.

∝∽

In the following example there was no easy compromise:

Marie, forty-four, married to Adam, has a thirteen-year-old, Grace,
from a previous relationship, who lives with them. Adam and his
mother Edith are close, but Edith does not speak to Marie. Edith has no
grandchildren from her two other unmarried sons. She wants Marie,
despite being premenopausal, to use extraordinary means to bear her a
biological grandchild. She is angry that Marie is not interested. Marie
wants Adam to stand up to his mother, but Adam is timid and non-
communicative in general, which is also a problem in the marriage.

Initially, the couple therapist empathized with Marie, acknowledging that Edith did seem to be a difficult woman. Edith not only
wanted Marie to go through an arduous process with no certainty of
results, but she was not accepting Grace into the family. He also
shared a sense that Adam has difficulty confronting his mother. He

suggested that Adam ask his mother to accept Marie's choice, because "it's important to me." After role playing with the therapist, Adam made the difficult call, and a date was set for the three to have dinner. Shortly afterward, Edith postponed until "after the Thanksgiving holiday."

Edith then invited Adam for Christmas dinner, with a begrudging "You can bring your wife" invitation to Marie. She never mentioned her step-granddaughter. The therapist still encouraged them to go and to bring Grace. Just before Christmas, Edith sent Adam and Marie an off-putting, provocative text message. Adam and Marie balked at going, but the therapist explained that sabotage is common in these situations and that they should "roll with the punches." Adam, Marie, and Grace enjoyed being with other family members and felt good about the prospects for Marie and Edith to reconnect. To date, though, it has been a long hard slog.

Interestingly, none of the strategies involved inviting the mother-in-law into a session. Edith was obviously upset that she might never have biological grandchildren and was probably unaware how much her behavior hurt Marie. She probably believed Marie did not understand what she was going through. She may not have been aware of her importance to Marie, and possibly also to Grace. It is also possible that the two could have actually shared a sense of loss—the absence of a new baby in Adam and Marie's marriage. Perhaps, if they could reach that level of understanding, if they could empathize, they might mourn together, and then move on to share Grace.

But there is more. Adam never mentioned it, but did he also want Marie to undergo extreme measures? Did he also desire his own biological child? Might Adam have unconsciously been letting his mother be his proxy pressuring Marie? It is not clear if the therapist ever directly explored this possible conflict between Adam and Marie. We only know for certain that Marie had one child and did not have a strong desire for another.

The strategies we recommend are intended to lower the reactive threshold of the cutoff parties in the long run, but in cases like this one, they may aggravate the situation in the short run. This was a deceptively simple case at first blush, but the intricacies and complexities were almost endless.

The following case of unmet expectations is simple in contrast:

Coptic Christians from Egypt, Amir and Justina met fleeing persecution. They were young, good looking, and instantly attracted to each other. A week after landing in Canada, they made a snap decision to marry. Justina had two daughters from her first marriage, so Amir became their stepfather. Amir, who had been first cellist in a Western classical music chamber orchestra in Alexandria, could not find work in Montreal, so he gave private lessons. Justina became a buyer for a department store. Their new lives were off to a good start, except that Justina was used to a high life and expected Amir to provide it. When Amir could not, she called her wealthy "ex," who always obliged.

This stressed Amir. He opened a business selling and repairing instruments, but it never got off the ground. They bought a house with money from the ex but could not afford the payments. Finally, during the 2009 recession, Justina had an affair, announced with no warning that the marriage was over, and left. Amir was devastated, suicidal, but recovered quickly with medication and support from his parents.

This is the context in which Amir related the story of bumping into Justina shortly after the divorce. When asked if they spoke, his reply was, "No, I pretended not to see her. Why would I speak to a cockroach?"

This is one of the few instances in which there did not seem to be a reason to reconnect. Nothing was holding this couple together. They did not know each other well when they married, they had no children together, their values were different, and they had moved on from the three things that had brought them together in the first place: sexual attraction, common ethnic and religious background, and the fact that they were refugees. Amir needed to work on himself. He had to control his temper and count the red flags he failed to see with Justina before going into another relationship. But repair of the cutoff was unnecessary.

ADOPTION, FOSTER CARE, AND DESERTION

Adoption, foster care, and desertion have in common that parents leave their children in the care of others. They usually do so because they are unable or not ready to care for a child or cannot afford to give a child a home. Separation is either formal, through governmental or private agencies, or informal, such as when an aunt or uncle takes in a niece or nephew during trying times for the parents or when a parent dies. We place these cases in our abandonment chapter even though many people surrender a child for adoption only as a last resort and suffer a lifetime of loss, regret, and self-recrimination. Regardless of the circumstances, it is usually still abandonment from the child's perspective, no matter how ambivalent or agonizing the decision was for the biological parents.

To be "surrendered," as it is known in adoption circles, is to be cut off from ones roots, "ripped" from the physiological, psychological womb, from the sights, sounds, smells, heartbeat of one's biological mother. Like adoptees, many foster children and those who have been deserted never fully recover.

Adoption

For some individuals the pain of surrendering a child reverberates throughout life, even when the event is supposedly "forgotten," "not very important," or explicitly denied.

Jenny at nineteen married Tim, who was ten years older. Twelve years later, they moved from Atlanta to New York for Jenny's job. Tim was excited about the chance to explore "the Big Apple," but Jenny had medical problems and was often unable to accompany him. She suffered migraines, IBS, and eczema that no treatment seemed to alleviate. She held a high-powered job but had no energy on weekends, was tired all the time. She was young and pretty, but with the demeanor and mindset of a much older woman.

The couple was close but had no children and no good friends. Jenny could sense Tim's growing impatience over her health issues. Her father had abandoned the family when she was eight and she worried that Tim would abandon her too. She was close to her mother and sister, who lived in Michigan, but had a dispute with her brother after his first son was born and cut him off.

Jenny also had a secret. At sixteen she became pregnant by her boyfriend and went to a home for unwed mothers. She could not remem-

ber who sent her or how she felt. She could not remember being there, except the birth itself, after which she mechanically signed papers. She never saw the baby; all she knew was that it was a girl.

The beginning of therapy was spent discussing Jenny's medical problems, helping her obtain better care. When the adoption secret was revealed, the therapist wondered aloud whether finding her daughter might help. After exploring the idea, though, it was evident that that period in Jenny's life was too painful and that she did not want to reopen the door. Out of her element in New York, and with no family or friends to support her, she relied completely on Tim and the therapist. One day, Tim had a stroke. Jenny called the therapist and asked her to come to the hospital. The therapist would have but literally couldn't. Jenny stopped therapy soon after.

The therapist was unable to help Jenny appraise the cutoffs in her life—the original cutoff by her father, the cutoff of her brother, and, at the heart of it, the surrender of her daughter—or their impact.

The therapist believed Jenny had made an unconscious punishing bargain with herself for having abandoned her child. The deal was "Since I did such a bad thing, getting pregnant and giving up [cutting off] my child, I'll atone by restricting my life. I'll have no other children, no joy." The guilt and sorrow were so deeply ingrained that Jenny was unable to unearth the bargain or forgive herself. Here is a perfect instance of Böszörményi-Nagy's and Spark's invisible loyalty (1973/1984), described in Chapter 1.

In contrast, the case of Marty and Joan gives the reader a sense of how reconnection and reconciliation in these primary cutoffs situations can be achieved:

Marty and Joan attended the same high school and then became college sweethearts. Sophomore year Joan became pregnant. Neither was ready to marry, much less start a family, but they were devout Catholics, so they decided Joan would complete the pregnancy and give the baby up for adoption. Atypically, the couple stayed together, eventually married, and had another child, a boy named Andrew. A happy ending—except that the baby they gave up haunted them, to the point where they started searching.

Eventually, they found Stuart, who agreed to meet with them. Over a year or more, there were visits. Then Andrew was brought into the process, and the secret of his biological older brother was revealed. Stuart had been raised by a good family and was a highly regarded in-house attorney with a family of his own. And there was an amazing coincidence. Andrew and Stuart, two years apart, had worked at the same pharmaceutical company in the same building in their first jobs, unbeknownst to each other. Andrew resented that his parents had withheld the knowledge of his brother for so long. He agreed to meet Stuart but was not sure he wanted a relationship.

Andrew had been a devoted son through some hard times and felt that his parents should understand his feelings. Marty and Joan felt that their relationship with Stuart was "from a different part of our lives" and should not be so upsetting to Andrew. The three of them could not discuss the matter without an argument, and at one point Andrew stopped speaking to Marty and Joan.

The cutoff lasted almost a year when all three realized they needed outside help. Their family therapist's stated goal was for the three to understand each other without judgment. No one was right or wrong, no one would win. The parents came to see the degree to which Andrew felt displaced. Andrew was able to understand what reuniting with Stuart meant to his parents and that it did not diminish their love for him. Andrew now attends the new, enlarged family gatherings, he is getting to know his brother, and peace prevails.

Here is an instance where repair of a primary cutoff by adoption was eminently successful and with the help of therapy prevented a permanent secondary cutoff between the parents and the biological son they raised. The case also elucidates how others not involved in the initial cutoff can be affected and also cut off. Therapists therefore need to be mindful of potential "collateral damage" and work with the family or individual to anticipate reactions of others to the "revealed family secret," the original cutoff as well as any reconnection.

From a child's perspective, the forced exit from the family of origin is a severe trauma. It certainly was for Halle:

At age eight, Halle was sent from Bogota, Colombia to New York by her mother to live with her father, his sister, and the sister's husband. The father had recently moved north, allegedly for work, but he actually had a mistress in New York. The mother's logic, according to Halle, was that he would remember his family if she sent the youngest child to remind him, and they would both return home. It was a desperate act that backfired, leaving Halle feeling unwanted and used. Days after she arrived, her father moved out and in with his mistress. Halle, left behind, was repeatedly sexually abused by her uncle, but fearing no one would believe her, kept it to herself.

Though her mother made some effort to keep in touch, in her teen years Halle refused to correspond or receive calls. She completed college and medical school and is remarkably well puts together considering the abandonment and sexual trauma in her past.

In couple therapy with Mel, her boyfriend of six years, Halle slowly accepted that although Mel professed love, he did not treat her well and was conflicted about marrying her. She realized he was like her father, who abandoned her at whim whenever the spirit moved him. Mel had broken up with her twice already. This time Halle ended it. Asked by the therapist how she found the courage after all the other losses, she spoke fondly of her grandfather. "I was his favorite, he treated me like gold." Here is proof that it doesn't have to be a parent, but it does have to be someone. Reminding clients of surrogate parents who cared for them is often a key to recovery.

While in therapy, Halle finally told her mother about her experience in the aunt's house. "You had a choice. Sending me away was selfish. I can move past it, but I'll never forget it." For five years, Halle's mother wrote apologies and tried to make amends. Halle has come around to some extent. Mother and daughter are in touch, though not close. Halle has moved on with her life.

✑✏

Hans's quirky story is remarkable in another way:

Hans grew up in Sweden. When he was five or six, his mother gave him up for adoption—and cut off contact—allegedly because she could not get him to stop peeking under her skirt! He was taken in by another family and put to work on their farm. One day, years later, while in the outhouse (reading torn-up newspaper used for toilet paper), Hans noticed an ad in which a mother was looking for her son. He somehow sensed it was his mother. He answered the ad, and a biological mother and son reunited.

We do not know what prompted Hans's mother's to search, except that as stated in the ad, she missed him. We also do not know what their relationship was like after they reconnected, but we can surmise that the mother had the classic "change of heart." This is probably an instance in which time worked its wonders, a phenomenon that needs to be recognized more in our work with clients.

In the last few decades the number of open or semi-open adoptions has been increasing, such that today the majority of adoptions are open (Siegel & Smith, 2012). This change reflects an expanding research literature that indicates better outcomes for both child and biological parent when there is some level of contact post-surrender (Child Welfare Information Gateway, 2013). However, as with closed adoptions, the desire for contact and the frequency and nature of contact may vary considerably over the life cycle. In cases where the adoption was secret, the biological parent, fearful of "recriminations," may want to keep the birth forever secret. And, the adoptive parents may claim that once a child has been surrendered, privacy needs to be maintained. In this mix the question that needs to be asked is "What about the child—what is in his or her best interest, and who decides?"

As therapists, we need to be mindful of these opposing perspectives and begin where our clients are, either to help them mourn the loss of their parent or child or help them move forward with a search. We also need to help our clients understand that the parent or child they seek may not welcome them and therefore they may experience yet another loss, this time of the hope of reconnection.

Foster Care

The pain of being a foster child, in contrast with adoption, is that you never quite know where you stand. You may know who you are but not where you are or where you're going: "This is not my family. This is not my home. I am an outsider. I don't know if I will ever go home. Do I even have a home? Who are these people? Will they be good to me? These other kids, how will they treat me? Why would they accept me? I wouldn't accept them if I were the 'real' son or daughter. Will my mother take me back? Do I want to go back? Maybe it's my fault. Maybe she doesn't want me anymore. Who can I trust?" Ambiguity reigns. This horrible childhood uncertainty poisons adult relationships. The story of Adina and Rani clearly is an example of such resonance.

❧

Some years ago, a therapist received a call from a woman about a problem she had with her boyfriend of many years. "I'm not sure you can help, but I'd like to meet you to see." Opening the door at the first appointment, he saw a small, spritely woman with an engaging smile and dreadlocks. African American he thought. She was actually from Yemen, and Jewish. In Yemen, where she was born, she was privileged. The family had servants. She had a private tutor and a good life, except that her parents fought and her father was abusive to her mother. She remembers him fondly, though, in terms of how he treated her and her brother. He was not home much and had other women on the side.

When she was eight, her father was imprisoned for political reasons. Her mother sent her and her brother to live with a foster family in Philadelphia. This was a "reasonable" foster situation, although Adina has vague recollection of being molested by a male relative of the foster family. She lived there for 3 years, at which time her mother came to the U.S. and took her brother to live with her, leaving Adina behind. When Adina's foster mother learned that Adina wanted to go "home," she promptly packed Adina's belongings and dropped her off on the mother's doorstep.

Although her mother did keep her, Adina never felt wanted. Luckily, she was intellectually gifted, excelled in school, and went to college and graduate school, where she met Rani, a Jordanian Muslim. They were together, on and off for 12 years even after Rani went back to Amman. He visited Philadelphia, she went to Jordan, and they took vacations together. Ten years into the relationship, Adina discovered that Rani had flirted with other women, once while he was staying with her. Adina was devastated. In response, Rani took two months' leave from his job to convince Adina to marry him.

During Rani's leave, they engaged in individual and couple therapy. At some point during her solo work, Adina realized there were other problems in the relationship. Although he professed love, he never introduced her to his parents, who he "knew" would disapprove. He did not live with her at a few points when he could have, and there they were, at age forty, on two sides of the planet. Adina was not convinced Rani really wanted to marry her. Rani was always afraid she would break up with him, which she often did, and he needed assurance that she would not leave him at the first provocation after they married. Adina could not promise she would not be bitter over the lost years, believing she would probably have to resign herself to not having children of her own.

Sometimes, Adina connected the rejection she experienced in childhood (starting with her mother and then her foster mother) to her conviction she was bound to be abandoned by Rani. Sometimes she realized that while Rani had flaws, she was possibly overreacting to them and preemptively cut him off in fear of being abandoned. But eventually, there was too much water under the bridge, and Adina cut him off again, this time for good.

This outcome, though a cutoff, still represents a partial solution to Adina's predicament. She wound up ending a relationship that had many positives but that had struck a too familiar chord. She was in constant limbo, just as she had been as a foster child. The therapist believed that Rani truly loved her but that he kept her on edge by being unable to commit. For Adina, the ambivalence and delaying tactics obliterated his love. Once she saw him as unfaithful, even if only by flirtation, she could never trust him again. No matter that some of his inability to commit was due to Adina's reactivity to small hints of rejection. In this sense the situation was circular and self-defeating. It was also true that Rani as a Muslim had to face his own ambivalence and family problems were he to marry a dark-skinned woman who was a Jew.

Looking back on this complex case, the therapist was satisfied that every effort was made to save the relationship and that the final cutoff at least enabled the couple, who had been locked in a perpetual cycle of cutting off and coming back, to move on.

⨳

Kenny's case continues the theme of unresolved childhood abandonment and its impact on adult well-being and the ability to trust. It also showcases the delicacy with which therapists need to approach clients with unabated rage. As clinicians, our inability to truly engage individuals with experiences of early abandonment may say less about our skills than about the fragility of these individuals and their absolute inability to trust, their fear of their own rage, and their tendency to reenact their primary abandonment.

> *Kenny told his new therapist that when he was four, his mother, Eva, placed him and his younger brother in foster care and left them there for ten years. His father, a schizophrenic, left the family early on and was not available either to Kenny or his brother.*
>
> *During their time in foster care and for the most part since, the two brothers refused any real contact with Eva. According to his current therapist, Kenny's experience in foster care framed his whole sense of self: "His identity is still that of foster kid." He cannot forgive his mother for making him vulnerable to stigmatization, which in his mind precluded him from ever having a normal life. He had been in therapy before, on and off, for fourteen years, but none of the prior work relieved his preoccupation with the past or freed him from feeling he was forever scarred.*
>
> *Kenny was bullied and teased in school. "Everybody hated me," says Kenny. His brother, Nick ("the only person who cared about me") became a homeless alcoholic who froze to death in a snowstorm. "The icing on the cake came later when I discovered that after me and my brother, my mother went on to have two more kids, and also abandoned them to the foster care system."*

Though he denies it, at least to others, Kenny appears to have transcended his childhood. At forty-five, he is a successful landscape architect, married with three children who are all doing well. Still, Kenny believes "everyone hates me" and remains angry and cut off from his mother.

Kenny's new therapist saw him as narcissistic and needy and believed his barely controlled anger pushed people away. She did not think she would ever have encouraged Kenny to contact his mother: "In cases like this, I would not push for reconciliation. I think it would not have been safe for the client; I thought the client would just get hurt again."

Instead, she tried to help Kenny deal with the pain of his abandonment and reframed his mother's abandonment as weakness, rather than rejection. She encouraged him to celebrate his accomplishments and his good life now: "I explained that rage and regret are not good for one's health, and encouraged him not to dwell on the past."

Given that Kenny soon cut her off too, the approach was probably suboptimal, but Kenny may never have been able to attach because the therapist is the same age as his mother!

An approach that may have succeeded would have been the exact opposite: to help Kenny give *more* voice to his pain. In the safety of her office, the therapist could reparent Kenny, witnessing and accepting his feelings, thereby also supporting individuation from his mother. Concurrent strategies would include exploring his idea about why his mother surrendered him and an estimate of her capacity to parent.

Over time, after Kenny fully expressed his anger and pain and was ready to reflect on his options, he might be ready to speak with his mother. He and the therapist could have role-played to prepare. Kenny could also write, revise, soften, and then send a letter. The outcome might be a final cutoff by Kenny, but by his adult self, or it might be a new relationship with his mother based in the present.

Some of our interviewees cautioned against letting clients hold out hope that their cutoff could be repaired. One said, "Misplaced hope can also lead to disappointment and hurt." When is hope realistic; when is it false? That is the question. As another therapist stated, "We always want the other to change, but happiness cannot depend on someone else's epiphany. If your happiness depends on someone else changing, you are screwed." In false hope situations, it is important to help clients adjust their expectations and reconcile issues internally, even if they cannot or should not recover the actual relationship. A proviso, however, is that the effort to protect clients from reopening a wound should not completely thwart their desire to attempt reconciliation. As long as their eyes are open to the possibility of failure, real-world rejection is usually tolerable, as long as someone—perhaps a therapist—is there to help mitigate it. For many people, the attempt itself is what matters most.

Desertion

Desertion is yet another form of abandonment. Sometimes, the person leaves with no warning, no explanation, and is gone forever. Often the remaining family members have no idea where the missing person is.

When Rosie was young, her mother told the story of their building superintendent who went out to buy a carton of milk and just disappeared, leaving his wife and children behind. That was why, her mother explained, "The leak from our bathroom faucet isn't getting fixed." This was frightening for an eight-year-old to hear, and Rosie struggled mightily to understand, until she worked up her courage to ask if that could happen to them: "Could it happen to us?" Her mother reassured her that it would not, and Rosie was able to let it go; but she never forgot the story.

Deserting one's family is an ever-present motif in plays and films, including Tennessee Williams's *Glass Menagerie* (1944/1998) in which the father, "a telephone man who fell in love with long distances; [he] gave up his job with the telephone company and tripped the light fantastic out of town" (Act 1, Scene 1). During the course of the play, his son Tom follows suit, leaving the weak and pitiable mother and daughter to fend for themselves.

The reasons people desert vary widely, but the impact on those left behind is the same: low self-esteem, hyper-vigilance, difficulty forming relationships. It is, therefore, critical for therapists to be alert to the possibility that a family member is losing his or her ability or will to cope and is contemplating escape.

Harriet was only in her twenties and not yet trained as a therapist when she met Bunny at the neighborhood gym.

Bunny was the eldest of five in her family of origin and was the designated "parental child." As such, she was in charge of younger siblings while her parents worked late. Her "way out" was to get pregnant at seventeen, marry her boyfriend, and have another child at nineteen.

Like many parental children, she tried to be a perfect parent to her own children. So Bunny became a classic "super-mom," completely devoted to them, with no time for herself. Not surprisingly, by the time she was twenty-eight Bunny had burned out, developing a severe psychosomatic skin condition requiring hospitalization.

Upon her release, she left her children with her husband and left town to find herself. She cut herself off from the children, reasoning or rationalizing that they would forget her in time, and she them. Any reminder would be too painful for them and for her.

Unfortunately, Bunny jumped into another relationship, immediately got pregnant and gave birth, but never fully bonded with her new husband or baby. "I heard she left town again, this time with her child, and became a Wiccan."

It is hard for Harriet to think back on this story through the lens of her now many years of experience as a therapist. Back then she had insufficient life experience from which to draw—not yet a parent, not yet a therapist. If Harriet were to meet Bunny today, she told us she would impress on Bunny the negative impact of desertion on children. She would press Bunny to restore contact for her own sake as well. In instances where children's well-being is at stake, we must inspire—implore—parents to do their best. Admittedly, the line between inspiring and judging is thin. That is where the art comes in.

The link between parental desertion and the ability of offspring to develop trust and engage in successful adult relationships is a focus in the following case. It exemplifies these dynamic intersections, as well as how the hope for reconnection can be energizing and potentially successful for some; but for others it may inhibit the development of their adult selves.

⁓⁓

Sara, a woman in her thirties, sought therapy because of ongoing problems in relationships with men. She had very low expectations and was constantly trying to please, changing her plans for them and expecting nothing back. In her current relationship, she had health problems she kept to herself.

Sara's parents divorced when she was in her twenties, and her father cut off from her and her sister entirely. He had a new wife, a new "set" of children, and did not respond to Sara's attempts to engage him. According to the therapist, Sara's older sister basically said "fuck you" to their father, but Sara will not give up. She is determined to at least understand why he disconnected.

Therapy focused on helping Sara make the connection between feeling abandoned by her father and her ongoing difficulties with men.

This client clearly needed to reevaluate her possibly vain effort to reestablish a relationship with her father. To decide whether to keep trying, the therapist encouraged her client to answer some key questions:

- What have you already tried?
- What is the relationship offering you? What are you getting emotionally or in tangible terms? What are you giving and getting?
- Are there benefits to staying cut off? In continuing to try to reconcile?
- What emotions are you experiencing toward the person: guilt, disappointment, anger, hurt, betrayal?

There are no easy answers to these questions. Instead, there are gradations with respect to costs and benefits, as well as what might be possible in the future. In these circumstances it may be less important to reclaim a past relationship than to help the client to understand the past and the person who abandoned him or her.

Through guided self-examination, Sara saw the pattern and connection between her relationship with her father and the relationship with her boyfriend. First, she began to assert herself with her boyfriend, and then, seeing the futility of her efforts at reestablishing a relationship with her father, she stopped contacting him. Six months later, in the midst of his second divorce, her father reached out. Here we see the pursuer-distancer pattern. When someone finally stops pursuing, the one who distanced sometimes comes back.

The importance of knowing the truth, the main reason Sara pursued her father, cannot be overstressed. In her father's case, it was guilt that led to consigning his first family to "my past life," also to oblige his second wife's insistence that he have no contact. The breakdown of that relationship enabled him to realize his terrible mistake. After a brief therapy with their father, Emily and Sara forgave him.

The ultimate cautionary tale supporting this point is of the young woman, Leah, we briefly mentioned in the Assessment chapter. She was told as a child that her father died, but later saw him on the street. As we indicated, she subsequently had a psychotic break and walked the corridors during her hospitalization repeating the title of a Broadway play, "Stop the world, I want to get off!"

Thus far, we have focused on parental desertion of children. In these cases we automatically empathize with the child and are challenged to empathize with the parent. But in the following email from a distraught mother, it is the parent we ache for. Here the challenge is to empathize with the child. The case, which unfortunately never materialized, is also a good example of third-party (therapist) hindrance of a potential reconciliation. Another therapist for the son might have found a way to bring mother and adult child together.

I am struggling through a rift with my thirty-year-old son that is breaking my heart. I'm so angry, I want to tell him to go to hell, but if I were to lose him completely, I couldn't bear it. I bounce between despair and determination to fix it. I don't even know where to begin, because he twists and distorts everything I say.

His therapist is the Gloria Steinem of the men's movement. He claims that men like my son's father abandon their children because women like me drive them crazy. He counsels clients to cut off from a narcissistic parent, so my son has abandoned me. I love him more than life itself and need help. Is this the kind of work you do?"

The next case is similar, except that this time the child was enmeshed with her mother and could not break away. Here the therapist had difficulty imagining any good in the parent.

When Natasha was seven, her mother suddenly moved from Russia to the United States, leaving Natasha behind with an aunt. She gave

Natasha no notice—did not even look back at her daughter or wave from the plane. There was no direct contact for three years. No presents, no letters, no nothing. When Natasha was ten, her mother sent for her.

At eighteen, Natasha, now a college student in Boston, started therapy in the wake of a devastating breakup with her boyfriend. Just a year before, after an argument with her mother, she had overdosed on drugs and alcohol. While recovering in the Emergency Room, she met the unreliable young man. He would break up and return, break up and return, but finally "dumped" her because she "wasn't good wife material." He wanted to be her whole world and rejected Natasha because "your first priority is your mother."

The therapist was undoubtedly right that Natasha was "brainwashed" and on a "tight leash." She was so tied to her mother that he believed she was "doomed" to choose men who would mistreat and then desert her, thus repeating her childhood experience. Further, "the mother saw her daughter as a "financial and emotional meal ticket. She actually wanted her daughter to marry the guy she met in the ER, somehow get his money, and dump him later on."

Despite this awful story, it is too bad no work took place with mother and daughter, but it is no wonder that the therapist did not suggest it, given the mother's terrible behavior. But had he held out hope that she had some redeeming qualities, it might have been different. Mother and daughter might have bonded over the early loss of the husband/father, and jointly recognized their shared struggle to survive. The mother might have been helped to express regret and apologize for leaving her daughter behind; hearing the reasons might have helped Natasha understand. The mother's insensitivity to her daughter coupled with the therapist's negative image precluded work with the mother-daughter pair, but one never knows. It is amazing how meeting and seeing the "guilty one" in the room can sometimes alter our perceptions.

⊷⊶

Chloe is a woman whose ex-husband controlled the money and power. His name, not hers, was on the deed to the house and on the bank accounts. At one point as they were separating, Chloe sought an order of protection because he was verbally abusive and becoming physically abusive as well. He undermined her attempts to discipline the children, and they stopped listening to her. Chloe, completely fed up, moved out and did not keep in touch, figuring the children would miss her. But, instead, they allied with the father against her. He claimed she was bipolar and obtained custody. He remarried and moved several towns away. Chloe has barely seen the children in years and cries constantly.

The therapist worked with Chloe to use the thread-bare connection to her children, encouraging her to take advantage of the rare opportunities her ex-husband allowed, making the little time she had with the children as enjoyable as possible, instead of blaming herself and them for not having more.

The therapist helped Chloe lower her expectations. Fixated on the past, Chloe wanted everything to be as it was before, wanted too much too fast. She finally saw that when she pushed, she was pushed away. The object was for her to gain control of her anger when things did not go her way. Chloe had to wait eons for the children to even notice the difference. She had to be patient and invest in a potential future response. Fortunately, as Chloe demanded less she began to have a better relationship with her estranged children. They now spend more time with her, they are more respectful, and she is more satisfied. With this deft therapeutic work, all was well enough in the end.

ILLNESS AND DEATH

Illness

Unlike death, with serious illness there is still hope for recovery, but in many cases death hovers in the wings, around the corner. Serious illness is therefore devastating not only for the afflicted one but also for others in the sick person's orbit as the following cases reveal.

Leo, a gifted young politician, literally bumped into Sandy, who was screaming outside the hotel at a conference in New Orleans. Someone had grabbed her purse. Leo ran down the street, caught up with the thief, and gallantly returned it. They had coffee, spent time, fell in love, married, and had two girls. He was Greek Orthodox; she was Jewish. Sandy converted over her parents' objections. While the couple was happy at first, underlying political and religious differences grew, and so did their emotional distance.

They stayed together into their forties until Leo contracted what they were told was a rare fatal disease. For whatever reason, this was the breaking point, and Sandy moved out. Sometime later, when the diagnosis proved incorrect and Leo survived, Sandy asked to come back. Leo debated, but in the end he took his mother's advice: "Move on and don't look back." Thus began the complete cutoff that has lasted to this day. Both Leo and Sandy remarried.

Although Leo and Sandy do not speak, the children are in contact with both parents through a court intermediary. Their good adjustment seems due in part to the fact that both stepparents want the children to have good relationships with their biological parents, and they encourage the contact. The stepparents have also bonded with the children. The value of a benign, understanding stepparent is immeasurable. We know about wicked ones, such as Cinderella's, but stepparents are just as often unsung heroes in a family who can be enlisted by therapists as constructive third parties to help a family of origin heal.

This case centers on the abandonment of one spouse by the other because death was thought to be impending. It was surely traumatic for Sandy as well as Leo and the children. Why Sandy could not handle it, we do not know, but we must pause to reflect that she must have had her reasons that, if brought to light, would surely cause us to judge her less harshly.

❧

The most poignant stories of abandonment begin and end when a parent dies, leaving a child behind. But Carrie's life exemplifies the ways in which abandonment in the form of a parent's serious illness can wreak havoc on a child. In this case, the therapist was able to engage the family to some extent, although it was paltry compared to what the client needed:

Carrie is a smart, creative woman in her early forties with a recent history of major depression and manic psychosis. She has also made sev-

eral suicide attempts and was hospitalized five times. In her twenties, Carrie functioned well, graduated from college, and married a steady guy. In her thirties, she realized the marriage was not working and decided to leave. Not long after, just before her self-described "breakdown," her ex-husband cut her off completely. He had a new relationship with a woman who insisted he not speak to Carrie, and he complied, breaking his promise that they would always be friends. This cutoff was the latest in a string of losses.

When Carrie was fifteen, after years of marital strife her father left the family to be with a woman he married. Carrie's parents stopped speaking, and her mother made a serious suicide attempt. Carrie found her in time, but the mother was then hospitalized for years. Carrie was "invited" to live with her father and stepmother but wanted to graduate from "her" high school, so her father left her in the house with an older sister, who it turned out could not effectively chaperone. Over the years, Carrie and her sister cut off from each other and from their parents. When Carrie became ill, her father was infirm, and although her mother tried to help by taking Carrie in, before long the mother collapsed again and was placed in a home.

Carrie has been in therapy for ten years. Early on, the therapist bore witness to the traumatic losses Carrie suffered and how little reliable parenting she had. It was not easy gaining her trust, but the therapist hoped that over time it would develop. Carrie did agree to a session with each parent that enabled her to ask for financial help from her father to get a master's degree in music, and she obtained a promise from her mother to stop complaining about her problems.

The accessibility of Carrie's therapist was essential. Lacking adequate family support and other compensatory relationships, she had no ability to master extremely painful feelings of abandonment, rage, and grief. Not every clinician is willing or able to give in this way, to extend boundaries beyond the ordinary. Sometimes the availability has to be 24/7 (though no one ever called us in the middle of the night). In any event, during the initial assessment of clients with complete abandonment issues, therapists have to assess whether they are prepared—within certain limits to be sure—to be a surrogate parent for a significant period of time.

When Carrie became ill, "losing her mind" she lost her livelihood, what she had in the way of family, and her friends, who did not understand her erratic behavior.

Realizing that the therapeutic alliance alone would not suffice, the plan shifted to finding other services to prevent Carrie from drowning in all the cutoffs—husband, mother's living death, father's unavailability, sister's unavailability, loss of friends, and loss of livelihood.

Through her therapist Carrie found and joined Fountain House. There, she received disability application assistance, got help with obtaining subsidized housing, received help in filing back taxes, gained transitional employment, and had an emotionally supportive community of staff members and friends. She also attended free support groups in the city. Through her primary care physician, Carrie also found a community psychiatrist "without whom I would never take meds." She is pulling herself together.

Testament to Carrie's progress is the fact that when her father became terminally ill, Carrie was there for him, visiting regularly despite needing to travel two hours on public transportation. It was painful visiting her mother in the nursing home which was too close a replay of her mother's mental illness years before.

The takeaway here is that even the best therapy is usually not enough to compensate for multiple cutoffs. The strategy, then, has to be acknowledgment by the therapist of the limitations of therapy and willingness to draw help from other sources.

Death

Although not always conceptualized as such, death is also a form of "cutoff." Most deaths are unintended. At times, despite their rational knowledge, those who remain may experience the loss as purposeful yet do not feel entitled to be angry at the person for leaving. Death is a cutoff like no other. Its finality makes it different even from adoption—one can search and hope to find one's child or one's mother. Dying is forever. Back to elemental aloneness. Such cutoffs are often so paralyzing that the associated emotions get shoved under the proverbial rug, buried for years.

Death of a parent is always traumatic. While usually less so in adulthood, for a child, a parent's death is devastating. When one parent dies, a child may also suffer a second psychological abandonment by the remaining parent if he or she is preoccupied with his or her own grief or the logistics that accompany a death. In these cases, again, someone needs to step in for a period of time, to be a surrogate. Ideally it is someone else in the family. But in Nora's case, there was no one until she was a troubled seventeen-year-old dragged into therapy by her father and stepmother. There Nora found a therapist who was available, willing, and able to help her mourn and provide some of the "mothering" Nora had not experienced when she was ten, or ever since.

♋

Nora's mother was sick for 6 years and died when she was ten. Nora does not remember that time. Her father soon remarried someone with three young children, and though Nora had room and board, her father had no time for her. She felt second class in the new family, "like Cinderella with a mean stepmother." The stepmother "told me my mother never really cared about me."

Predictably, Nora acted up. She disobeyed rules regarding curfew, noise, cleaning her room. She embraced "goth," got piercings and tattoos, drank, smoked, and announced she was a lesbian. She ran away multiple times and was completely out of control. By the time the family brought her in for therapy, she was ostracized by everyone in the household, considered "no good," "crazy," persona non grata. They could not wait for her to leave, and she knew it.

What Nora needed was respect paid to the loss of her mother, help in honoring her memory. She needed to know that she could both miss her mother and be angry for being abandoned. Nora also needed to express her rage at her father for neglecting her, for him to apologize, and to achieve some level of repair of their relationship. It was too late in the game, though. The couple labeled her hopeless and wanted her gone. Nora descended into a suicidal depression and was hospitalized for several weeks. No one visited.

Upon Nora's release, she moved out and stayed with a friend, and the therapist saw her individually until she moved away. For twenty years, Nora would occasionally call the therapist out of the blue, recounting romances, breakups, jobs, school, general survival stories, asking for advice, always longing for a loving relationship and a stable home.

She recontacted the therapist as she turned forty. Back in the area, she was determined to learn the truth about her mother. She found her mother's closest friend and learned how much her mother had loved Nora, how worried her mother had been about how Nora would fare after her death. The friend apologized for not keeping an eye on Nora. Nora cried on and off for months. She "conversed" with her mother, and felt her mother's presence. She set a new career direction and formed a stable relationship. She has some contact with her father, but "no expectations."

We conclude this chapter with one more story, about how a parent's death knocked a reasonably solid young man off course. With a therapist's help, he got back on track in time to have his own life.

∽⌒∾

Walter, a human rights lawyer, has no problem excelling at work. But something else weighs him down. He cannot decide whether to return to Belgium or stay in the U.S. He is also beside himself because he cannot stop thinking about an English girl he met on vacation. Walter is thirty-five and feels ready to have a family of his own. Giselle, however, is "confused," not sure she is interested, and will not commit to seeing him on any regular basis. Walter's obsession is so intense he cannot sleep, has lost his appetite, cannot concentrate at work and is afraid of losing his job. The therapist is worried enough to refer him for a medication evaluation.

While Walter had been "prized" as the only son, he was sheltered and unused to adversity. But when he was nineteen, his father died, and as the one closest to his mother, he instinctively slipped into his father's role. He arranged the funeral, took care of his father's estate, wrapped up his father's affairs, even slept on his father's side of the bed for a while.

Despite his problems, Walter is an outgoing, charming young man. His friends love him, and he could easily have someone, but he has never had a significant relationship. Ever the dutiful son, Walter Skypes with his mother twice a day.

Walter's six-month therapy began with an exploration of the role he took on as head of the family when his father died. His father was "easygoing, almost too passive," his mother was "boss." To her, failing or performing poorly was not an option. After her husband, who kept her steady, died, she was highly anxious and could not calm down. Walter tried to reassure her, but because he was a worrier too, he couldn't.

In the course of therapy, Walter gradually saw that he had unwittingly stepped into his father's shoes. He did not mourn, and although he physically left home, he never claimed his own developmentally appropriate independence. He also realized that Giselle's lack of commitment served a purpose. Since Giselle was not really available, Walter could still keep his relationship with his mother, who would tell him not to call so often but berate him when he did not. In a sense, he was being toyed with by both women.

The therapist commented that it was amazing how quickly Walter regrouped once he connected his obsession with Giselle to how he felt in his relationship with his mother: "In both cases, I never really feel secure." He still wanted to go "home" but decided not to live with his mother. Because this was a relatively functional family until the father's death, his mother ultimately accepted Walter's fewer Skype sessions and his gradual disengagement, saying, "Though it's hard to let you go, I've always said you should have your own life, and not worry so much about me." Walter also decided he did not want to be with Giselle or anyone so unpredictable, and he stopped trying to convince her of anything. He wanted a woman who wanted him.

Having examined the various types of cutoffs that occur as a result of feeling abandoned, we will leave feelings of sadness, depression, and loneliness to explore a more active, energizing emotion: jealousy. But in so doing, keep the words of this Arab proverb in mind, "Jealousy is nothing more than the fear of abandonment."

Chapter 4

JEALOUSY AND ENVY

> O! beware, my lord, of jealousy;
> It is the green-eyed monster which doth mock
> The meat it feeds on.
> Shakespeare, *Othello* (III.iii.165–171)

In his novel *1984*, George Orwell (1949/1969) wrote about "thought crimes"—unspoken, punishable ideas, beliefs, or doubts that oppose or question authority. We call jealousy and envy "feeling crimes." People are carefully taught—at home, in school, and in the community—that such feelings are bad. So instead of acknowledging them, using them to understand ourselves and what is missing in our lives, we suppress jealousy and envy, bar them from consciousness, until these emotions either spill over into acts of betrayal, or cutoffs.

Jealousy and envy are closely related emotions, at times overlapping or intertwined. But they are not the same. Envy refers to another's good fortune in general, whereas jealousy is the desire to have someone else's significant other, position, or possession.

The following example may help. A single man is *envious* of a friend who is married because he has *a* wife, whereas the same single man would be *jealous* if he wanted the friend's *particular* wife! In the first instance, there is no competition because there are other potential wives. Envy is painful enough. Jealousy is worse—hotter and more insidious.

Both are probably built into the psyche from birth. Sybil Hart found that children show jealousy as early as six months if their mothers pay attention to a life-size doll (Hart & Carrington, 2002). Hart's research could also explain why children may show distress when a sibling is born, creating the foundation for sibling rivalry (Hart et al., 2004), and Douglas Mock (2004) provides countless examples of sibling competition among animals in the wild to explain how it actually serves an evolutionary function.

Even if not inborn, two quotations suggest that envy and jealousy are universal:

"Envy assails the noblest: the winds howl around the highest peaks." (Ovid)

"If envy were a fever, all the world would be ill." (Danish proverb)

And, if further proof is necessary, when life deals a loved one a blow, many people find themselves deriving secret satisfaction from the suffering. One composite word in German, *schadenfreude* (taking pleasure in someone else's misery), captures this unfortunate, too human tendency.

Parents exacerbate jealousy and envy. Many would contend that parents are the source, and that at the heart of jealousy is how individuals were treated by parents and other caregivers. Subtle and blatant forms of abuse or neglect (including favoritism) are usually at work beneath the surface when pernicious sibling rivalry persists into adulthood.

People envy others for what their parents taught was important to possess. Unless parents are unusually gifted at hiding it, if they valued money and the child hasn't made it, he or she likely envies others who possess it. If the parents valued beauty, the child will suffer for lack of it. If parents valued girls, a boy will be jealous of his sister. We can be pretty sure that even if parental favoritism among siblings (not to mention parents' preference for each other to the exclusion of their children) goes underground, it will likely reappear in tortured romantic jealousy in adulthood.

The green-eyed monster is so overpowering that once the jealousy switch is turned on, it can overwhelm mature individuals who are not normally given to it. Even Othello, a steady, trustworthy, and trusting soul, could be convinced that his wife, Desdemona, whom he *knew* to be devoted, was unfaithful.

The fear of acting on these emotions is so strong that people apparently need religious admonitions to avoid it. "Thou shalt not covet" is writ in Ten Commandments stone. We also have the Christian seven deadly sins, among them *invidia* or "envy," and corresponding warnings in Hindu, Buddhist, and Islamic traditions. All have Leviathan images, such as in Job of a scaly monster of supernatural strength, breathing smoke from his nostrils, flames blazing from his mouth.

As intense as jealousy and envy may be, we are still only talking about feelings and wishes. Most people live with these uneasy feelings. They do not destroy individuals or their relationships. How do most people control them? Why are these all-too-human emotions sometimes intolerable? When do these hostile feelings convert to action? Why do some people cross the line?

The first answer is that jealousy and envy usually prey on the most vulnerable. Low self-esteem is the major intervening variable between thought and action. If one is insecure, the fear of abandonment is paramount. The slightest interest a lover shows in someone or something else is taken as proof of unworthiness, that one could never prevail in a competitive situation, that he or she is sure to be deserted in the end.

Furthermore, insecure people cannot accept the idea that someone else may actually be preferred over them and may exaggerate the import of very slight rejections as further proof of their own inferiority. Simply put, the insecure are easily "hijacked," to borrow Daniel Goleman's (2005) word. Jealousy and envy overpower the rational mind, distort perspective, undercut self-control, and incite violence.

&

This is what happened to Dylan, who spent the greater part of his adult life consumed with envy of a neighbor who became financially successful beyond even his own wildest dreams. Dylan's parents held the neighbor up as a shining example, which was especially hurtful because Dylan helped the neighbor develop his ideas and was neither acknowledged nor given a piece of the pie.

Dylan's own dream of becoming a symphony conductor was dashed when his parents refused to pay for conservatory training, and the neighbor would not lend him the money. Dylan dropped out of college and embarked on a bitter path to oblivion. Now fifty, often stoned, he has no steady employment, no career or family of his own. His childhood envy still poisons his life, as do his many grudges. He no longer speaks to the old neighbor, and he cannot get through a therapy hour without raging about his family, the neighbor, and his lost opportunities.

Dylan has managed to control his vengeful thoughts thus far, but his therapist worries about his potential for violence. The cutoff from the neighbor is at this point helping, and that is why he did it.

Besides underlying insecurity, there is a systemic element to be factored in. It is the question of balance in a relationship. Most close relationships are founded on some form of parity, sense of equality, or reciprocity. Friends feel they have more or less equal standing and equal power to determine the course of the relationship. One party may have more money, but the other may be more accomplished. The same is ideally true with siblings, though in many cases the eldest or the eldest male has greater delegated power from the parents. In marriage, historically, traditional male dominance was offset by reciprocal exchange for protecting his wife. Parent-child relationships are supposed to be reciprocal over time; initially parents have the power and responsibility for care of children, but toward the end of parents' lives, children care for them. It is the unwritten contract, the "deal," the payback, a balancing out.

But then sometimes something happens. There is an undoing of the delicate balance. A change of status occurs, and the parties are no longer in sync. A backstage mother finds herself resentful of a child who accomplishes what she was unable to, such as in the film *Black Swan,* and the mother undermines rather than enjoys her daughter's success.

Some athletes, such as tennis player Mary Pierce, have cut off from over-involved or abusive parents (Jones, 2000). A friend gets a promotion or a close friend at work gets the promotion one wanted, a sibling wins the lottery, or—the ultimate example—a divorce is amicable until one former spouse has a new love, and suddenly, nothing is the same.

The reactions to jealousy and envy occur along a continuum. The person first registers the feeling, either consciously or subconsciously. He or she tries to live with it. If the person cannot, the feelings become acute or intolerable, and he or she may decide to cut off, or will be cut off. Alternatively, the person may seek to equalize the relationship by punishing the one who has caused the anguish by betraying him or her somehow, from harmful gossip to murder. A key factor causing spillover into action is the way a suddenly more successful person handles his or her success. The individual is either sensitive or insensitive to the other person's feelings and how the success might affect the other person. In any case, when *invidia* enters, kindness and empathy—*humanitas*—is out the door.

In an attempt to distinguish between jealousy and envy, and as we move into case discussion, remember that we will reserve jealousy for romantic feelings and for material objects that cannot be replaced. In those instances, where there is only one "object," the desire is to possess that particular person or thing, and ultimately to deprive the other person of it. Where there is no attachment to a particular person or object, and where, say, one party would be satisfied by having a different, equally wonderful partner and the person is only upset that the other party has obtained a material or psychological advantage, we call it envy.

ROMANTIC JEALOUSY

As the attachment literature suggests, romantic jealousy may be the grown-up version of sibling rivalry for parental affection. If those childhood experiences were especially problematic or painful, they tend to be recapitulated, even magnified in adulthood. This is why romantic jealousy has such an obsessional quality to it.

We can predict, therefore, that a cutoff resulting from intense romantic jealousy will be hard to fix. As the following example of two brothers shows, however, resolution is always possible.

⚭

Max had a history of emotional difficulties and led a hermit-like existence on a small inheritance and governmental disability that Carl helped secure. The brothers had good times, but Max long resented

Carl for being overbearing and belittling his ideas, and Max envied Carl's professional success.

When Carl and Max were in their forties, Carl flew from Philadelphia to the Oregon woods to see his brother. A neighbor had called to say that Max did not seem right. Carl's attempt to convince Max to try yet another therapist failed. The "conversation" wound up with Max shoving Carl "off my property." There was less communication afterward, but no official cutoff.

The following year, Carl visited again, this time surprising Max by bringing his new wife. Janice resembled their mother, a beautiful woman who had died when the boys were in their twenties. Although Max said nothing, it was clear he was not happy to see Carl or to meet Janice. A year later, their sister Liza, who lived in England, came to the U.S. for her birthday, which she hoped to celebrate with her brothers. Max told her in unequivocal terms that "if Carl comes, I won't." Thus began a fifteen-year complete cutoff.

Carl made overtures to Max, sending presents and emails. The presents went unacknowledged, and the emails were blocked. Though she had her own resentments and sided with Max, on her next visit Liza stayed with Carl and Janice.

Janice could feel the tension and asked the siblings to talk. She helped Liza express her feeling that Carl had "lorded" his academic success over her. She asked Carl to understand Max's jealousy, especially now that Carl had Janice. Liza shared her sense that Max was taken with Janice. Carl finally understood the reason for his brother's cutoff and vowed to stop taking the rejection so personally. He apologized for his behavior toward Liza, and Liza tried—unsuccessfully—to get Max to soften. But, Janice's intervention did work in that a cutoff between Carl and Liza was averted.

Janice, for her part, called Max once in a while "on instinct," to keep hope alive for the brothers' relationship, and because Max would always talk to her. He was so willing to talk that it surprised her. He was sweet and it felt a little like flirting.

When the brothers were nearing sixty, Janice put in a call to Max. To a simple "How are you?" Max replied, "Oh, okay, I guess." They spoke for a few minutes about nothing in particular, but the "I guess" stuck in Janice's mind. She circled back to ask what "I guess" meant. "'I guess' means I've got lung cancer, and I'm dying is all," Max replied. After commiserating, Janice asked if he would be willing to see Carl. Without hesitating, Max said, "Yes, that's in the past now." So Carl went. Nothing deep, nothing terribly personal was dredged up. They just "hung out" like they used to.

An imminent death can definitely put a cutoff in perspective, allowing grudges to be dropped and resentments to be let go. Perhaps Carl's original efforts and Liza's and Janice's third-party interventions that seemed futile at the time did gradually combine to convince Max of his brother's sincerity. Perhaps once Max was ill and out of time, the efforts were sufficient to override Max's jealousy.

Had Max not been terminally ill, it is unclear whether or when the brothers would have managed to surmount the imbalances in their lives. We know of other instances in which tremendous sibling inequities such as these cannot be bridged—especially if there is only one woman in question, and the more successful brother has her.

Surely there were red flags prior to the cutoff. Carl was the unabashed favorite, and Max had shown signs of being jealous of their parents' preference for Carl before. But, the actual cutoff happened only after Carl married Janice. Neither Liza nor Max was married, and neither had children. Neither had any money to speak of. By marrying, Carl upped the ante on his prior comparative success. He not only married but found a woman who looked like their mother, had some means, and had three children, making Carl a stepfather too. Before Janice, Max had managed to keep his resentment under wraps. It was this status change that had tipped the balance and produced the cutoff.

☙❧

Not all jealousy cutoffs stem from competition between contemporaries. Both romantic and maternal jealousies collided when MaryAnn and her mother-in-law, Bea, competed for precious time with Julio. Julio had undergone surgery to correct a minor problem. Now he lay comatose in the hospital with a poor prognosis after a tragic surgical mistake.

MaryAnn and Bea encamped in Julio's hospital room day and night for a week. Julio was Bea's only child, and, as she was recently wid-

owed, he was all she had. MaryAnn, young and married only 5 years, was about to lose her husband. MaryAnn gently asked Bea for some time alone with Julio. Bea heard the request as MaryAnn "kicking me out of the room." Bea stopped speaking to MaryAnn, a silence Mary-Ann said was "deafening."

MaryAnn was initially incensed but realized that Bea was understandably jealous of her relationship with Julio. Bea needed to defend her maternal prerogative, while MaryAnn needed to exercise her marital one. In addition, MaryAnn grasped that they were competing for the last days with Julio, that they were both stressed to the limit and therefore likely to misinterpret each other's feelings and requests.

Pushing past her own pain, MaryAnn apologized. Though she was not sure she had done anything wrong, she decided it was worth it for family peace: "I'm sorry. Let's look at it this way. We both love Julio, we are both about to lose him, we have to be there for each other, and it would be good if we can cut each other some slack." Bea accepted the apology, and relented.

Here is an instance in which one of the cutoff parties had presence of mind in a horrible situation, and the communication skills to match. MaryAnn used the same approach a good clinician would, including a clarification of the women's different, but equally important roles in Julio's life—no need for a therapist here.

One teenage boy gave his mother something like that to hold onto when she half kiddingly warned him it would be hard to accept his someday having another woman in his life. "Yes, it's true," he said. "But just remember that you will always be my first." This little vignette contains good advice for a therapist contending with a client cutoff over intergenerational jealousy. Help articulate the roles of mother and daughter-in-law contemporaneously, so that each has a defined and secure role and place.

PARENTAL FAVORITISM

Favoring one child over another is problematic for both children. The favored one comes to believe he or she is entitled and superior, or feels guilty and undeserving. The other one feels inferior, unworthy, and jealous. The following is a case in point.

❦

Wendy is a fifty-year-old single woman. Her mother, Francine, had an illegitimate son but later married and had Wendy. Wendy is angry at her mother for favoring Oscar, when Wendy is the one who cares more. Wendy's mother is a strict Catholic who still feels guilty about her son's illegitimacy. As a result she is too lenient and gives Oscar everything he wants.

Oscar, fifty-five and single, is highly dysfunctional. He doesn't work and rarely visits his mother. Although Wendy and Oscar were close as children, they now barely speak. Wendy thinks Oscar is a sociopath. When she has to see him at their mother's house, their mother hovers over him. Wendy fumes and is afraid she is going crazy. Once, prior to starting therapy, Wendy complained to her mother about the preferential treatment of Oscar. Francine defended herself by saying that Wendy was at least legitimate and treated well enough.

The therapist who provided this case focused on trying to help Wendy decrease her anger, not on Wendy's relationships with Francine or Oscar, which the therapist believed were hopeless.

To be sure, this is a family stuck in family-of-origin mode. Neither adult child is able to "differentiate," to emotionally leave the nest; the siblings remain locked in battle for their mother's attention. They are stuck, but not hopeless. To break the deadlock, the therapist could ask the client's permission to shift from individual to family therapy. She could help Wendy confront her mother constructively, by expressing her hurt directly. Since there was an injustice in how Wendy was treated, this truth would have to be acknowledged before Wendy could ever decrease her anger, or even consider connecting with Oscar. Francine could be asked about her own life and guided to understand her daughter's hurt, even to making an apology.

MONEY

To avoid envying someone close who has more money, we tend to choose friends in similar circumstances, or as the lyrics for *West Side Story*'s "A Boy Like That" go, "stick to your own kind." So, once again, whether it is friends or family, close relationships tend to be balanced until something changes. And, when it does, especially when a monetary imbalance becomes too great, the parties can wind up in court.

✎ ✎

Ron and Cynthia were twins. After their father's funeral, Cynthia realized that Ron was not going to return her share of the money he had "borrowed" from their father. Cynthia cut Ron off and sued him. According to Cynthia, whenever Ron was low in cash or in trouble, he would "twist our father's arm." Over the years, Ron "extracted" $500,000. Although reimbursement was not addressed in the will, Cynthia thought it would be only fair. There were other issues, including that Ron was the father's favorite, that he was a pretty mean brother, and that success in this family was measured by money.

Cynthia lost the suit and did not speak to Ron for ten years. He cajoled her to no avail. Ron's position was that Cynthia was much better off than he was and that if their father did not equalize the situation in his will, it was because he was mindful of that.

Ron's therapist advised him to back off and give both himself and Cynthia time to recover from the stress of the lawsuit. This was not easy for Ron, who was extremely anxious, always feeling he needed immediate resolution to any problem. But the cooling off gave Ron time to explore the meaning of money in the family and to feel better about his professional and athletic accomplishments, besides making money. He grasped that even though Cynthia had money, she still felt devalued and deprived in the family they came from. And last, the therapist pointed out that siblings often rediscover each other in later life—when their children leave, when spouses or friends die—and that in old age relationships often come to matter more than money.

The outcome was exactly as the therapist had predicted. Cynthia's first husband died, and her adult sons moved away and no longer needed her. Depressed and lonely, she woke up one morning and realized she wanted to see her brother.

OBJECTS/PROPERTY/LAND

Objects and property, like romantic jealousy, differ from money in that it is often not possible to duplicate or replace an object or piece of land. They tend to have specific symbolic value, either in them-selves or because they belonged to someone important to the person who wants it. When two people who are close both want the same thing, it adds another layer of difficulty to a sibling inheritance situ-ation, a stepfamily prenuptial, or a divorce. As we have seen, money is symbolic as well, but at least in theory, more can be obtained. There is only one house in that specific location with that particular view, but there are many thousand-dollar bills.

Objects are also specific in that they will often be a stand in for the person who originally owned them and who may be gone. You never hear someone say they think of their mother whenever they see a ten-dollar bill, whereas you often hear people say something like "I think of my father whenever I walk past his house, or when I wear one of his ties." The point is that objects and property may have sentimental—or irreplaceable aesthetic—value beyond their actual monetary worth.

Melissa is the oldest of five. For as long as she can remember, she was the parental child, taking care not only of her siblings but also her mother, who was mentally ill and frequently hospitalized. Melissa's father tried his best to keep the family together, but he yelled at Melissa whenever she "slipped up again," starting when she was eight.

Melissa did what she could to help her mother, whose rare smiles she treasured, but she was never close to her sibs. When she was older, though, and had no children of her own, she gave substantial gifts to her nieces and nephews. She knew she was compensating for the dis-tance she kept from her siblings, but still, it made her feel good.

When Melissa's mother died, a fight ensued. Melissa wanted a pearl necklace her mother had worn on festive occasions; her sisters wanted it too. One brother, the executor, refused to give the necklace to anyone and placed it in a safe. The necklace had little monetary value, but it reminded Melissa of the few good times with her mother. The sisters' stated position was that family jewelry should be passed down through the generations. Melissa has no children; therefore, she should not have the necklace.

Melissa saw her family only on Christmas and Easter. Apart from these holidays there was little contact. When Melissa hosted her father's seventy-fifth birthday party, she sat alone much of the evening, and none of her siblings thanked her.

Melissa's therapist helped her mourn her mother and the childhood she never had. She saw her siblings living an ideal life with work and family, whereas she had work but no social life. The therapist asked if she would be happier completely cut off. Melissa resisted this drastic step, but sensed that in that low moment. She decided to stay connected but that something had to change.

The therapist never argued with Melissa about her wish to have the necklace. On the contrary, she encouraged her to be more assertive about it. They practiced what Melissa would say to her siblings, how she could explain what the necklace meant. She gathered her courage, spoke with her brother first, and then called a family meeting. When she spoke firmly and from the heart, the family understood. Melissa would have the necklace as long as she agreed not to sell it or give it away. She agreed to pass it on to a niece in her will.

From necklace to clock:

Two brothers, Daniel and Darrell, stopped speaking because Darrell always wanted the family grandfather clock, but somehow Daniel "wound up" with it when their parents' estate was settled. Years passed, but neither brother could let go of the issue. Daniel maintained he loved the clock, too, and that their parents obviously wanted him to have it, and Darrell held that Daniel always knew how much Darrell wanted it. Eventually, Daniel wanted to end the cut off. An opportunity arose when they were both invited to a family wedding. After the ceremony, without speaking, Daniel took his brother by the hand and walked him over to his SUV. In the back was the grandfather clock. Reconciliation was immediate.

Daniel relinquished the contested object realizing that a relationship with his brother was more important than the clock. Sometimes this kind of clarity is not easy for a client to reach. In the difficult cases, we assess the siblings' relationship and their relationship with their parents prior to the precipitating incident. Is this struggle another reflection of unspoken jealousy going back to childhood? Is each sibling aware of how the other feels? Does each know or understand the value the other places in the artifacts of their parents' lives? Can they discuss the meaning of these objects without flying off the handle?

A therapist with whom we shared this case came up with other options. The siblings could take turns having the clock, thus both enjoying it. If they could not agree on who should have it, they could sell it or give it away. They could flip a coin, but then the underlying issues might not be dealt with and new struggles could emerge. The point is that such disputes can often be resolved by helping the parties loosen up, brainstorm, and think outside the box.

Ideally, we want to help each party understand the other's perspective and that by improving the relationship in this way, the "clock" and where it will go become less important.

BEAUTY

Beauty may be a cultural construct, but its power seems to be universal. Some think being beautiful bestows special status, or perceived entry into a more privileged life. The corollary is that if one lacks beauty, one is left out, marginalized. Such was the experience of Joyce.

✎∾✍

It took Joyce a lifetime to understand why she felt unloved. She came to see it through the lens of beauty. Until she was four, she was mostly cared for by a loving nanny and led a charmed life. When the nanny left, Joyce was bereft. She grabbed a pair of scissors, stood in front of the mirror in her room, and cut off her long hair. Her mother, Rosalyn—pregnant, self-absorbed, and unable to empathize—told friends and family in Joyce's presence that Joyce was an "impossible" child.

The new baby, Maddy, was cute, with blond curly hair. Rosalyn called her "my baby." Joyce felt left out or in the way. Joyce, at age thirty, showed to her therapist a family photo taken when Joyce was six. Off to the side, Joyce looks unhappy, awkward, and alone. Maddy, leaning against her mother, is indeed adorable, bubbly, confident, and, given Rosalyn's adoring look, the apple of her mother's eye.

To Joyce, Maddy was pretty and had exquisite taste, attributes that mattered. Backhanded compliments and invidious comparisons were plentiful. Maddy was "beautiful," Joyce "handsome"; Maddy's hands were "graceful," Joyce's "useful." Upon discovering an old report card, Rosalyn was surprised because "I didn't realize you got good grades too." And, finally, "That's a nice outfit. I never knew you could put yourself together so well."

As an adult, Joyce had an epiphany. She dealt with her jealousy by internalizing Maddy, trying to "be" Maddy. Whether shopping for clothes, furniture, or an apartment, she would wonder, "Would Maddy approve?" There was Maddy, in Joyce's head, like it or not.

After leaving home, the sisters kept in superficial touch. Then Maddy married Martin, a rising attorney with a huge inheritance. Maddy's status changed completely, further unbalancing the sisters' tenuous relationship. Now Maddy had travel, a country mansion, expensive clothes, jewelry, spa treatments, a chauffeur, a private plane, plastic surgery, dental implants, and so on while Joyce would only grow old "naturally." Despite her many professional accomplishments and good looks, when she was around Maddy, Joyce always felt inferior.

One day Martin took Joyce aside and berated her—for being divorced, for being a "terrible sister," the sole cause of Maddy's problems. At that time, Martin was the most powerful person in the family. Everyone, especially Rosalyn, idolized him. No one knew Maddy was miserable in their marriage and that she would eventually divorce him.

The "conversation" with Martin hurt Joyce tremendously. "I have to take a stand," she told her therapist. She invoked a conditional cutoff from Martin—and from Maddy, because Maddy did not take him to task. A few months later, Joyce refused to attend Rosalyn's holiday dinner, without an apology from Martin. At Rosalyn's behest, Martin apologized, and Joyce accepted it. It was the Jewish New Year, at which time animosities from the past year are supposed to be resolved. After Maddy's divorce, a semblance of balance was restored, and the sisters, beauty fading, drew closer as they aged.

FAMILY

In this section we discuss envy of one party in a relationship toward the other for having family, or more family. It can be envy that crops up when a friend gets married and acquires a mate, or it can be when a friend has a baby while the other has fertility problems. It can be an older parent who envies his friends with grandchildren if his own children, despite best efforts to hurry them along, show no signs of "delivering."

These feelings can run deep, sometimes to the point of absurdity to an outsider. To wit:

∽∾

A young couple wrote to Philip Galanes (2012), the New York Times *Social Qs columnist complaining about friends who threatened "never to speak to them again" if they "stole" the baby name the friends were planning to use. Apparently, this happened on four different occasions, and the couple added that "some of these friends are still single!"*

Such a threat, especially coming from single friends, few of whom are likely to have children anytime soon, does seem ridiculous. It is not as though there is a law restricting friends from using the same names for their children, or as if the single friend's opportunity to use that name is forever lost. But the incipient cutoff demand is understandable as an oblique expression of a single friend's envy of the married friend, who not only has a relationship but is also about to have a child. It could also be about identity theft, or sibling rivalry, as in who will be first to have a child. Finally, the cutoff threat is about the profound status change that takes place when someone has a child and leaves a single friend behind. There are countless examples of cutoffs that occur when children, if not children's names, come between friends.

Had these friends discussed the issue, perhaps the envy of the still-single friend could be mollified. The woman about to give birth could empathize with her friend's feelings and explain that the same name can be used twice. One author's grandchildren are Sophie and Sam, names at or close to the top of current most popular names in America lists. This means we cannot call to either one in the playground without five other kids turning around. But Sophie and Sam are delighted their names are so popular; they show no sign of feeling diminished by sharing their names.

There is no humor though, in the following situation that ended in a cutoff between one woman and her close college friends.

❦

Andrea came from a secure, trouble-free middle-class family. One dream was to be a field anthropologist, the other to marry a journalist who would publicize her findings and whose career she would support. Her own career was sidelined when she met Jason, a novelist. They moved to Washington, DC, where she worked as a medical secretary, earning just enough to keep them afloat. They had one child, then twins two years later.

Jason was not the easiest husband or father. He was moody, had writer's block, and would retreat to his study for weeks. Their friends, mostly hers, loved both Andrea and Jason. However, it was clear Andrea resented Jason for his lack of productivity and she envied her friends' easier path. Nevertheless, the friends remained close through their twenties and well into their thirties.

Jason always believed he would die young, which he did on his thirty-eighth birthday—run over by an elderly driver who "did not see him." Because Jason had been unhappy and they had marital problems, Andrea believed the "accident" had a suicidal component. This left a badly shaken Andrea alone to raise their three young children. Her parents helped, and the friends rallied round. At first, everyone was welcome. But soon, Andrea stopped returning phone calls and started refusing invitations. When one friend asked why, she explained. "My life is a mess. It's too hard to be around all of you when you're doing so well. I'll never marry again; you all have each other."

In essence, Andrea's status changed and she couldn't handle the discrepancy in fortune between herself and her friends or the new level of envy she experienced.

The friends honored Andrea's request for a temporary cutoff, giving her time. Perhaps her request was a reaction to the trauma and part of the mourning process. Her therapist supported the retreat but also encouraged her to explicitly state that it would be temporary.

In the cutoff period, the therapist provided a long-range perspective and challenged Andrea's idea that she was destined to be alone forever. She explained that people's fortunes "turn on a dime," and while it was certainly Andrea's "turn" to suffer, circumstances change. Something happens to alter one's life course, and over time misfortunes often have a way of balancing out. If these friends are valuable, keep them. Yes, they are luckier now, but they are also there for her now. Andrea can be there for them when her life improves.

At the same time, this therapist helped Andrea begin to be proud of her strength as a single widow, and see that these friends would be the first to introduce her to a single man if or when she was ready. The cutoff lasted three months, after which Andrea called her friends and asked to get together.

Next we see how a primary parent-child cutoff ripples through a family like a giant wave; in this case affecting all of the siblings in secondary breaks, and moving on to the next generation as well.

⧼⧽

Isabelle and Jules are the parents of four children in their twenties. Two years ago, Mimi, twenty-three, joined a cult and shut off contact with the family. No one knew where she was, and according to their therapist, the parents spent a fortune on a private investigator trying to find her, with no success. To Gabby, twenty-five, it was "ridiculous." She was angry and jealous because her parents seemed to care more about Mimi, who had deserted the family, than about her and the other two who were "loyal."

One day when Gabby was visiting from Atlanta, Isabelle and Jules mentioned a new way to search for Mimi. Gabby blew up, ran out, and has not spoken with her parents since. Gabby then persuaded her sister Zoey to cut off their brother Simon, the only child still speaking to the parents. Gabby then cut off Zoey and Simon who were close to one another. Before all this took place, Isabelle and Jules had flown to Atlanta every few months to see Gabby and her son, but no longer. Recently, Gabby had a daughter whom Isabelle and Jules have never seen.

The therapist's tack was to console the parents, to encourage them to make the most of the relationship they still had with Simon, and to focus on other aspects of their lives. But before long, the couple stopped coming.

The clinician might have suggested a meeting with the parents and Simon, who, caught in the middle, would likely have echoed Gabby's feeling that the parents forgot the other siblings in their panic over Mimi. The therapist could suggest the parents write to their daughters promising not to discuss the search for Mimi in their presence and to enjoy the blessings they still had.

If this effort failed, the parents could ask Gabby, Zoey, and Simon to meet with the therapist or a colleague to explain their point of view and impose any conditions they want met in order to reconcile. The siblings would probably agree to meet, because they too no doubt were suffering from the disconnection, no matter what they said.

If reconciliation was impossible at the time, the goal would be to leave the door open for reconsideration at a specified time, perhaps in a year. In any case, the parents' job would be to refocus on the three children and reassure them of their equal love for all. If Mimi was the favorite, the parents would have to work hard to rebalance the family.

In the interim, the parents must ask themselves what went gone wrong in their relationship with Mimi. The therapist could explain that joining a cult is some naive young adults' bizarre way of transitioning from home to independence. To a floundering young adult, an extremely restrictive replacement structure has a certain appeal. There is apparently no point in disparaging the cult, which many parents are understandably inclined to do, because it only produces more resistance on the part of the child. They could join a support group for parents who similarly "lost" a child. But, the surest path toward reconciliation is continuing to search for the child, and once he or she is found, to never stop telling the child he or she is loved and can come home anytime, no questions asked (Bardin, 2000).

YOUTH

The fallout from parental mishandling of a child's need for independence extends to collegial relationships and can be seen in the often torturous breakups of mentors and disciples. The mentor's envy of the disciple's youth and ascendency are at the heart of the matter, and some of the best examples involve role reversal, instances in which a young protégé is given to understand that he or she is being groomed to replace, or at least join, the mentor at the head of the table. For these relationships to end well, the mentor has to be ready to pass the baton, to graciously move aside. At the same time it is incumbent on the protégé to be sensitive to the loss of status and power of the mentor. In the sense that the mentor is a professional parent, his or her job is not only to back off, but to do so at the right time. For a real parent it is the period of late adolescence and early adulthood. For a mentor, the job is usually done by the time the mentee approaches forty (Levinson, 1986). The time may vary, but cutoffs predictably result from the inability of the mentor to transcend his or her jealousy and often pure narcissism and to adapt to the inevitable status change.

Sigmund Freud was fifty-one and Carl Jung thirty-one when the two psychoanalytic giants met; Freud was at his professional peak, and Jung was a young psychiatrist of "unusual promise" (Davis, 1997). A classic mentor-protégé relationship was established, with Freud seeing Jung's potential and tapping him as a possible successor. Though the friendship lasted 7 years, it may have been doomed from the start. Freud demanded complete loyalty from all his students, but Jung had increasing difficulty submitting to Freud's demands. Not surprisingly, when the break finally occurred, Jung was nearing forty.

Especially exasperating to Jung was Freud's interpretation of any deviation from his position as neurotic. Jung says as much in an angry missive to Freud, which produced the enduring rift:

> May I say a few words to you in earnest? I admit the ambivalence of my feelings toward you, but am inclined to take an honest and absolutely straightforward view of the situation. If you doubt my word, so much the worse for you . . . your technique of treating your pupils like patients is a blunder. In that way you produce either slavish sons or impudent puppies . . . I am objective enough to see through your little trick. You go about sniffing out all the symptomatic actions in your vicinity, thus reducing everyone to the level of sons and daughters who blushingly admit the existence of their faults. Meanwhile you remain on top as the father, sitting pretty . . . nobody dares to pluck the prophet by the beard and inquire for once what you would say to a patient with a tendency to analyze the analyst instead of himself. You would certainly ask him: "Who's got the neurosis?" (McGuire, 1974/1994, pp. 534–535)

One wishes that some third party had intervened to help Jung understand Freud's difficulty letting go, and the affront to his status as Jung ascended. Freud also needed support in coming to terms with the end of his sole reign over the new field. If such had been the case, the two men might have recast their relationship to remain appreciative, respectful colleagues or friends.

Had Freud lived longer, he might have extended his development stages into adolescence, adulthood, and old age. Were they alive today, Freud and Jung might have taken—or developed—an adult development course incorporating the challenges inherent in the mentor-disciple relationship. They might have anticipated the trouble and been more mature in how they handled themselves. However, not knowing the true strength of Freud's ego, the success of any primary or secondary intervention is only speculation. We will return to Freud and Jung's cutoff in the chapter on Principle.

In the play *Collected Stories* by Donald Margulies (1998), we have a dramatic version of the classic mentor-protégé relationship, this time between two women. In the beginning, Lisa, the young student writer, and Ruth, the revered published author, are singing in perfect harmony. Lisa worships Ruth, and each is comfortable in her position. But during the course of the play, roles reverse. Lisa matures as a writer, gains recognition. Ruth experiences a descent into relative obscurity, which she cannot tolerate. The relationship strained, Ruth accuses Lisa of having stolen her next big idea:

Ruth: Go home.
Lisa: What?
Ruth: I can't talk to you anymore.
Lisa: Don't say that.
Ruth: I feel like I've been bugged. My dear young friend turned
   out to be a spy. A spy who sold my secrets.
Lisa: Ruth, please. We can talk about this.
Ruth: Look, do me a favor, take out the trash with you, I've got a
   leaky bag.
Lisa: Ruth?
Ruth: Go home.

(*Margulies*, 1998 Act 2 Scene 3 p 60)

There are many examples from film, literature, and life that explore the mentor-protégé role-reversal theme (such as *All About Eve*, *The Dresser*), and they all end badly.

When the situation is familial, when a child overtakes a parent, it is often no different—a fact to which any child who has dared to compete with, or overtake, a self-centered, ego-driven parent can attest. In the same vein, we know a concert pianist who won't let her son take lessons and a professional baseball player who won't practice with his son, though he knows his son wants to follow in his footsteps.

For parents who have difficulty enjoying their children's success, we tell the following story:

Richard was a chess enthusiast who lived for the game. He wanted to be a professional and rose in the amateur ranks, but he stopped competing when his wife, Chris's mother, left the family. Chris was two. Richard worked as a carpenter to support Chris and himself and played chess on the side. Chris took an interest in the game when he was very young and studied his father's every move. One day, as he was turning four, he asked his father to teach him. Delighted, Richard taught Chris as quickly as he could learn.

Soon Chris had gotten everything he could from his father, so Richard took him to a professional. Chris lived with Dimitri for a year, after which he announced his intention to go professional too. Dimitri thought it was possible. On arriving home, Chris challenged his father, who had never lost to his son before, and Chris won. Richard reported that the day Chris surpassed him was the happiest one of his life.

In telling clients this story we do not drill the point. Rather than criticizing the clients/parents' past actions, we simply ask if they think the story is true. If they cannot conceive of it, we confirm that it happened and ask if they can imagine feeling this way toward their child. Some say they can or want to; others say they cannot. In the latter case, we explore the block. It is usually regret, resentment toward their parents, or a circumstance that prevented them from realizing a dream. We then delve deeper into the regret until it dissipates. Sometimes this process enables them to return to, or restart a career they abandoned long ago. Then they can let their children thrive.

FRIENDS

In this section we will be discussing envy of friends who have more friends. The example we provide did not wind up in a cutoff but almost did, and the pain Judy experienced was significant enough to prompt a discussion with her therapist. We include this case because such situations are common and may at first seem unworthy of serious discussion. However, listening closely to friend-envy stories usually provides another window into earlier issues for the client.

Karen and Judy were close friends who lost touch after college. They reunited years later when Judy recognized Karen in line at a local deli. They had much in common: they were mothers, married with three teenage children. Also, economically on a par, they lived near each other and got together often. Both women loved art and design. Karen's husband, Lucas, a physician, and Judy's husband, Zach, a basic scientist, could talk for hours. The only significant difference was that Judy had a career.

At some point though, Karen and Lucas had less weekend time. They were always "booked," and Judy noticed that they were not invited to join Karen and Lucas with other friends. Still, Karen and Lucas always seemed happy to see them during the week and acted as if nothing was wrong.

Meanwhile, though, some of Judy and Zach's other friends moved away, and Judy's closest friend died. Judy and Zach felt lonely at times, and Judy realized she was envious of Karen and Lucas's many social engagements. This was all the more upsetting because Judy and Zach had added Karen and Lucas to a regular foursome they had before the third couple moved away.

The situation came to a head when Judy heard from a mutual friend that Karen and Lucas were hosting several dinner parties over the next couple of months, none of which Judy and Zach were invited to.

Judy was so hurt she couldn't sleep that night and wondered if she should simply end the relationship. Her therapist persuaded her to hold off, first so they could understand Judy's reactions and then to understand why Karen and Lucas were behaving this way. They realized that while Judy was actually left out by Karen, her hurt was over-determined by her family-of-origin experience. Her older sisters never included her either; she was jealous that her sisters had more friends and that they were closer to each other than to Judy. Remembering her history enabled Judy to attach less importance to Karen, and Karen's behavior. Judy was able to disengage and gain perspective. Whatever Karen did, mattered less.

Judy also began to understand what might explain Karen's actions. Karen was an only child, unused to sharing, but was basically a good person. She was sweet and loyal, but also anxious and inflexible when it came to not knowing her plans, changing plans, or not having any plans. Karen's social life was extremely important to her, one of the ways she measured her success in life. Perhaps it was to overcome loneliness she felt as a child.

By enumerating Karen's good qualities, Judy was able to take Karen's actions in stride. She also suddenly recalled the mutual friend saying that the three parties were to repay friends who had recently invited them. Judy and Zach were so busy professionally they had not had company over for quite a while. Karen and Lucas may have felt hurt about that. Judy, more spontaneous, would call Karen at what must have seemed like the last minute. Judy had to concede that a busy social life was less important to her than to Karen, and at the end of the day it was okay for Karen to win the "competition" for friends.

In this case, a cutoff was averted because Judy's hurt was replaced by her own feeling of being remiss. Instead of cutting off, she reversed course and invited Karen and Lucas for dinner. Three months later, Karen invited Judy and Zach to a party. Ideally, close friends should be able to discuss these things. But it is also true that some people have difficulty, and Judy's estimate was that with Karen it would be better to let corrective action speak and leave well enough alone!

ACCOMPLISHMENTS

Though jealousy among siblings exists in nature, human parents, with the advantage of consciousness, can mitigate its effects before they become toxic to the point of a cutoff. Henry and Harry, brothers with strong personalities, had great difficulty bridging their divide, in part because of a turf war over accomplishments to which their parents were largely oblivious.

Henry is four years older than Harry. Both brothers were well loved by their well-intentioned, well-educated, parents, Maurice and Dominique, who were also heavily invested in their own careers. Having emigrated from France, both were Romance language specialists. They spent "quality time" with the children, but not enough. They were stressed by career demands; nannies came and went.

When the children were fourteen and ten, the slowly unraveling marriage fell apart. The parents lived near each other; the children went back and forth. At that time, children were believed to escape unscathed as long as parents behaved reasonably well.

Both children were bilingual. Henry was a star in school, especially at learning languages and on the track. Harry was also smart, was good at languages, and emulated Henry every way possible. Harry signed up for track and, like Henry, took Latin and Greek. After school, Henry was often left in charge. Unbeknownst to Maurice and Dominique, Harry's resentment for "babysitting" spilled over to Henry. Because he was younger, Harry couldn't keep pace with Henry. So in adolescence he became sullen and stopped performing in school. Henry, the "good boy," believed his parents were too soft, treating Harry equally despite his bad behavior. Meanwhile, Harry embraced the "bad boy" role.

A standoff continued with the brothers maintaining superficial contact, until Henry married into a prominent political family in his midthirties. At that point, Harry's jealousy exploded. He refused to speak or see Henry. Everyone tried to persuade Harry to change his mind. Everyone tried to get Henry to ask Harry why he was so angry. Neither one budged. What finally broke the ice was Harry's own sense of accomplishment. He achieved significant success in a business he built from scratch. One day, Harry copied his parents on an email asking Harry "Can we be friends?" "Yes, I'd love that," Henry wrote back.

Having seen the film *Darjeeling Express,* Harry came up with a wonderful strategy. He suggested that he and Henry go mountain climbing, something they were both experienced at. The climb required them to cooperate and trust each other's goodwill, which set them on a path to reconciliation. Neither raised the issue of the cutoff.

Speculation about what caused the rift always came back to accomplishments. So a clinician analyzing this type of cutoff would do well to think about ways parents could help their "acting out" child feel better about himself. Perhaps the decision to let Harry follow Henry was a mistake. Did Harry think he had to compete with Henry to be loved, that he couldn't be himself? Perhaps the rift could only have been resolved by Harry finding his own identity and sense of accomplishment. Some credit also goes to the parents who never gave up on Harry, even during his most difficult adolescent period. A therapist friend of Harry's father offered the following perspective, which clinicians can pass on to other parents in this predicament: "You always say it's your fault that Harry is in such trouble. But think of it this way. If it weren't for you and Dominique, it could be worse. Harry might be out on the street. As long as he has you, it'll turn out all right." Essentially, the advice was to stay connected, never cut off. This was a case in which one cutoff in the family did not lead to another.

HEALTH

Envy of someone else's health when one becomes compromised is almost inevitable, unbalancing even the solidest relationships.

⁂

Larry, now seventy, complained to his therapist that George, his life-long friend, was not answering his emails, not picking up the phone. Five years prior, George had survived a plane crash but was left a paraplegic. Larry recently moved to Miami, while George was back in Baltimore, so opportunities to be together were only occasional. Also, since the accident, Larry did all the traveling.

Larry was perplexed, but put the matter aside until George wrote that he didn't want to see Larry anymore. Larry was hurt, figuring he'd done something wrong but didn't know what, or what to do. He worried he simply wasn't interesting enough or doing a good enough job of distracting George, who brooded endlessly about his medical problems. Larry always worried about being interesting enough, since his only sibling was a brilliant Broadway actor who always "stole the show."

The therapist first commiserated and then asked Larry to speculate why George might have cut off. Larry generated a sizable list including that George found it difficult to be with him. Larry was in perfect health and George might be envious. Finding the cutoff understandable, Larry decided to contact George. George did not respond at first, but with persistence George finally confided that it was too painful to recall the past, which Larry brought up whenever they were together. George also insisted he didn't need anyone to "cheer him up." George believed Larry had no idea what he was going through.

Larry, who is actually a thoughtful introspective man, realized he tried too hard to bolster George with stories about his own life, and that was not what George needed. Larry corrected his approach, listened more and commiserated plenty. George gradually let Larry back in his life.

MEANING

Loss of meaning, or purpose, is a hallmark of depression and much has been written about this form of anguish within and outside the mental health arena. Lack of meaning plagues people who are only "normally depressed" as well as clients who come for help.

Intellectual communities have been built on it. First it was existentialism, then the *nouvelle vague*. Now some environmentalists contend that it is too late to worry about meaning or a course correction, because the end of the world is nigh. It is hard, given the evidence piling up, for—maybe especially for—reasonably upbeat people to find a point, to discover true meaning in life.

༺࿐༻

Two good friends since elementary school are walking down the street, talking about their lives. Francesca muses aloud that although she likes being a doctor, maybe she should have chosen a different field. "I didn't realize how boring medicine can be; it's just a trade, not much creativity to it."

Nina, manager of the sales division of a major pharmaceutical company, suddenly stopped, put an arm around Francesca, and blurted out, "Francesca, please don't complain to me. I'm so envious, because there is so much meaning in what you do. You're helping people every day; I only push drugs, most of which don't work, and take people's money. What satisfaction is there in that?" Soon afterward, Nina stopped having time for lunch with (i.e. cut off from) Francesca. She told her therapist she was miserable in her work and wished she had done something else with her life.

Nina's therapist interpreted Nina's frustration as an existential crisis. She understood that Nina lacked a sense of meaning and felt that this was not just depression, but a worthy topic in and of itself. In effect, she put Nina's envy to good use. Instead of trying to help her reduce her envy, which would probably not work, she helped Nina understand why she was envious. This led to a discussion of the lack of meaning in Nina's life.

Nina reexamined the career decision she had made and began to consider what course correction she could now make. She revisited interests she had set aside and came back to one she had abandoned early on. She used some of her savings to return to school. She is now a dedicated music therapist, employing her love of music, her analytic, interpretive abilities, and her finely tuned empathy. She has also reconnected with Francesca and brought her up to speed.

POWER

On the surface, the following case could easily be mistaken for a cutoff about money, but it is more about power—the power one man has over another. Money is the weapon, but the urge for power is the motivator. It is hard not to be blinded by the vast amounts of money some clients have and not see that for some clients, some cutoffs, it is not the money that matters.

✸

Phil and Debra were married for thirty years and had three children. Debra's father, Warren, used the little money he had to control Debra, his only child. According to a friend of Phil's, Debra "was married to her parents." From the beginning, Warren disapproved of Phil, alleg-

edly because he did not have the money he thought his daughter deserved, but primarily because Debra had someone besides her father in her life. Afraid to alienate her father, Debra rarely stood by Phil.

Phil was also jealous of Warren, for his power over Debra. Warren owned their house, the Mercedes, everything it seemed. Debra, torn between father and husband, unable to assert herself with either, went shopping to cool her nerves. Sometimes Phil couldn't pay the bills.

This went on for twenty years, when suddenly everything changed. Warren won "gobs" of money in the State lottery. To pay down the debt Debra had accumulated, Phil asked Warren for help to expand his business. Warren asked for a business plan; Phil sent one. Warren's response was a dismissive "not interested."

Phil emotionally withdrew. Debra requested he move out and filed for divorce. Soon after the divorce, however, Debra was diagnosed with a life-threatening illness and asked Phil to move back in. Warren opposed it, but this time Debra held her ground. Warren ostracized Phil for three years, did not acknowledge him at Debra's funeral, and barred him from the house afterward.

Phil discovered his true calling in caring for Debra. He is now in nursing school. Warren recently contacted Phil to make peace. Phil debates whether to invite Warren to a session with his therapist.

Here Phil is the client, and the therapist does not know much about Warren other than that he is a "control freak" according to Phil, Phil's extended family, and his grandchildren. From Phil, she also knows that Warren vehemently opposed the idea of couple therapy for Debra and Phil and considers all therapists charlatans. She knows that Phil is easily overpowered by Warren, so it is not necessarily a good idea for the two men to "meet for drinks," Phil's first idea.

This was never a close relationship, and with Debra gone, Phil hesitates to reconcile, but he and the therapist agree it is worth considering. First, Phil wants to voice his anger at the way he was treated by Warren, and hopefully receive an apology. The major goal would then be to help the children, who have lost their mother and are left with two cutoff male relatives and no sense of family. The relationship does not have to be close. The first hurdle is simply being in the same room and being civil.

The danger in encouraging a meeting might be that Phil would be overpowered again. Warren could be defensive and go on the attack.

If little or nothing were accomplished, the cutoff might be sealed. Mitigating the therapist's concern is that a year has passed since Debra's death and everyone has had a chance to reflect. Also, Phil has a rich network of family and friends and has found himself as a result of the ordeal of caring for his ex-wife. He is sturdy enough for the encounter.

The meeting played out as planned. Phil articulated his resentment over Warren's "misuse of power," his "interference" in their marriage. Warren explained that watching Phil care for Debra slowly convinced him that Phil loved his daughter and was not just after Warren's money, which is what Warren had always feared. They bonded over their mutual loss to some extent. Warren did not fully apologize for his past behavior, and Phil did not insist, but the session ended with the two men agreeing to be "respectful" in the future. The following week, Phil received a check from his father-in-law "for school." Phil is not sure if he should keep it, wondering whether strings could be attached. Still, what a gift!

SATISFACTION

If parents teach children the importance of attaining their own goals, they will be satisfied reaching the goals, whether the bar is high or low. What becomes stressful is the situation in which parents set the goals, usually high ones, and the children feel compelled to reach them. Failing to reach these goals makes them likely to envy others who do. Few people have learned that striving itself is worthy, but those lucky ones who have, know that satisfaction comes simply from having tried.

People who reach their goals, however modest, are satisfied and are likely to be envied by those whose goals are out of reach. This is often the case with first and second children, because parents tend to expect more of the first.

⋙⋘

Neica is a firstborn who was taught that setting and meeting high standards is of the utmost importance. She was a serious girl who spent countless hours studying, way more than her friends did. She suffered from test anxiety and would pull all-nighters in middle school. Her parents realized they had overemphasized achievement and vowed to treat Neica's younger sister differently. They taught Barbara that it was important to enjoy life and not to worry much about school or work. "Family and friends matter most," they counseled.

Having received different messages, both girls went on to pursue their ends. Neica set her sights on medical school and got in, but not to her first choice. Although at the top of her premed class in college, she found herself just an average performer in medical school and couldn't accept that. Barbara, on the other hand, went to community college, married her high school boyfriend, and had two children. She never questioned her modest goals or looked back. But Neica, despite her own significant accomplishments, found herself envying her sister's happiness. She didn't envy Barbara's life, just her easily won satisfaction. She pulled away from Barbara, using a cool "too busy with school" as a virtual cutoff. Barbara felt rejected and wished their relationship could be as it was before.

Barbara discussed her angst with a friend who happened to be a family therapy master's degree student. Together they constructed a genogram. One insight gleaned was Barbara's recollection that their mother wanted to be a doctor but that her own parents had supported her brother instead. Barbara's epiphany was that there was intense pressure on Neica to go into medicine "for" their mother. Barbara began to empathize with Neica.

In the summer between her first and second year of medical school, Neica came home. Barbara took her out for dinner and let Neica talk about the stress of school and how easy Barbara's life seemed in comparison. Barbara shared difficulties raising her children, and that marriage was not "a walk in the park." This revelation rebalanced the relationship in Neica's eyes. Barbara shared her experience of the family genogram and her realization of how differently their parents had treated them. Neica responded beautifully, vowing to her sister that she would reduce the stress she heaped on herself, and the two sisters were in emotional synchrony again.

PUBLIC RECOGNITION

We have two cutoffs under this rubric. Since we cannot breach the anonymity of well-known clients, we have chosen those who already have public profiles. The first example showcases scientific colleagues who were friends, the second an interfamilial example of cutoff sisters, both famous actors.

In a 1981 *New York Times* book review of Donald Johanson's and Maitland Edey's book, *Lucy: The Beginnings of Humankind,* Boyce Rensberger, a highly regarded science writer, observed that the evolution of humans from "apelike animals living millions of years ago . . . is one of the great scientific epics of all time" and that the discovery of "Lucy" had provided an important contribution to a field in which there was much debate: how to explain human evolution from the fossil record. To Rensberger, Johanson's unearthing of the three-million-year-old Lucy had "forced a major reinterpretation of the early stages of human evolution."

Lucy's four-foot skeleton brought much public fame to Johanson. His contemporary and sometime colleague, Richard Leakey, well known in academic circles and anthropological field exploration, had not experienced the same level of recognition when he discovered a two-million-year-old fossil. The men's on-again, off-again friendship finally blew up in a live *Cronkite's Universe* TV program filmed at the New York Museum of Natural History. During the program, Leakey disagreed with some of Johanson's claims about Lucy. Some believed his disagreements to be the result of professional jealousy, not scientific evidence. After the program, Leakey did not speak to Johanson for thirty years (Bowman-Kruhm, 2010; Lewin, 1997).

One wonders if Leakey's reaction to Johanson, was in part the outgrowth of living in the shadow of his famous parents, the paleontologists Louis and Mary Leakey. To be again overshadowed, this time by a friend, may have been too much to bear.

When one sibling or friend far outstrips the other, envy is not hard to comprehend. Therapists expect it and can readily empathize. But when siblings or friends are both highly successful in the public eye, we have a harder time. The case of sisters Olivia de Havilland and Joan Fontaine is legendary, even for Hollywood. Well into their nineties, when Joan died in 2013, the two had not spoken since 1975.

꧁꧂

Although there had been a long history of rivalry as children, the public feud started early in their careers when one or the other was nominated or won an academy award. Although Olivia won two Academy Awards, she never forgave Joan for winning first. Joan believed that Olivia was their mother's favorite because she was forbidden to use their biological father's name. Others said the sisters were set up as children by the mother's invidious comparisons. In any event, the sisters clearly competed on every front—film roles, men, and their mother's love and attention.

The final break came when Joan missed their mother's funeral. Allegedly Olivia had not informed her in time. Joan is quoted as saying she "could not remember a time when she was treated well by her older sister." When asked if she cared to reconcile, Olivia retorted "better not." She had reached out once or twice over the years and was rebuffed. (Soares, 2013)

A therapist who has not personally experienced unrelenting jealousy or envy will be hard pressed to empathize with either sister. Even so, were we to have such a case, and most therapists will, we have to try. Reiterating what one of our clinician interviewees wisely pointed out, "There will inevitably be counter-transference when a client has a cutoff. We have to make a habit of checking ourselves and our reactions. Envy of this sort is difficult to fathom; digging deep is important." This "case" would be challenging indeed.

We have completed our discussion of jealousy and envy as possible reasons people cut off. We identified various forms (romantic jealousy, money, objects, youth, beauty, accomplishments, meaning, health, family, friends, power, satisfaction, public recognition) and suggested strategies for the clinical cases and other examples provided. In cases where no clinician was involved, for those personal, public, or literary stories, we commented on what we would consider trying were the cases ours or were the literary characters to anthropomorphize and knock on our office door.

In the next chapter, we explore the subject of betrayal. This happens when jealousy goes awry, causing people to overreact, lose their reason, resort to revenge. In escalating fashion, it becomes an eye for an eye, or a perhaps worse, cutting off with the finality of murder or suicide.

Chapter 5

BETRAYAL

Before you embark on a journey of revenge, dig
two graves.

Confucius

This chapter considers betrayal as a reason people sever a significant relationship. Dante, in his *Inferno*, parsed punishment for sins like no one before or since. Betrayers of family, community, or "benefactor" (mentor)—not just those without remorse—are placed in the lowest ring of hell. There, in the Ninth Circle, they are frozen in a lake of ice. Below them lies Satan, who betrayed God.

Of particular relevance to our topic, Dante also distinguished betrayal from fraud, which he found slightly less sinful (just an Eighth Circle offense) because fraud is (usually) a sin committed against a stranger, whereas in betrayal one turns against someone who is close. This distinction still holds, explaining why betrayal elicits more extreme reactions. Further, the glue of family and society is the ability to trust that the other will not render harm. Without trust there can be no community or society. This is another reason betrayal has been placed in the lowest circle, and presents the most difficult context for reconciliation.

Dante described many kinds of betrayal, not all of which we see in our clients or their significant others. But the commonality they share is that most forms of betrayal involve sins of commission, as opposed to say, jealousy, which involves "coveting," ill will, "feeling crimes." Coveting and ill will are intense emotions, but are nevertheless, only feelings. In almost all instances of betrayal, there is a breach of faith, either an implicit covenant or understanding or an explicitly stated one. Unlike "feeling crimes," betrayal presumes taking an action that crosses the line.

WHY PEOPLE BETRAY

As we shall see in the cases provided, people who feel betrayed respond in a variety of ways. They may walk away, or retaliate in kind. They may also escalate and in some cases react violently, by committing murder or suicide. These are the ultimate cutoffs, from which there is no return.

On the other hand, people who commit acts of betrayal are themselves motivated by powerful forces. They may be driven by factors external to the relationship, such as their own ambition, that have nothing to do with the particular person they betray or anything that person may have done to deserve the betrayal. They may also betray out of jealousy, feeling abandoned, feeling betrayed themselves by the other person in the relationship and decide to return the favor. It is up to the therapist to identify where, when and how the chain started and how to help clients avoid escalating or engaging in extreme behavior.

In all cases of betrayal, the person who betrays crosses a line that the other person considers of critical importance. And it is this boundary crossing that causes the other to end the relationship. The boundary may be customary or tacitly understood as unacceptable, such as theft or incest; or it could be a broken agreement, such as divulging a secret or publically humiliating a spouse. We must also remember that betrayal, like jealousy or abandonment, will be all the more abhorrent if the one betrayed is experiencing or perceiving it as a repeat offense or as reminiscent of an earlier betrayal. We will see an excellent example of this in the case of Hope and Randy.

What follows examines various kinds of betrayal. Where possible, we offer strategies that were used successfully or suggest what a therapist might try in a given situation. However, some insoluble cases serve as a reminder that not all cutoffs can (or should) be resolved.

As one clinician wisely said to us, "You can only do what you can do!"

DIVULGING SECRETS OR WITHHOLDING INFORMATION

This clinical case is a variant of the parental favoritism theme. Here, one adult sibling, Clarence, feeling betrayed, took revenge on his sister, Claire, when he learned she had withheld critical information.

༶

Claire is the daughter of a woman who cut her son, Clarence, out of her will. This, according to Claire, was because Clarence didn't help their mother in her old age. The therapist believed that "the brother was actually the mother's favorite, but the favorite of a dragon!" Clarence and Claire were jealous of each other and highly competitive throughout their lives.

The immediate problem was that the mother had told Claire she had cut Clarence out, but Claire never gave Clarence the heads up. Clarence informed Claire in writing that he didn't care about the money because he had plenty, but he was cutting her off because she knew their mother's intentions and had not warned him.

Claire is not married and has no children, so for Claire, Clarence's family is very important. Yet, Clarence's three children also cut off from Claire. She has not seen them in ten years.

The cutoff with her brother was not Claire's presenting problem. Rather, she came to discuss her difficulty with retiring. She felt it was "time" and had other interests she wanted to pursue, but she was afraid and did not know why. She had anxiety dreams about dying alone at her desk.

In hearing a casual remark about being cut off from her brother, the therapist grasped its significance and helped Claire connect it to the potential loss of work structure. Next, he delicately explained that Clarence's sense of betrayal was understandable. Even though it wasn't fair, Clarence had always been the mother's favorite. Now not only did their mother dethrone him, Claire made it worse by not alerting him. To Clarence, Claire's withholding of information about the will was a hostile act. Claire finally saw Clarence's point. She had passively accepted the cutoff though it made her miserable. Now the therapist encouraged her to be proactive, to ask herself what was in her heart and in everyone's best interests.

Claire sent a gift. She also left a voicemail message. Neither gesture was acknowledged. She then reached out to her nephew. The nephew would see her, but only after she made peace with their father, her brother. Back to square one.

Claire and the therapist brainstormed the possibilities: giving up again, making another apology, asking Clarence what it would take for him to end the cutoff, offering Clarence half the mother's estate as restitution after the fact. Claire decided not to give up until she had tried all of the above.

Interestingly, as soon as she offered restitution, Clarence relented because "I finally feel you understand." Once the relationship was restored, Claire retired in a year.

In the following case, a secret becomes a toxin in both the immediate and extended family:

Paul, a thirty-seven-year old African American man in Chicago, never told his parents he was gay. However, when he was thirty, his father, a prominent member of the business community, suddenly divulged to Paul that he had a gay lover and had contracted AIDS. Paul's mother was told that her husband had sex with a female prostitute, and she stayed with him. However, when Paul learned the truth, he was furious that his father had never confided in him. He cut his father off and later boycotted his funeral. His mother was mystified about the cutoff. When the extended family heard about the father and Paul being gay, they wrote to Paul severing all ties. This drove Paul into therapy.

Paul's therapist understood that his father's coming out stirred up Paul's own identity issues and regretted that Paul never had a positive role model for being gay. Instead, the father's lifelong secret about his sexual orientation conveyed a "message" that Paul should be ashamed. Paul was actually doubly betrayed, first by his father and then by the extended family.

The extended family also felt betrayed by the gay revelations in their midst. Like the Jewish immigrant family in the Preface, the whole family was bent on upward mobility and "knew" it could not afford "black marks" on their reputation. In this case, the extended family was not the client, but clinicians see this problem every day, so we must find ways to empathize with the shattering of a dearly held myth of perfection, however unpalatable.

The therapist modeled acceptance of Paul's sexual identity. She asked about his secret life and romantic relationships. She encouraged him to be himself with his mother. Eventually, Paul opened up. His mother was upset to hear the truth about her husband and this second revelation about Paul, but she told Paul she would pray for tolerance and would try to accept him.

Paul often expressed "a longing for family and home." The therapist probed to see if he wanted to contact the extended family. Paul shot back, "They don't deserve it." So the therapist let it go. Paul remains in therapy but has made little progress. He continues to feel angry and depressed.

This therapist commented that she may have backed off too soon, perhaps a counter-transference reaction to Paul's unremitting anger. She decided in the interview that she would broach the subject again and hoped that this time he would give voice, mourn his father, and heal.

❧

Parental alienation, a type of forced cutoff, frames the following case:

> Alfred was two when his parents divorced. His father, Bob, left, and Alfred did not hear from him. Susan, his mother, feeling deeply hurt and rejected, kept Bob away from "her" son. Susan returned unopened letters from Bob without ever telling Alfred and cashed child support checks while badmouthing Bob for not paying his share. Alfred believed Bob had abandoned him, when in actuality Bob had tried his best.
>
> When Alfred was nineteen, after no contact for years, Bob finally reached out to his son. When Alfred told his mother he'd seen Bob, she threatened to cut Alfred off. "She didn't care about me, because she kept me from my father," Alfred told his therapist. "From that moment on, I hated my mother's guts. I stopped speaking to her and did not relent even when she was dying."

At the time of the cutoff, Alfred's girlfriend's mother took him in. They married two years later, but divorced five years after. Alfred's forced cutoff from his father and the unresolved cutoff with his mother took a tremendous toll. He was emotionally stuck and had a host of physical symptoms.

Alfred undertook therapy in four rounds; each time the therapist encouraged him to work through the cutoffs in his life, as Alfred kept repeating his cutoff with his mother with other women. Over the years, the therapist had to keep her eye on the issues beneath the presenting problem, and it was only during his fourth round of sessions that Alfred was finally able to access his feelings, and begin to heal.

Alfred's presenting problems were as follows:

- At twenty-four, he worried about his marriage was in trouble
- At twenty-seven, he was consumed by "white liquid rage" at his ex-wife
- At thirty-four, he had issues with a girlfriend twenty years older
- At thirty-nine, he was ready to tackle his mother's death and all the cutoffs in his life

In the fourth set of sessions, Alfred saw the repetitive pattern in the cutoffs from his ex-wife, mother, and older "surrogate mother." He acknowledged the good in his marriage and also recognized that his ex-wife had certain things in common with his mother that were not healthy for him.

The therapist helped Alfred express sadness at the breakup of his marriage, and the loss of dreams they had. The therapist helped him develop a goodbye ritual. He wrote to his ex-wife, enclosed certain photos she wanted, and found a song to capture his feelings about letting go. Alfred's last decision in therapy was to visit his mother's grave, to try to forgive her betrayal and make peace.

During the last round of therapy, Alfred's physical symptoms diminished. He reported "no more nightmares . . . sleeping like a baby, floating on air."

In reviewing this successful outcome with us, the therapist still questioned herself. "Maybe I should have pushed Alfred sooner to address the cutoff with his mother even though he might not have been ready to handle it. It has always been sad to me that he never got a chance to reconcile before she died."

Interestingly, like the therapist who was blind to a cutoff in his own family, this therapist did not recall this client's cutoff from his mother until we were well into the interview and constructed a genogram! She had selected this case only because of the forced cutoff from the father. We will speculate about the reasons for these peculiar ellipses in the Conclusion of the book.

BROKEN PROMISES

The three cases that follow involve a breach of faith or trust.

Raphael entered therapy after breaking up with Carmen. His problem was "making decisions" and he regretted keeping her too long. "She was thirty-five and I don't want to do that to anyone again." Months later, Raphael laid eyes on Lucy during a concert intermission, and instantly thought, "Wow, she's the one!" After they dated briefly, Lucy invited him to move in. His therapist recognized that although intellectually gifted, Raphael was very naive about relationships. She suggested he get to know Lucy better before moving in, but as he was "in love," there was no stopping him.

Trouble started immediately. Lucy had no room in her closet and would not let Raphael bring his desk. She did not like his dog. More worrisome, Lucy was unmotivated at work, avoided meeting Raphael's friends, and seemed to have no interests of her own. The worst was that instead of resolving an argument, Lucy sulked. Still, Raphael wanted "to work things out."

He insisted on a serious talk. Lucy confessed that at thirty, she was feeling insecure. Being married was critical and she was still single. Raphael was ready but questioned whether Lucy really loved him or whether she just needed to be married. The following week, Lucy came home distraught. Her younger sister Elaine was engaged. As teenagers, Elaine had promised not to marry before her, so now Lucy felt betrayed. She told Raphael if he was not ready to propose, she would stop speaking to Elaine and would refuse any role in the wedding unless she

herself was at least engaged at the time. The pressure on Raphael was
unbearable, so he moved out.

This case is an excellent example of a broken promise that led to a
cascade of cutoffs. Elaine certainly should not have promised Lucy in
the first place, but Elaine was fourteen at the time. Were Lucy the
client, or Lucy and Raphael the couple, the therapist could empathize with Lucy's sense of betrayal and her embarrassment at being
the older, still-single sister. Lucy's therapist might also introduce a
social perspective, that getting married at a certain age, even if cul-
turally prescribed, is not essential and that not marrying at all is no
shame either.

If Lucy's hypothetical therapist went further, he would help Lucy
see that the issue is not just societal, but also familial. For instance,
for Lucy's mother, having her daughters married, and marrying well,
was the primary marker of her success as a parent. She unwittingly
let her daughters compete over clothes, boyfriends, and popularity,
rarely encouraging school or their own individuality or interests.
The mother herself had not developed her own talents and could not
impart self-confidence to her daughters. Thus, it became only about
marrying, and Lucy could not see beyond it.

Raphael, on the other hand, like Henry and Harry, learned that
accomplishments were critical. He might marry and have a family,
but that would only be the icing on the cake. A gender difference for
sure, but also a difference in values and goals. No wonder Raphael
and Lucy had problems. As tensions escalated, the therapist and
Raphael explored the ways Raphael had been drawn into the sisters'
competitive struggle. They also saw how Lucy had in some ways
contributed to her own betrayal. Her request for her sister to wait
called for a potentially huge sacrifice from Elaine, since neither one
could know what the future would hold.

Identifying the source of Lucy's "crisis" and Lucy's own role, the
therapist asked Raphael to look back at his own family of origin to
see whether his relationship with Lucy seemed familiar. "Oh my
god," he exclaimed, "my mother was so critical of me, my father
also. Lucy fits perfectly into my family." He also realized that the distance he put between himself and his family explained his rush to
find love elsewhere, which inevitably backfired. With these new

insights, Raphael could leave Lucy, vowing never to rush into a relationship again, to let love come slowly.

≫ ≪

Keith was eight when his parents divorced. He spent the rest of his childhood shuttling back and forth between two homes and adjusting to two stepparents.

When Keith was twenty-five he lent his father, Herb, a substantial amount of money that he had inherited from a maternal uncle. Occasionally, he would ask when Herb would repay him, but his father always had a reason. Feeling increasingly frustrated and betrayed, at thirty-five, Keith cut his father off. After five years of not speaking, Keith, more and more depressed over the impasse and some other problems, began to see a therapist.

In the initial consultation the therapist noted Keith's cutoff with his father. However, assessing that Keith was too vulnerable in other domains to explore his relationship with Herb, the therapist focused his early work with Keith on marital and work issues. An age peer of Keith's father, the therapist observed himself "bonding" with Keith. The work progressed well, and Keith began to make important strides in communicating his wants and needs both at home and at work. He also began to rethink his career decision. Only at this point did the therapist encourage Keith to explore the cutoff from his father.

Keith was raised to "respect your elders" and above all to never challenge his father. The therapist reminded him that he had disagreed and even got angry in sessions, and that it had been okay. The therapist had Keith reflect on what exactly the dictum "respect your elders" meant in 2013. Moving from an abstract dictum to his own life, Keith decided that respect was a two-way street and that although he was nervous, he was ready to confront his father and express his outrage at the betrayal.

The therapist worked with Keith on his approach. They carefully assessed Keith's readiness, going so far as imagining how he would feel if his father refused. Keith decided he could handle a refusal and wrote a letter asking his father to come for a therapy session when he was next in town for business. Herb agreed, and they sat in the therapist's office for over an hour, while Keith expressed his anger and disappointment that his father had not even made an effort to pay him back.

Herb apologized but stated unequivocally that there was no way he could ever repay the debt. Herb explained that his business was failing, and Keith (though far from financially secure himself) should understand that he actually had more resources than his father had. Moreover, Herb's second wife had spent much of Keith's money. Keith stood his ground. In fact, knowing about his stepmother made matters worse, not better. He added that he didn't think he'd ever fully forgive his father for this betrayal of trust and a broken promise but that he would try to move on. Although he never recouped the loss, Keith was finally able to "let it go." Such is the power of giving voice to one's grievance.

⧼◦⧽

The outcome of Hope's story is almost predictable, given that she had told her fiancé in no uncertain terms that their marriage would be forever—except for one "deal breaker."

In the initial session, Hope described having had a rough childhood. Her parents fought constantly and finally divorced when she was eleven. Her father had cheated on her mother from the start and had walked away with most of the money for which the working-class couple had worked so hard. Hope decided she would never marry without a solemn vow from a prospective partner to be faithful to the end.

Randy promised. They married and had eight good years before having a child. Hope had a difficult pregnancy and struggled—successfully—to continue excelling in her highly remunerative job. She expected Randy, whose job was less demanding, to "step up" on the home front, and railed at him when he resisted. Randy worried about how they would manage family and work. Already getting less attention from Hope, he wondered what would happen once the baby arrived.

One day shortly after giving birth, Hope received a letter from the "other woman" saying that she had been with Randy throughout the pregnancy. Hope was devastated. Randy wanted to keep the marriage and begged her to go into couple therapy. Hope refused. Instead, she went into individual therapy to double-check her leaning toward divorce. She ordered Randy to move out and stopped speaking to him.

She did let him see the baby, but communicated only by text or through the nanny.

Of course this case is about extra-familial infidelity. However, Hope repeatedly told her therapist that the affair was not the problem, it was that Randy had broken his solemn promise to her. That was what was "killing her." Randy's promise was a contract, the foundation of their marriage. Now the contract was broken and "the deal is off."

Hope would not agree to couple therapy but asked her therapist to meet with Randy alone. In a one-on-one, Randy might reveal what had happened and provide the therapist "a sense of Randy" and what might be possible for the couple going forward. The therapist hoped that the threat of divorce would motivate Randy to commit to serious introspection. Unfortunately, this was not the case. Randy was unable to grasp why Hope was so enraged, since "we had so many other good years together." He had apologized and had sworn "it" would not happen again.

Hope, a strong personality, had dictated most of the terms of their relationship. Moreover, she over-functioned in the marriage while Randy under-functioned. In fact, it seemed that he had become passive-aggressive and then verbally abusive whenever he felt his masculinity challenged.

The therapist gently explained this no-win dynamic to Randy and explored the nature of his apology. He had said he was sorry, but only for the affair. He had not apologized for his broken promise. When the therapist emphasized that this might be keeping Hope from speaking to him, he apologized again, this time for the promise he broke.

The therapist then urged Hope to take in the apology and find ways to maintain a relationship with Randy for the sake of their baby. She gave Hope reading material about the importance of co-parenting between former spouses (Ahrons, 2005). Hope resumed speaking to Randy, and vowed she would keep in touch regardless of their differences.

We consider this case to have been quite successful even though the couple divorced. A cutoff that would have hurt their innocent child was averted, and the couple found a way to successfully co-parent after the divorce.

LYING OR UNDERMINING

The next form of betrayal is about lying to or about someone close. In this section we also include deliberate undermining of another person to destroy their self-confidence or credibility. The film *Gaslight* is a haunting portrayal of how pernicious undermining can disturb a spouse's sense of self and reality.

∞

A less dramatic yet still painful cutoff occurred between two men we know. Like the case of Keith and Herb, this cutoff involved non-payment of a loan, but the underlying issue was different.

Peter and Leo became friends in the 1960s when Leo, his new downstairs neighbor, helped him carry some belongings up to his new apartment. Both young men were struggling—Leo, an actor; Peter, a graphic designer. They were handsome, ambitious, and confident. They had the world at their feet and loved their bohemian lives in Haight-Ashbury.

As years went by, both had disappointments. Leo's first marriage collapsed, and he lost custody of his children. Peter had a string of failed relationships and was not making it as a designer. He took a sales job that he hated, to support himself. The two men commiserated.

And so it went until Leo met and married Connie. Neither had money and they struggled together. At one point Leo pumped gas. Peter finally landed a job with excellent benefits, and Elsa, who had steady employment and family money, came into his life. Their bohemian life became a distant memory. Peter and Elsa lived in a style far above what Connie and Leo could afford. Peter lent Leo money on three occasions; Peter obtained promissory notes. After the third loan, Peter refused a fourth request and asked Leo to start repayment. Leo did not "remember" one of the loans and insisted on seeing his signature on the note.

For whatever reason, Peter could not find that note, but Elsa remembered the time, place, and amount. Did Peter misplace it feeling guilty about exceeding his friend? Perhaps, but in their next interaction Leo further claimed he had never borrowed the money in the first place. Peter knew Leo was lying. He told him it was one thing not to repay the debt, another thing to lie about it. He would forgo the debt if

NOT ON SPEAKING TERMS

Leo acknowledged it. The lie was the thing. Leo refused, and Peter has not spoken to him since.

This relationship soured for a number of reasons, starting with sibling-like jealousy. Both men had siblings, with whom they were in conflict. Their own relationship worked as long as it was in balance. Once Peter's fortunes changed and he outstripped Leo financially, Leo's envy went haywire. It was mollified by the various loans, but once the spigot was turned off, the envy became too much.

Leo's adult son saved the day—a beautiful example of a third party facilitating rather than wrecking a relationship. Functioning as a therapist, he contacted Peter on his own initiative, knowing his father was still upset at the loss of Peter's friendship. He invited Peter to Leo's sixtieth birthday party. Peter agreed to go, but asked him to convince his father to admit borrowing the money. At the party Peter and Leo agreed to talk, and they had dinner a few weeks later. Leo went so far as to say he "guessed" he had borrowed the money, but that it was a terrible time for him, all a blur. That was good enough for Peter—apology accepted. Peter admitted to not having been sensitive enough about Leo's struggles and thought perhaps he should have simply let the debt go.

⸙

The following case illustrates how a single lie can have devastating effects on all members of a family:

Tom and his wife, Bess, were married for 7 years and then divorced. During the marriage they had two sons, Alan and Bruce. Both parents were extremely involved with the boys, so they agreed to joint custody. However, 2 years later, after Tom remarried, Bess accused Tom of sexually abusing their sons. Family Court found against the father, even though no physical exam of the boys was performed, and suspicious interviewing techniques (gold stars each time the boys gave a "right" answer) were employed. While Tom was not charged with a crime, the subsequent order of protection stipulated that Tom was to have no contact whatsoever, not even to say hello, though the sons lived few blocks away and Tom sometimes passed them on the street.

Tom failed to have the court order overturned and "coped" with his frustration by increasing his intake of alcohol and cocaine. But he also sought psychotherapy. People in the neighborhood reported that Bess was a "raging, fall-down alcoholic."

Tom had no real contact with his sons until Alan, the oldest, was eighteen at which time Tom was released from the restraining order. As the boys' contact with their father, who always financially supported them, increased, their relationship with Bess worsened. So Tom withdrew again, this time on his own volition.

After years of depression, Alan committed suicide. Tom now sees Bruce infrequently and thinks it best to have no contact with Bess—to "let sleeping dogs lie."

Tom initially came into therapy to deal with his ongoing upset over the order of protection. The work focused on helping him regain a sense of himself, his integrity, and his standing in the community. Tom wanted his sons to see him as someone other than the ogre portrayed by Bess and the Court.

While the above approach was certainly appropriate, the therapist might have tried other strategies as well. The father also needed to discuss, own, and work through the abuse if it actually happened, or, if not, he needed strength and stamina to fight the court order (and advised to retain a lawyer). Perhaps the therapist thought it was too late. One can't help wishing the couple or the family had sought a therapist prior to the divorce, or at least while there was joint custody.

This couple desperately needed help to transition through the father's remarriage, which was the "status change" that ignited the mother's jealousy and led to the court order. If the pair had met periodically with a therapist to manage their relationship and their sons' problems, the court order and cutoff might not have happened. It is even conceivable that Alan's suicide might have been prevented.

THEFT

The public drama of the Madoff family showcases the inconsolable pain that financial betrayal mixed with public humiliation can cause. As you may remember, subsequent to Mark Madoff and his brother disclosing their father's multi-million-dollar Ponzi scheme, Mark completely cut himself off from anyone who stood by Bernie. We will revisit this story in Chapter 7.

But as the next two cases also reveal, such betrayals and the breaking of trust are rarely mended.

∽∼

When Clem died, he left twice as much money to his son, Matt, as to his daughter, Fiona, explaining in the will his belief that a girl's husband, not her father, should provide for her. Since the father had always considered his daughter's husband a "loser" and had never stopped reminding her of it, he was in effect punishing his daughter from the grave for having married someone he disapproved of.

Clem's second wife, Lena, was approximately the same age as his children, and he left the bulk of his estate to her, including his deceased first wife's jewelry. When Lena, despite Matt's repeated requests, would not return some of "their" money, Matt cut her off completely.

Matt entered therapy a year after his father's death to deal with his rage and sense of being betrayed by his father. When the therapist asked Matt what he could do, Matt came up with equalizing the money he and Fiona had inherited. At least he could look at himself in the mirror and break the chain of vindictive selfishness his father had so wantonly displayed. After sharing his inheritance with Fiona, he reported feeling better.

The therapist then worked with Matt to explore the perspective of the father and Lena. In the process, Matt recalled that Lena had no children of her own. Matt and Fiona were each happily married and had full lives with their children. Could the larger inheritance for Lena be a consolation prize from her husband? With this reframing of what had seemed like a conspiracy of the father and stepmother against the adult children, Matt calmed down. It took a while, but he eventually contacted Lena and apologized.

∽∼

Nathaniel met Sam when he was twenty and Sam was turning forty. Nathaniel was a street-smart young man who marched to his own drummer. He had dropped out of school but had a knack for business, which his highly educated physician parents did not realize. Nathaniel loved motorcycles and bought an old Harley that Sam, a topnotch mechanic, refurbished. Nathaniel began to work for Sam, helping him buy old cycles that Sam fixed and resold, paying Nathaniel a percentage. Sam had a son from whom he was estranged and glommed onto Nathaniel, fancying himself a surrogate parent. Nathaniel, for his part, felt misunderstood and unable to live up to his family's expectations. He loved Sam's imagination and his acceptance, which he had trouble getting at home.

With a small inheritance from his grandparents, Nathaniel bought a sleepy truck stop that unexpectedly became a wildly popular restaurant. Meanwhile, Sam's motorcycle business failed in the 2009 recession. Sam borrowed money, a substantial amount, from Nathaniel to "tide himself over" until he sold his house. Nathaniel also hired him at the restaurant. When the house sold, Sam repaid other debts but "postponed" repayment to Nathaniel because "you don't need the money." The friendship deteriorated from there. In an effort to salvage it, Nathaniel forgave half the debt.

The end came after Nathaniel invited Sam on a one-week road trip, all expenses paid. Upon their return and still wanting to trust Sam, Nathaniel asked him to deposit some cash into the restaurant bank account. Sam put the money into a safety deposit box "somewhere" and left town. He kept one key and sent Nathaniel the other one but wouldn't say where the box was! Nathaniel begged Sam in a series of emails to reveal the location. Sam wrote back explaining why he wouldn't. Nathaniel threatened to sue but decided in the end to simply cut Sam off. The two have not spoken for years, but Sam contacts Nathaniel by email now and then asking to renew the friendship.

As we thought about this story, we wondered what we might have done had this been our clinical case. The "key" would have been to assess Nathaniel's motivation and reasons for remaining in the friendship and continue to trust Sam. If he was eager, we would have asked him to examine Sam's behavior. How good a friend was Sam, really? Had not Sam disrespected Nathaniel from the start? There was a clear red flag in Sam's unilateral declaration that Nathaniel "did not need the money."

Nathaniel needed to ask himself how he became so attached to Sam in the first place. He had very likely taken Sam's "acceptance" at face value and failed to see the deviousness in his dealings. He needed to connect his relationship with Sam to his distanced relationship with his family. We would encourage Sam to reconnect with his family of origin rather than with Sam, a poor substitute.

We now turn to three kinds of betrayal (enmeshment, incest and extra-familial infidelity) all involve crossing of emotional and/or sexual lines.

ENMESHMENT

The term *enmeshment* is most associated with, if not coined by Minuchin (1974), whose contribution to theory was discussed in Chapter 1. As a reminder, enmeshment refers to a systemic process by which family members are so entwined that no one has a separate identity or sense of themselves as individuals. To some extent, enmeshment may be a cultural phenomenon, more commonly seen in socio-centric (versus egocentric) cultures, in which the family takes precedence over the individual. Enmeshment, however, goes further, in that it denies any space between individuals, to a point where there are no boundaries and thus none to be crossed. Denying a loved one's separateness, his or her right to independence of mind and movement, amounts to betrayal.

This problem is exemplified in the following story of Ruby.

Ruby, fifty-four, looking every bit like a bag lady despite her upper-middle-class background, was brought to the first appointment by her parents. Ruby lived with Heather, her sixteen-year-old daughter from a brief marriage. Ruby's parents were worried because Heather was "throwing things" at her mother and threatening to kill her. Ruby refused the idea of calling the police should she need to. And Heather refused to see a therapist, or even join a session with her mother.

So Ruby was the client, with occasional participation of her parents. The father was extremely controlling, using money to goad family members to do his bidding. A sad but amusing example of Ruby's inability to see herself as an individual was how she dismissed her frequent stomachaches. She complained but avoided the doctor because "everyone in my family gets stomach aches. My mother, my aunt, my grandmother, me, we all have the exact same thing!" The not-so-amusing fact is that Ruby's sister died of stomach cancer two months before Ruby started therapy.

One of very few signs of health, Ruby had left home at thirty-five to marry and have a child "before it was too late." When the marriage ended, Heather became her whole life. Ruby spent most of the money her father gave her on Heather's clothes. Ruby described Heather as "a little doll." They went everywhere together: "I'd keep her home from school so we could shop and do things together; she was my best friend. Now she won't even talk to me."

Because it was a crisis, there was no time to slowly work through the mother-daughter issues. Instead, the therapist instructed Ruby to stop trying to engage Heather in discussions beyond day-to-day necessity. The therapist regularly reminded Ruby that when she begged and tried to ingratiate herself, the result was a scene, and nothing was accomplished. This educational point was a means to quickly reorient Ruby away from being Heather's "peer" to her more-appropriate role as mother of a teenager—to explain and normalize the separation process, and the need to start letting go.

This was all new to Ruby, but she latched onto the advice, and Heather stopped threatening and throwing things. But silence prevailed. Heather barely spoke to Ruby for the next 2 years. At eighteen Heather moved in with her boyfriend, Greg, a carpenter who lived in a working-class neighborhood. The day Heather left, Ruby mused to her therapist, "Why would a kid born in a mink coat long for such an ordinary life?"

The therapist encouraged Ruby to ask. Heather explained that Greg left her alone. With Greg she could be her own person. As Ruby talked with her therapist about Heather's response, she realized that unlike her experience with her parents and despite their conflict, somehow Heather had managed to establish a sense of self, while Ruby was not sure who she herself was. The therapist encouraged Ruby to take heart in Heather's ability to separate, while acknowledging Ruby's pain at Heather's refusal to see her.

Therapy sessions now focused on providing Ruby with an opportunity to discover herself. The therapist encouraged Ruby to see herself as an independent person who could envision and shape her own life. She suggested Ruby see her parents less often and refrain from meeting their demands. She wanted Ruby to fill her life with a variety of activities and friends, and maybe even a new man. However, "Ruby even resisted the thought of implementing her own ideas." It was "yes, but"—and no action. Fortunately, instead of expressing frustration and repeating the pattern of shaping Ruby to her expectations, the therapist caught herself and removed the pressure to change. Be patient, she told herself. This is Ruby's rebirth; let her emerge in her own time.

By holding back, by not attempting to force change, the therapist allowed Ruby to take some control, beginning with her power to say "no." The theory was that as Ruby took charge of her own life she would be less intrusive and clinging with Heather. The hope was that Heather would see that Ruby no longer needed her so desperately and that Heather would begin to reengage.

The therapist shared that if one had been a fly on the wall in her office, one would not see reparenting in the sessions. Instead, what they would see looked more like friendship. Ruby already had parents who loved her, albeit in a domineering way. What she needed was respectful friendship. Further, the therapist confided, "We had fun together. We discussed movies, books, clothes, fashion, and laughed a lot. But make no mistake, we got serious too."

One day Ruby reported that for the first time ever, she stopped her father from yelling at her. She also told her therapist, "Even though I don't always respond, I hear everything you say. It's working."

When Ruby talked about her non-communicative daughter, the therapist sometimes commiserated. Enmeshment with a child and reactive distance on the part of the child is a common pattern in single-parent families: "I revealed some of my frustration with my sometimes uncommunicative daughter." This was a strategic decision to normalize the problem. It also gave Ruby the experience of being treated as an equal, the knowledge that she can have a relationship in which neither party is exploited.

Though Ruby made few observable strides, by the time she decided to terminate she felt immeasurably better. She was no longer being assaulted by her daughter and was able to stand up to her parents to some extent. She called the therapist a year later to report that Heather had contacted her and come for a visit.

With Ruby, and in many other cases, it is often best to take baby steps or none at all, to provide the client with empathy and support, but not to push. This case is a good example of the critical importance of clinicians' self-reflection and observation—are we acting because it is right for the client, or because we need results now?

⚬⚬

The following case is similar in many ways to both Ruby's and Heather's in that there is an enmeshed mother with an adult daughter who refuses to speak to her. The difference is the long-term, abiding presence of a stepfather who helps defuse the situation, an in-house third party who helps them come together. This is also a case in which the parents were able to look at themselves, as could the daughter. Albeit with different levels of motivation, all three family members met with a therapist to solve the problem.

Anita met and married Bradley when her daughter Tanya was five. Prior to Bradley coming into their lives, Anita and Tanya had been very close—some would say too close. Anita had separated from Tanya's father when Tanya was one. He moved back to Hungary and did not keep in touch. They did not know where he was, and Tanya was not interested, because "I consider Bradley my real father." She admired him, and felt he was the more reasonable of her parents. Anita was a "wonderful mother in most ways, but I feel I have to be perfect to please her."

In her twenties, Tanya rebelled and had less and less to do with Anita. A classical string player, Tanya found "professional parents" whom she latched onto instead. Bradley and Anita thought Tanya was being exploited. She was the professional parents' assistant and junior teacher, for too little remuneration.

At thirty, with her partner, Colin, Tanya had Cal. The couple parted amicably shortly after Cal was born. Like mother, like daughter. The grandparents, Anita and Bradley, adore Cal. Tanya gave them easy access while barely speaking to either of her parents herself. Then, on Cal's fourth birthday, after what seemed like a minor blowup to Anita, Tanya cut off entirely. For more than four months, Anita and Bradley had no contact with Tanya or Cal. Anita was beside herself and found a family therapist online. Bradley agreed to go. They emailed Tanya, who, Anita reported to the therapist, very hesitantly said she would attend one session and "see."

Anita scheduled an initial family consultation. Since Tanya was not sure she still wanted a relationship with her parents, not at all sure she was "into" family therapy the therapist's inclination was to connect with Tanya individually first. She asked Anita's permission to call Tanya in advance, which Anita agreed to: "I'll do anything to get my daughter in the room." In that critical first call, the therapist told Tanya how brave she was to even consider family therapy and said she would be there for her if she felt "odd woman out." So strategy number one was to connect as soon as possible with the most reluctant participant. In this case it was Tanya, who had initiated the cutoff.

The therapist's second move was to propose a series of meetings, some individual, some subgroup pairs, and all three together. All parties agreed to this up front, and also to the idea that the particular configuration for the next meeting would be decided at the end of the previous one. To build Tanya's trust, the therapist alerted Anita in an individual session that she would need to temporarily ally with Tanya and asked Anita if she could tolerate it. She promised to try.

When the family was together in the room, the therapist sat next to Tanya and helped her to express her point of view. This maneuver was delicate, because the therapist knew she risked antagonizing Anita. She also might be perceived as usurping Anita's place with Tanya, along with implied criticism of Anita as a parent. Tanya for her part had cut off over what she experienced as criticism from her mother about how to raise Cal, her work at the music school, and her choice in men.

Anita was distraught about the cutoff from Tanya and about being unable to see her grandson. Tanya was gradually helped by Bradley and the therapist to empathize with her mother's anguish. Tanya told her mother she felt like she was "walking on eggshells," constantly judged through verbal and nonverbal messages that she was not measuring up. Up to this point, neither Bradley nor Anita had understood the reasons Tanya had distanced herself.

In the sessions, Anita and Bradley explained that they had not meant to be critical but were worried about Tanya managing her life as a single mother, about her earning enough to support herself and Cal. While they were happy to help financially, they were nearing retirement, and realized they would not be able to contribute as much in the future. Tanya stated she knew she couldn't keep relying on them.

While the family was in therapy, six sessions in all, Tanya gained a seat with a major orchestra, solving the family's financial concerns. Bradley commented that Tanya had seemed so mean and withholding to them, but he now gathered that she felt powerless too, "odd woman out" in their little extended family, that to Tanya neither parent seemed to respect her ability, judgment, or point of view.

With the air a little less tense, the therapist picked up on Anita's mournful "We used to have such a good time." It turned out their best times were sharing their love of nature and photography. Tanya explained that she could never keep up with Anita verbally—"Who could keep up with a Classics professor?" She preferred doing, rather than discussing things with her mother. To Anita, this was a major revelation. On the spot, mother and daughter decided to take a one-week summer photography class in Maine. As they left, the therapist saw Tanya give her mother a big hug. The family came once more after the summer and reported being "back on track." Case closed.

INCEST

As we have seen, enmeshment is about crossing an emotional boundary *in* the family, compromising a family member's integrity, an intrusion upon his or her emotional "space."

Incest is like enmeshment in that it is clearly a boundary violation as well as a threat to the integrity of the victim's self. However, it has the added aggressive feature of being a literal invasion if not assault upon the body. Also unlike enmeshment, adults who cross that boundary absolutely know they are doing something considered wrong. Consequently, most people who commit incest suffer tremendous guilt, however they rationalize it. In many if not most cases, an act of betrayal in the form of incest leads to either an immediate or a delayed cutoff that is too often left unresolved. Incest is also still a subject many therapists are afraid to touch.

                                                  Chelsea's parents, Winston and Diane, scheduled an appointment with a family therapist because their daughter announced she was dropping out of college and moving to Paris with her forty-five-year-

old boyfriend, Roger. This was the first the parents had heard about Chelsea's relationship. Chelsea had met Roger a year before in Aix en Provence on a summer exchange program. Roger was an up-and-coming art dealer, but Chelsea slipped and told her parents that he once trafficked in cocaine. She was twenty and a university student in the United States. She was in love, and if her parents tried to stop her, she would cut them off completely. Roger no longer used drugs. Chelsea was an innocent as far as drugs were concerned.

Chelsea stopped speaking to her father when he attacked this "insane" idea and threatened to cut her off financially. Winston wants to "speak" to the boyfriend "man to man." Compounding Winston's incredulity at the age difference was rage that Chelsea had not informed her parents until now and anger at her for even thinking she could leave school when her parents had poured their savings into her education. Diane believed that if Chelsea pursued this relationship, she would be "dragged into the mud," ruined for life.

Diane contacted a therapist to help her and Winston cope with this situation. The therapist asked to include Chelsea, stating that they would probably have better luck if Chelsea participated. The therapist suggested that Diane ask Chelsea to attend three sessions before deciding to leave school. Chelsea agreed to meet first alone and then with her mother and/or the therapist three times, but not with her father.

Chelsea told the therapist in that first one-on-one meeting that her father was too demanding, that his expectations were "over the moon," and that he came close to sexually abusing her as a teenager. She "hated" him, and her relationship with an older man was his punishment. She needed someone like Roger because she'd never had a "real" father.

The therapist proceeded step by step. Chelsea agreed to a session with her mother to explain why she was not speaking to her father. The therapist obtained the father's permission, stating her belief that the mother-daughter session could serve as a prelude to including him and ending the cutoff. As was the case with Anita, this therapist told us she'd never had a parent refuse a properly explained request, even if it meant exclusion of a key family player.

Diane was torn between loyalty to husband and daughter. She briefly contemplated divorce but believed Winston would do whatever it took to keep the family together. The therapist recommended that Diane explain Chelsea's feelings to Winston in a session.

In a subsequent meeting of Winston and therapist, the therapist repeated Chelsea's feeling that her father had occasionally stepped over the line. He denied it, and the therapist did not argue. She simply stated that it was critical not to allow even the perception to continue. At the same time, the therapist empathized with this father's obvious love for his daughter. They discussed the fact that attraction of fathers to daughters is common, thereby normalizing the feelings but not the behavior.

Winston wrote a letter of apology, at the same time begging Chelsea not to leave school. Chelsea compromised. She would stay with Roger over the summer but return to finish her senior year. Her father backed off, and Chelsea slowly began to contact him—at first just about her allowance! Though Winston was upset that Chelsea was brief and cool toward him, at least they were communicating again. Chelsea went to Paris and returned on schedule. The relationship with Roger cooled. She went home for the summer after graduation and called the therapist to say that her father was no longer yelling, their relationship was much improved, and "I'm not afraid of him anymore."

⚬⚬⚬

The case below involves sibling incest, a brief, but catastrophic episode for both children. Because it was buried for so many years, it led to seemingly insoluble marital problems and misery for all concerned.

Jared and Louise had a long, often stormy marriage. Jared admits to having a bad temper, but much more in the past than the present. Years ago, he hit Louise, but was remorseful, and swears he would never touch her now. Still, she is afraid. Arguments start when he wants to be close or intimate, and they escalate when she pulls away. She comes from a family that never fought and buried problems under the rug; battles were the norm in Jared's family.

By the time they came for therapy, Louise was emotionally gone. She viewed Jared as "sick" and claimed she stayed mostly out of pity. It was at times a volatile situation. Jared related that when he was growing up, there was little love, no praise, and a lot of criticism. He hoped to have a loving marriage and was bitterly disappointed that his wife was so distant. He considered leaving, but loves Louise and feels he cannot be alone.

They worked on the marriage for at least a year, making small strides, but it was too often one step forward and two back. Louise decided to stop. But she wanted Jared to "keep working on his anger," which he reluctantly did.

Attending sessions individually allowed Jared to express his frustration about his marriage and his family of origin. He felt solely responsible for the sorry state of the marriage and felt he had to defend himself all the time. He also saw himself as the problem kid in his family of origin. Since his parents died, his brother was not speaking to him, and his sister avoided him completely. Louise told the therapist the problem was his temper.

No matter what Jared did—controlling his temper, not asking for sex—there seemed no way to reengage his wife. Too much water had gone under the bridge and Louise was still afraid. They were both miserable, but could not separate. It was deeply ironic to the therapist that Jared was consummately patient as a researcher, taking years to write a book, but was always desperate for an immediate positive response from people closest to him.

On the theory that Jared needed more support to undertake another round of therapy with his wife, the therapist suggested that he might let the marriage be for a while and detour to work on his relationships with his siblings. He might then either have the strength to work even harder on the marriage or to summon the courage to leave.

During one of their sessions, Jared revealed a suicide attempt at twelve after he was caught stealing five dollars from a classmate. Asked why he wanted to die, he responded, "I knew my father would find out and beat the crap out of me; zero tolerance for bad behavior in my house." No one asked why he stole the money, which as it happened, was to buy food for a stray dog he had adopted and kept hidden in a neighbor's stable. He then volunteered that the night after the attempt, he crawled into bed with his sister—initially for solace, but then he also attempted to have sex. The sister initially repressed the memory, but eventually remembered and cut Jared off.

When he first agreed to individual therapy, it was to appease his wife. At a certain point the focus changed. He was there for himself and finally grasped that he was basically a good, intelligent man with a problem. He agreed to keep a record of his thoughts in a notebook whenever he felt his anger rising, and he learned to meditate.

Jared sent a brief letter to his sister, something short of a full apology, with a copy to his brother. The brother reported that the sister was not prepared to see him now but might be in the future. He told Jared he loved him, and in a visit that ensued, the brother advised Jared not to worry so much about the past.

After a year of individual work, Jared persuaded Louise to return to therapy with him. She recognized some progress and may slowly be reinvesting in the relationship. Incest was at the core of Jared's low self-image. Once he began to forgive himself, his temper abated and most of his relationships improved. The therapist believes he will eventually recontact his sister with a deeper, more specific apology.

Mother-daughter incest is far less common than father-daughter, but it does happen. And when it does, it is just as likely to produce a cutoff:

Nadia, twenty-eight, was referred to a therapist by her internist. She was having trouble urinating, and a urologist found nothing anatomically or medically wrong. Nadia was a bright, somewhat shy young woman who had excelled in college. She loved animals large and small and loved the idea of travel, but she had never been anywhere. She lived with her parents, Marshall and Stella, in their one-bedroom, one-bathroom apartment and was close to her mother, but she and her father had not spoken for six months.

Marshall had initiated the cutoff. Nadia thought it was because she always challenged him and would not leave him alone. She did not understand why she yelled at him, but speculated it was because "he doesn't pay attention to me." An assistant in an accounting office, Nadia "hated" her job and was recently fired.

Nadia was eager to have a life larger than her parents' but had no idea how to go about it. Her parents had met as petty bureaucrats in the post office, settled down, had one child, and (according to Nadia) had no motivation to go anywhere or do anything. As Nadia got comfortable in therapy, she talked about how little she had in common with them. One time she laughingly confided that she sometimes thought of them as aliens, "maybe from Mars!"

As Nadia described her childhood and her living situation, a theme emerged. She had no privacy. Her parents had the bedroom; Nadia's "bedroom" was a section in the living room with no door. She had occasional sex with boyfriends but now wanted a "real relationship." She would invite young men to the apartment but had to be on the alert for interruption from her parents. When her parents had sex, they would sometimes leave their door open, and she could hear it. Then, and at other times, they would hurry her out of the bathroom. This pressure from her parents had never occurred to Nadia as the source of her difficulty urinating.

Early in therapy Nadia worked up her courage to ask for a door, which the parents agreed to install. Finally, after a year in therapy, Nadia revealed a persistent memory of her mother fondling her inappropriately when she was around ten. After school, she and her mother would get into bed. Her mother would read stories, and touch her. She doesn't remember details, but the thought of it disgusts her now. She also realized what her anger at her father was about, because he was sometimes home when this went on. She blamed him for not paying attention to what was happening in the house. When she understood that her deeper upset was with her mother, she reached out to her father in small ways, and he started speaking to her again.

The therapist suggested that Nadia bring her mother to one of the sessions. It took Nadia a while, but she did agree to it. The therapist was amazed that this supposedly timid young woman spoke to her mother in such a mature, non-confrontational way. Her mother owned up and apologized to a degree, but was also understandably defensive, replying "Remember, you wanted me to read to you and kiss you the way the Prince did." Nadia's simple reply was, "You were the adult; you should have set the limits."

By the time she finished therapy, Nadia was urinating normally. She also began traveling. She went to Africa for a month by herself, to the Caribbean, and to Scandinavia. She got a job with an animal rights organization, made new friends, and got her own apartment.

This case is interesting especially in that Nadia stopped speaking to her father, who was not the main offender. But she had unwittingly discovered the fact that in many cases of incest—and other forms of abuse—the silent parent functions as a "co-conspirator" with the person involved and may be viewed somehow as the safer focus for anger, reflecting the mechanism of displacement.

EXTRA-FAMILIAL INFIDELITY

Extra familial infidelity crosses the invisible, and at least tacitly understood boundary that encircles most marriages or committed relationships. Someone within the family breaks the rule and "goes outside." In these instances, the betrayal may be emotional, and is almost always sexual.

Euripides's ancient Greek masterpiece, *Medea*, is as fine an example of a tragic (and hijacked) response to extra-familial infidelity as exists in Western literature. Medea's husband, Jason, leaves her for another woman, the king's daughter, to enhance his status in society. He also banishes Medea to prevent her from taking revenge. Medea leaves Corinth, but only after murdering their children and Jason's new bride.

Horrific as the story is, it is emblematic of the jealous rage that can boil over with extra-familial infidelity. In this instance, we have an explosive combination of extreme personal rejection, romantic jealousy, loss of country, loss of children, and loss of social status and social support. Unfortunately, similar stories still occasionally appear in the news.

Ever since Medea, and probably before, we bemoan each and every occurrence of filicide, a parent murdering his or her own child. While we don't know exactly what recently prompted two mothers, Andrea Yates and Susan Smith to kill their young children (Sher & Braswell, 2010)—or whether infidelity was involved—their actions remind us that murder of one's own offspring, however primitive, still happens with some regularity, in animal as well as human communities (Mock, 2004). Therefore, when a fragile client experiences

a devastating betrayal such as extramarital infidelity without sufficient social support, therapists should be aware that reason can van-
ish in a heartbeat and that murderous cutoffs may result.

Betrayal in the form of infidelity is not only committed by adults.
In the novel *Mildred Pierce* by James M. Cain (1941/2003), we have
a rare instance of a child's intentional, exceptionally cruel and
incestuous extra familial affair. Veda, Mildred's narcissistic daughter, seduces and then runs away with Monty, her mother's live-in
lover. In retaliation, Mildred whose "only crime, if she had committed one, was that she loved this girl too well," completely cuts Veda
off. "To hell with her," Mildred rationalizes, but we know there will
be no end to the pain.

In the clinical example that follows, we see what early intervention can do to prevent such an outcome. Alec heard a therapist speak
at a coffeehouse gathering and approached him afterward. Alec was
in "terrible shape" and couldn't eat or sleep. Could he come in the
following day? Here is Alec's story:

*Just before I came to the coffeehouse yesterday, my fiancee, Felice (guess
she's not my fiancee anymore) left me a text saying she does not want to
hear from me again. I should stop bothering her and "get a life." I
can't wrap my mind around the fact that she's done. We've known
each other since primary school. Over this whole past winter she strung
me along saying she was confused, that she couldn't see me because she
had to study for the Medical College Admissions Test.*

*I tried to leave her alone but I called sometimes just to see if there
was anything I could do for her. She put me off. Then, six weeks ago, I
found out from a friend that she was going out with someone else the
entire time. They are serious and she may marry him. I was ready to
do anything for her, including adopting her 6 year old daughter, but
she never gave me a chance, and now won't even meet to help me get
closure. I've called multiple times. She won't pick up the phone. Sometimes I'm so upset that I imagine killing her and her daughter. Would
you call and ask her to meet me, or come to one session, please?*

The manner of a breakup especially if it is delivered callously can
set the stage for revenge. Sadly, Felice mishandled the situation by
inching her way out of the relationship, never telling the truth. Had

she been forthcoming about seeing someone else, Alec might have ended the relationship himself and would not have become so anxious, angry, and obsessed. In any event, when a breakup comes as a result of infidelity and is as devastating as Alec's was, the therapist must take it seriously and probe for underlying cutoffs in the client's past.

The therapist wrestled with Alec's request for him to call Felice. Alec needed face-to-face closure. If the therapist refused, he might lose Alec, who was clearly in trouble. But the therapist also knew that calling Felice was not only a questionable move clinically, but also might backfire. So he suggested postponing the decision, explaining that before he could agree it was important to know more about the situation and why Alec was having so much trouble letting go. The therapist also instructed Alec that if he could not control an impulse to call Felice, to call him instead. This alternative helped Alex, and he did call, but just once or twice at night.

It turned out that Alec cut off from his parents. They were alcoholics and verbally abusive. As the eldest, Alec tried to protect his siblings but could not, so he left town after high school. He maintained a passion for the justice he never experienced as a child and therefore could not live with the fact that he was treated unjustly again, this time by Felice, to whom he had given his heart. Adding insult to injury, Alec was convinced that even after betraying him, Felice would lead a happy life unfazed, while he was destined to be unhappy, alone, a loser.

Step two was to shore up Alec's confidence. The therapist drew attention to red flags in Felice's behavior that should have made Alec more cautious. She had a mean streak (like his mother) that had never been directed at him but that Alec observed in the way she treated others. She was obsessed with money and status. Her goal was to be a plastic surgeon and the highest earner in the area. Her values differed markedly from Alec's. How would they be compatible? Alec had a job and friends, but no money, and didn't care!

Step three was to support Alec's own idea to write a letter to Felice enumerating the ways she betrayed him. He composed it, reported that he felt better, and never needed to mail it. By the way, the therapist eventually did call Felice. She initially balked, but finally met with Alec six months later. Alec voiced his feelings and was able to let go.

VERBAL CRUELTY AND PUBLIC HUMILIATION

The difficulty with verbal cruelty is that words once spoken, even in private, are hard to take back. Public humiliation cuts like a knife. Even on a short list of devastating public remarks, author Mary McCarthy's (*The Group*) is a standout, guaranteed to provoke a sense of betrayal of expected respect as well as a cutoff. McCarthy and author Lillian Hellman (*The Little Foxes, Pentimento*) had much in common as smart successful women in a man's world. They knew each other's work, knew they held radically opposing political views, and knew that at different times they had been interested in the same man. So, while they were not close friends in the literal sense, they certainly knew each other.

Responding to questions from Dick Cavett in a 1980 televised interview, McCarthy not only called Hellman "overrated" but then blew her away with the now-legendary declaration that "everything . . . every word she writes is a lie, including *and* and *the*!" (quoted in Mahon, 2008). Hellman retaliated with a $2 million lawsuit that she won and that McCarthy could not afford to lose.

There are many such outlandish, funny, sad, fascinating public figure betrayals that cause irreparable cutoffs. Take the riveting televised Casey Anthony murder trial. While press and public "convicted" Casey, Jose Baez, her defense lawyer, swore that Casey had actually been "thrown under the bus" by her father, who essentially testified against his daughter by hiding his own complicity in the accidental drowning of Casey's daughter. Casey has not spoken to him since the trial ended (Baez & Golenbock, 2012).

A happier ending occurred for Angelina Jolie and her father, actor Jon Voight. Their cutoff had been precipitated by Voight's public comment that he hoped his daughter would get help for her "mental problems." At least partial credit for Angelina's willingness to reconcile was due to Brad Pitt, who encouraged it, another good example of the positive influence a third party can have.

৵৶

The next clinical case also depicts a father-daughter rift, no less painful or disruptive because the public in question was "only" the family. This and the following case are also examples of partial reconciliation effected by third parties, in this instance a therapist.

In the chapter on Abandonment we discussed cases in which a parent was absent when the client was a child as "sins of omission." In this case, Ann Marie's father was very much present.

Ann Marie's father, Malcolm, was verbally abusive, especially when he drank. Ann Marie remembers spelling and math tests at the dinner table. If she gave an incorrect answer, she was "stupid" or "hopeless." She also remembers when she forgot to return something to a neighbor: "In front of the whole family he called me an 'irresponsible little bitch' and asked why couldn't I be more like my sister." That is when Ann Marie first stopped speaking to him.

Malcolm quit drinking when Ann Marie was a senior in high school and gained better control of his temper. But she could not forgive him for the past and has kept her distance for thirty years. This was a partial cutoff, as Ann Marie has maintained minimal contact. Her father lives in a neighboring community.

Ann Marie's mother died when she was in graduate school and her father never remarried. In his eighties, Malcolm was not well. When he tripped over an area rug, fell, and broke his ankle, he wrote to Ann Marie asking to stay with her "just until my ankle is better." At that point, Ann Marie had not spoken to him for two years. She was not sure what he wanted or needed but was angry that he even asked. Though she refused, she felt guilty and thought it was probably her duty to help.

A single mother with two teenagers at home and a full-time job, Ann Marie had no time for herself. Her sister lives three hours away. The ambivalence and internal conflict about what to do made Ann Marie anxious and depressed, so she sought out a therapist.

The therapist cautioned the client—and us—that "if someone is toxic it is important to carefully monitor and control the relationship." However, by so quickly labeling the father, the therapist missed giving Ann Marie a chance to consider how her father felt and whether he might have matured over the years. The label preempted any motivation Ann Marie might still have to rethink her relationship with her father. It also precluded the therapist suggesting a joint session with Malcolm. Nevertheless, the therapist did do some important preparatory work.

She asked Ann Marie what kind of relationship she wished she had with her father, and they briefly revisited her childhood. This allowed the therapist to "bear witness" to what Ann Marie lived through and affirm that Malcolm's behavior clearly betrayed Ann Marie's sense of safety and trust. Having been "heard," by the therapist, Ann Marie realized for the first time that the treatment she received was not her fault, that her father's accusations were not proof she was an unworthy child.

With this insight, Ann Marie asked herself what she should do—stand firm with a refusal to help her father, or "cave"? The therapist gave her perspective by asking Ann Marie to consider the two possibilities as if she could look back years from now. How would she feel about either decision? Neither felt right. The therapist then asked if there was some in-between action she could take, a gesture that would both help her father and not compromise her.

Ann Marie wanted not to feel guilty if she declined to help her father. She also wanted to "take the high road," though she felt he did not entirely deserve it. Ultimately, she decided to help, less for duty's sake than for her own sense of herself. The therapist empathized with Ann Marie's fear that her father would move in and never leave of his own accord. So the question became "What kind of contact do I want now, and what can I realistically expect of myself and him?"

The answers came easily once Ann Marie asked the right questions. She called her father, reiterated that she could not take him in, but that she would help him get visiting nurse services and would stop in regularly to see how he was doing. When he commented that she was doing "the minimum," she countered with, "I'm doing what I can, Dad. Let's start there." Ann Marie also told him that if this period went well, they could continue rebuilding a relationship—a partial reconciliation.

With that, Ann Marie reached the goal she and the therapist had set, to help without sacrificing too much of herself, to set a boundary, and recover her own compassion, despite her father's mistakes.

PHYSICAL ABUSE

Our last category, physical abuse, is a serious invasion of one's person, of one's body. It is painful, frightening, and leaves the victim feeling vulnerable and unprotected. It also makes them angry, often unbearably. While people who experience emotional abuse swear they would take physical abuse "any day," we wonder. It has to depend on the particular circumstances, the people involved, and the nuances of behavior in each situation. At the end of the day, we think it best to leave it that both are damaging—all the more so if uncompensated for by expressions of love, affection, or repara-tion.

Physical punishment might be tolerated occasionally if it is pre-dictable—such as if a child knows he will be spanked for breaking an established rule—but not if it is frequent, extreme, or if one has to be constantly on guard. In the latter cases, cutting off at least temporar-ily may be necessary. It bears repeating here that therapists should always probe a cutoff to see if physical abuse is involved before pressing for reconciliation. In such cases, therapist and client have to consider the benefits, if any, for reconciliation versus maintaining the cutoff and helping the client move on.

David, forty-two, consulted a therapist on the advice of his girlfriend because he was obsessed with a family problem. He couldn't sleep, and she was worried about him. He'd recently had another altercation with his brother-in-law, Joey. This time it came to blows, though no one was hurt. David stopped speaking to Joey and his father. He believed his father sided with his sister and with Joey,"betraying me."

The family owns a five-screen movie theater. While David's father, Manny, is no longer involved in day-to-day operations, he still has "moral authority." But David told the therapist, "Joey acts as if he's the boss and my Dad won't tell him he's not, or put me in charge. No one is really in charge, and my Dad says he just wants us all to get along." David believed his father didn't care if Joey beat him up: "It's just a continuation of what my father used to do to me himself."

Joey is married to David's sister, Renee, the youngest sibling. Manny always had a soft spot for his only daughter. But he "whipped out the belt" at the slightest infraction from David. To this day, David has the marks on his back. He felt his father's resentment stemmed from the fact that David was the brightest of the four children and stood up to him. He was also first in the family with a college degree, while his father had dropped out of high school to run the family business.

Sadly, David has not developed his considerable intellectual gifts; he manages equipment at the theater.

The therapist could feel David's frustration and saw ways David could handle the situation differently, but David was initially too embroiled in the family drama to contemplate change. Fortunately, the therapist caught himself in time and converted his own frustration to empathy for David, who had clearly been mistreated. "Putting myself in your shoes," the therapist said, "I see no way out either. It feels like glue." He asked David how he had come to be so stuck and got the immediate answer, "I guess I'm still waiting for my father to approve of me." That was something they could work on.

Hearing himself say it, David realized the futility of waiting for Manny's approval and began to brainstorm with the therapist. He could press charges against Joey; he could meet with Joey, with or without the therapist. He could meet with his sister to discuss the problem either on his own or with the therapist. He could meet with his father, with or without the therapist. He could leave the family business, even though he might lose his inheritance. The options now seemed endless.

After discussing pros and cons, David invited his father to a session. If nothing came of it, David would consider leaving the family business. In the joint session, David told his father why he had stopped speaking to him, that he was always afraid of him. He felt his father had never treated him properly or ever taken his side. "I've spent my life seeking your approval, and never got it."

Manny was stunned but said he didn't want to go to his grave with David hating him. He didn't exactly apologize, but he did agree that Joey was "a problem." He also agreed to speak to Renee about Joey, and then to Joey as well. Finally, he would tell Joey and Renee that David was in charge.

While none of those promises were kept, David realized that his father simply could not decide which child to place in charge, that his father's non-support was not personal. But it did leave the door open for Joey. Of utmost importance, he saw his father's behavior as weakness and indecisiveness, rather than deviousness. He stopped looking to his father for solutions and is now debating next moves. But as he does, he is speaking to his father again, with less anger in his tone.

The next case could just as easily fit in the next chapter, on Principle. We placed it here because of the surprising eruption of violence in an otherwise controlled family environment.

Claudia and Santiago have two adult children, thirty-two-year-old Woody and twenty-nine-year-old Jewel. Woody is a successful film sound editor with a steady girlfriend and his own therapist. He had not seen or spoken to his mother for many years. His parents' relationship was frayed, and they had only a tenuous one with their daughter, Jewel, and her husband. Claudia tried to preserve a sense of togetherness without Woody, at least a facade during the holidays, but sadness pervaded. In individual therapy, Claudia decided she is ready to repair her relationship with Woody. She asked him to engage in family therapy with her. He agreed.

In the first joint session, Woody easily expressed love for his mother, but in the same breath he "hit her" with his deep pain. He reminded her how unhappy she had been when he was a child and how she had lashed out at the slightest thing, usually at him. On one occasion, she completely "lost it," hitting him so hard he was briefly unconscious. She had forgotten that incident.

Claudia apologized profusely for her past behavior, vowing she would never hurt him now, either physically or emotionally. Having had years of therapy, she was a different person. Woody believed she meant well, but he was still afraid. She wanted him to come home for a visit. He wasn't ready to see her outside the therapy room but said he would work up to it. Maybe they could have lunch, maybe then he could visit. This was October.

Woody relented at Christmas, primarily because his girlfriend would be out of town with her family and he did not want to be alone. The first thing he did upon arrival was to turn on the stereo, selecting Bach's "Christmas Oratorio." It was to calm his nerves, but Claudia ordered him to turn it off. When she was a child, her father, long gone now, had a rule that there was to be no music at Christmas. He was very religious, and it was a serious day. Claudia was determined to honor his memory, and Woody was being rude.

Upon hearing this, the therapist suggested that Claudia might want to choose her son's needs over her father's decree. Her father was dead; her son was alive and hopefully back in her life. Woody felt he had stretched himself to honor his mother's wish that he visit, and he was upset she could not understand his anxiety or respect his feelings. Besides, Woody argued, the piece he had selected was utterly "appropriate," couldn't she see?

Perhaps it was too soon for them to come together informally. Clients with such inflexibility are unable to yield, even when the stakes are high. Surely, Claudia's adherence to her dead father's "rule" did not help her relationship with her son. Perhaps the therapist erred in not helping them prepare enough. In any event, there was a lucky break. Woody's sister's husband suggested a compromise. Bach before dinner and after; no music during the meal. Claudia and Woody accepted the friendly suggestion, a disaster was avoided, and once again a third party saved the day.

This physical abuse case clearly involves a matter of principle in the rule cherished by Claudia, and we will revisit these principles and how they relate to cutoffs in the next chapter.

Chapter 6

PRINCIPLE

If only I could throw away the urge to trace my
patterns in your heart, I could really see you.
Brandon (1978, p. 47)

Principles are cognitive beliefs based on research, life experience, or values—"truths" that shape thinking and actions (Rabinowitz, n.d.). At times *principles* and *values* are used interchangeably. However, they are somewhat different. While both provide a litmus test for right or wrong behavior, principles are more intractable, structured in their expression and articulated under the rubric of a scientific theory, religious tenet, political belief or ideology. Values, on the other hand, are more emotional and immediate, more individualistic in how they shape one's perceptions of others and the world.

In this chapter, we focus on principles people use to explain a cutoff. At the same time, we examine the values and other contextual issues that contribute to people's inability to resolve perceived breaches.

To determine points of intervention, we discuss the ways in which individuals explain their principles and how they respond to a perceived violation by someone close to them. For instance, some individuals have deeply held principles and also respect other people's actions or beliefs, even if they do not agree. In fact, there may be some explicit agreement about incompatibility in values and beliefs, followed by a modification of the relationship, but not a cutoff.

When, however, the transgression has to do with a principle one person believes embodies immutable truth—say the law of God—emotions may flare. In these situations, other characteristics—in effect, the wholeness of the other person—may be submerged. The transgression of boundaries ascends in significance and obscures other aspects of the relationship. Many times, cutoffs based on principle cross a previously established line and are experienced as a betrayal by one or both parties. One believes the principle under which he or she thought they were both operating is violated. The other believes that the one with the principle betrayed him or her by judging the relationship solely through the prism of the principle.

Honor killings are an extreme example of this fusion of principle and betrayal. Historically, and still in some places, women are considered property, reflecting the family's prestige or wealth. Modesty and chastity are prized. Even if a woman is raped and thus loses her virginity through no fault of her own, she is nevertheless "polluted" and loses her value to the family. Even if she simply marries below the family's station, she contaminates the family or clan And the ultimate solution in some places is to cut off the contaminant by killing her. In these cases, the family believes that by "sacrificing" the daughter or sister, the family is purified and regains its honor. Some believe the killing to be ultimately protective, even an act of mercy.

As some of the cases in previous chapters revealed, concern about "contamination" or "purity" may also surface when a child marries out of the family's class, faith, race, or ethnicity. Similarly, subscription to "fundamental" religious principles or cultural tenets is reflected in family cutoffs when a son or daughter reveals that he or she is gay, lesbian, or transgendered. In these situations the individual who cuts off believes he or she is obeying the laws of God as manifested in the Bible, Qur'an, Talmud, or other religious text. These texts, and the guidance of religious leaders and scholars, are said to be the foundation upon which the individual builds his or her life and which guide both action and response to the actions of others. For these individuals, principles are not subject to modification according to individual conscience, life experience, or the dynamics of cultural and social change. They cling to literal meaning rather than the spirit of the law, with no room to reinterpret in the light of social and economic evolution.

In contrast to absolute adherence to religious and cultural principle is the approach exemplified by Baruch Spinoza, the seventeenth-century Dutch Jewish philosopher whose work in ethics continues to animate religious, philosophical, and social discourse. According to Spinoza:

> every person is duty bound to adapt . . . religious dogmas to his own understanding and to interpret them for himself in whatever way makes him feel that he can the more readily accept them with full confidence and conviction. (quoted by Nadler, 2013)

Spinoza offers a very liberal approach to the Bible that allows for differences in belief and multiple interpretations of a single text or tenet. If multiple equally valid interpretations exist, by extension, they must somehow coexist. To do so, there must be some level of tolerance, acceptance of that which is different, without judgment. One can have tolerance without forgiveness, but the two are often interwoven, for to accept difference in belief or action—to believe that someone else is wrong, but still acceptable—suggests that one is able to set aside or forgive the action while accepting the person. In fact, in his oft-quoted comment, Alexander Pope, the seventeenth-century English author, implied that error is part of one's humanity and that forgiveness stretches us even beyond that: "To err is human; to forgive is divine."

However, is there in fact some higher truth through which one can measure all action, and which ultimately limits one's ability to be tolerant? Are there certain universal human rights such as preservation of life and dignity, self-determination, and freedom from oppression? Do individuals or societies have the responsibility, at some level, to intervene, to not tolerate actions that threaten life, social bonds, or a society's capacity to preserve itself? And who should decide? The American philosopher John Rawls (1971/1999) believes that social preservation trumps the principle of tolerance and that:

> an intolerant sect does not itself have title to complain of intolerance, its freedom should be restricted only when the tolerant sincerely and with reason believe that their own security and that of the institutions of liberty are in danger (p. 220).

Rawls's focus is on society at large; similarly as clinicians, our focus is on individual and family relationships. As such, we believe that in most cases family preservation trumps principle. Although a clinician in the west would not ordinarily encounter an honor killing in the course of a career, clients do come to us with cutoffs that amount to a death in the family, some even ritualized as such—e.g., sitting Shiva because someone did not live within or up to a given value or principle. Honor killings aside, we clinicians have to develop perspectives and strategies that can be used to assist or mediate a cutoff that presents as one of principle, even including the symbolic death of one or both parties.

"Death," honor killings, the sense of absolute right or wrong— this chapter will no doubt create some discomfort as it stirs up our own conflicts, confusion, and contradictions, made all the more difficult if there are significant differences between our clients' worldview and the religious or ideological tenets with which we were raised. Some of the issues will stir deep emotions in the reader as they have us. As clinicians, we need to be mindful of our own principles and monitor the elasticity of our tolerance. Failure to work on these issues will limit our capacity to hear our clients—their pain and frustration. And, it will limit our ability to help.

In the following pages, we observe how principles shape choices and how, at times, a stated principle camouflages other underlying issues in a relationship. As we explore these dynamics we identify and discuss specific strategies that echo and build from the basic ones presented in the Strategies chapter.

We begin with a brief discussion of cutoffs associated with theoretical and scientific principles. This is followed by an exploration of cutoffs based on national and ethnic differences, often transformed into political differences. Religious and cultural principles, so often intertwined, are the next thematic category. Cutoffs resulting from the violation of social principles will then be explored.

THEORY

The irony is not lost on us that our discussion of scientific or theoretical principles starts with a brief return to the cutoff that occurred between two major figures of psychoanalysis, Freud and Jung.

As discussed in the Jealousy chapter, the infamous cutoff between Freud and Jung was in part about a mentor who could not relinquish control and celebrate the new-found success of his mentee. Jung not only refused to embrace Freud's libido theory, concept of repressed memory, and other aspects of psychoanalytic theory, but he proceeded to develop his own theory about the collective unconscious. For Freud, this was unacceptable, intellectual heresy.

We include Freud and Jung in this chapter not to debate the merits of their respective theories or to psychoanalyze their relationship. Rather, we use it to illustrate how a principle or intellectual disagreement may overlap, even obscure the mentee-mentor relationship, and result in a cutoff.

In these kinds of situations, and as Bowen taught us, clinicians find it helpful to re-conceptualize the cutoff and explore the mentee's feelings about the process of separation and individuation from parents. The focus is not on the principles or the theories, but rather on helping the client to appreciate his or her own personal identity and professional growth, and distinguish them from the response of others.

Once the mentee feels more secure, he or she can decide whether to reach out to the mentor and explicitly state how important the relationship has been and that while their work may no longer be congruent, he or she wants to stay in contact. The emphasis is on the intellectual nurturing that enabled the success of the mentee. The outreach focuses on the mentee's appreciation of the mentor. It requests a change in their relationship—for the mentee to move from novice to colleague or friend—and separates the relationship from the intellectual or theoretical conflict.

Mentors who recognize that developmental tensions are disguised under intellectual ones may be open to moving forward in a restructured relationship. However, if the senior colleague is unable to be consoled by and take pride in his or her success as a mentor, the junior colleague has to move forward alone. In such situations it is critical for a therapist to affirm the growth and success of the mentee, to be the supportive enabling parent, and to counter the hurt of the abandoning one.

It is equally important to help the mentee mourn the relationship, as well as the mentor as an individual—to reflect on the past and decide what he or she wishes to bring into the future. Only through affirmation of the loss can he or she move on. Failure to do so can stymie the client's future intellectual growth and achievement as well as interactions with other colleagues.

In leaving this section, we feel compelled to add that a young professional without a mentor often feels like a motherless child, adrift in the world of work. This may bring being cut off by a mentor into perspective: It is better to have been mentored and lost than never to have been mentored at all.

IDEOLOGY AND POLITICS

Ideological cutoffs may occur when a perceived greater good trumps a relationship. What first comes to mind is Brutus's conspiring to assassinate Caesar, his patron and friend, when he believes Caesar's grab for power threatens the Roman republic. While this assassination is surely an extreme betrayal-of-friendship cutoff, principle is the primary motivation. Brutus is grief stricken and guilt ridden but rationalizes the murder by proclaiming it was "not that I loved Caesar less, but that I loved Rome more" (Shakespeare, *Julius Caesar,* III.ii).

Fears for personal or family safety may also trigger a cutoff based on ideology or politics. In the United States, the post–World War II years witnessed growing anti-Soviet sentiment, the emergence of a second Red Scare, and the rise of McCarthyism. Freedom of belief and association were in jeopardy.

৯৵৶

The following case reflects not only differences in belief but also a betrayal of friendship based on the differences. As we shall see, Janet believed that attendance at a meeting had the potential to threaten her and her family's well-being.

During World War II, Janet became close friends with her neighbor, Sadie. They often talked about the war and when the Allies were victorious jointly celebrated with their families. Over the next few years the women continued to discuss politics. Sadie knew that Janet was a staunch Roosevelt Democrat, worried about the rise of communism and fearful of the Soviet Union. Sometime in the early 1950s Sadie invited Janet to a speaking event that turned out to be a communist recruit-

ment forum. Janet felt Sadie was dishonest in not disclosing the pur-
pose of the meeting in advance. She stormed out and never spoke to
Sadie again.

In this example from one of our parents' lives, it is unclear
whether either woman would have sought out a therapist's help. To
repair the relationship, Sadie would need to focus on the sense of
threat experienced by Janet. For Janet, it would be the sense of
betrayal that a friend had knowingly misled her and thereby put her
in harm's way. A third party might have helped Sadie apologize for
not giving advance warning and helped both women understand the
other's political position and what it meant to each of them, the goal
being for each to empathize with the other.

༄༅

The next case also demonstrates the need to look beyond the
stated difference of principle to the impact of that principle within
the life of the individual, the community, or the society.

Just before the 2012 election on a National Public Radio show, This
American Life, *Ira Glass and his colleagues interviewed two men
whose friendship had been fractured over their choices of president. As
Glass noted, "It's not just that they have different solutions to the country's problems. They don't even agree on what the problems are."
Charles's choice of Barack Obama was personal; he had significant
health problems and absolutely required ongoing access to health care.
Frank's passionate support of Mitt Romney reflected his "love of country." "The stakes are too high," Charles commented, "to consider it
simply as agree to disagree. I don't agree to disagree. Frank needs to
change his opinion because his view on the conduct of this society will
kill it."*

The question relevant to our own practices is: Can individuals
who vehemently disagree politically or ideologically overcome their
differences? A book co-authored by writers at opposite ends of the
political spectrum, Phil Neisser and Jacob Hess's *You're Not as Crazy as
I Thought (But You're Still Wrong): Conversations Between a Die-Hard Liberal and a Devoted Conservative* (2012) suggests that it is possible. The
authors state that it is not about agreeing to disagree, convincing the

other person that he or she is wrong, or changing the other's opinion. Rather, the object of the dialogue is to "understand what the
person believes and why he or she believes it. The other person does
the same for you." This is a powerful concept—to help someone step
back and truly listen to how the other person constructs his reality
and how the person arrived at his or her perspective.

Can this strategy work beyond the political landscape? We believe
it can, because the essence of this strategy is the process of helping
the other to move from object to a fully dimensional human being.
The other's reality may be different from yours, but he or she can
still be well meaning, of goodwill toward you. What was it that originally brought the two of you together? What was the attraction
before the politics or principle got "in the way"? Sometimes bringing
the history of the relationship to the fore during a conflict is enough
to motivate the parties to keep their cool and salvage the relationship.

Think of people you know—friends, couples, and families—who
manage to agree to disagree or place a boundary around a contentious area. The political strategists James Carville (Democrat) and
Mary Matalan (Republican) have asserted numerous times over
their nineteen-year marriage that they "do not talk politics at home."
While we cannot help wondering what does go on at the family dinner table and how a discussion about current events is eschewed,
they are still together.

ETHNICITY AND RELIGION

As observed in Chapter 1, being a Hatfield or McCoy, a Montague or
Capulet has become shorthand for intractable family boundaries
not to be crossed. In literature and history, these boundaries may
exist because of an ancestral past insult, betrayal, jealousy, even
murder.

In some cases, descendants try to ignore inherited rules of affiliation, such as young people falling in love. In literature and life many
of these attempts seem cursed, as in the tragic deaths of Romeo and
Juliet. On a much larger scale, the "tribe" creates a new boundary
between it and the errant couple, detaching themselves from their
existence. We will see how this is ritualized by some religions.

Clan or family grudges based on affiliation can spiral out of control when played out in a sociopolitical arena. Over the past two decades we have seen ethnic wars flare up across the globe—for example, between the Hutus and Tutsis in Rwanda and between the Serbs and Croatians in the former Yugoslavia. The civil war between the Hausa and the Igbos in Nigeria is also called to mind by one of the authors, who engaged in volunteer efforts to end the starvation of Biafran children. In these tribal or ethnic wars, cutoff by annihilation seems to be the goal. The individual ceases to exist and becomes the *other*, objectified, dehumanized, devoid of personal history, no more than a symbol. Few of us work on the international scene mediating these conflicts or even tending to people physically or psychological maimed by them. However, we can still learn from them.

The objectification of the other opens the door wide for cutoffs between people and between family and social groups. When one or another aspect of an individual becomes the dominant characteristic through which all else is seen, the person ceases to exist. What remains is the characteristic detached from the individual's particular history, personality, and sensibilities. The person's individuality is reduced to a stereotype despite tremendous diversity of characteristics within the clan.

The group attempts to maintain a sense of oneness for its identity and ability to survive over time. Difference in thought, but especially action, may not be tolerated. The family or clan may cast off by shunning or by sitting Shiva for those who do not conform. A clan principle, such as purity or honor, is ostensibly the precipitant for the cutoff, but in the end it is really the principle of absolute loyalty to the family or clan. In sum, the crossing of a boundary becomes the main issue as well as the principle itself.

We can look at this in another way. Individuals who "simply" violate a principle may feel guilty and seek redemption or forgiveness, although some do manage to shrug off the transgression and move on. However, when an individual violates a group principle and is cut off, the focus becomes the new status of the individual and far less the principle violated.

In some instances, the client who seeks therapy is uninterested in reconnecting with the group as a whole, yet feels the loss of former individual attachments. Just as often, however, the client seeks our help because he or she wants to rejoin the community or family, or wants to broker a middle ground, to be part of the group, yet also be apart or deviate in some way. The therapist has to help the client determine which of the two outcomes the client really wants and be ready to support either direction. In these situations our clinical work involves two overlapping phases: (1) exploration of the client's identification with the family or community including his or her perspective about the violation of boundaries; and (2) a negotiated or mediated process in which others need to be engaged.

To begin the first phase, some of the following questions should be asked:

- What has family/community/group identification meant to the client?
- To what degree did he or she ever subscribe to the boundary, and why?
- How would he or she explain or define the principle behind the boundary, its function for the family/community/clan?
- What made him or her cross the boundary?
- How did he or she expect the family or group or community to react?
- Can he or she understand the concern and the impact or meaning of the "betrayal" to the family/community/group?
- Where is his or her primary loyalty now—to the family or group or the world beyond?
- What will be the benefits and sacrifices related to his or her decision?
- Can he or she somehow maintain contact without belonging to the family or group?

If desired, the next step is reaching out to the family or community, or its representatives. As described in the Strategies chapter, the purpose of the joint meeting is not to prove one right or the other wrong. Rather, the focus of the session or sessions is to acknowledge the sense of loss and betrayal, to open up communication, to facilitate each party hearing what the other has to say, to explore perspectives, and to discuss ongoing expectations.

In all likelihood, the specific principle violated will need to be aired. However, the clinician has to move the discussion back to the issue of inclusion and exclusion, and the impact and meaning for each party. What is being sacrificed or gained by the individual or the family or group? Here we return to the objectification of the other. Can the family or group see the wholeness of the individual who violated the principle—or only the principle? How will the violation affect the family or group if the individual is permitted to return to the fold without a change in behavior? Is there some middle ground or compromise—to agree not to agree and recognize that the loss is greater than the "rightness" of either position?

No doubt, in some sessions, tempers will ignite. The anger exhibited will often mask underlying pain and hurt, and thus needs to be unearthed—both the failure to subscribe to the group and the failure to be recognized as a multifaceted individual who may match the group in many ways, but who also differs.

If re-inclusion or connection seems remote, whether because of a failure to get the family or group representative to engage with the client or an impasse in the conjoint work, our aim with the client shifts. It now focuses on the client's capacity to mourn his or her group identification and helping the client develop a new identity. This new identity may retain many characteristics of the family or group, including its beliefs and principles. However, the client must accept that publicly he or she is no longer a member.

In our clinical work, the principle of affiliation frequently presents itself in situations of intermarriage. With the exception of strategic marriages performed to build political alliances, intermarriage has long been perceived as a direct threat to the social and economic continuity of a community. It has a tragic history in terms of laws based on a belief in racial purity and the related desire to perpetuate a group without dilution of its gene pool.

In Germany under the Nazis, Gentiles and Jews were forbidden to marry. In the United States, anti-miscegenation laws—the prohibition of marriage between blacks and whites and even their cohabitation—existed in state law until 1967, when the Supreme Court wrote its decision on *Loving v. Virginia*. In South Africa, it was only in 1985 that anti-miscegenation laws were repealed. While these laws are no longer applicable, the emotional residue remains strong for many people.

Among the cutoff cases clinicians shared were two about inter-marriage. In one, a mother would not accept her daughter's Muslim husband. In the other, a father cut off his daughter after she married a non-Jew. In each of these cases we see how the principle of loyalty both camouflaged and embodied other issues.

Charlotte was a divorced, psychotically depressed woman, hospitalized in her twenties and then again after her divorce in her late forties. In the course of therapy Charlotte revealed that her twenty-five-year old daughter Sharon had met and married Aariz, a Muslim man. Charlotte obsessed about Sharon's choice and insisted her daughter break it off. Sharon refused. In response, Charlotte continually berated Sharon for choosing Aariz. "How could you choose a Muslim especially after 9/11!" Angered by the continued harassment, Sharon stopped speaking to her mother, slamming down the phone each time her mother called and avoiding family events if her mother was to be present.

As the years of estrangement multiplied, Charlotte stated her wish to reconcile with her daughter. However, she was adamant she could not accept a Muslim son-in-law into a family of churchgoing Protestants. Thus, despite her stated desire to reconnect with her daughter and see her grandchildren, Charlotte continued to criticize Sharon for her choice of husband. Sharon was happy in her marriage. She and her new family enjoyed celebrating both Christian and Muslim holidays. She had no interest in resolving the conflict with her mother unless her mother accepted Aariz.

This conditional cutoff case illustrates how principles function to distract from other underlying issues. Charlotte's focus was her daughter's intermarriage, but in the therapist's work with Charlotte, the principle of religious loyalty was not addressed. Nor was Charlotte's concern about the faith of her son-in-law and the failure of Sharon to baptize her children. Instead, the clinician, recognizing Charlotte's long history of mental instability, focused on her sense of loss and her desire to reconnect with her daughter. The clinician then addressed Charlotte's psychological fusion with her daughter, like the case of Ruby in Betrayal chapter, and her need to distinguish her needs from her daughter's. For Charlotte, Aariz's religion meant the destruction of her own identity, and she believed Sharon's choice represented a purposeful betrayal of the world Charlotte relied upon to function.

Therapy, which included cognitive behavioral strategies, focused on decreasing Charlotte's ceaseless calls to her daughter. At the same time, the therapist encouraged her to construct a positive self-image based on her own talents and abilities, rather than on whether Sharon appreciated her.

We want to note here that Sharon's choice of husband may well have been an unconscious or conscious rejection of her mother's world. But it was not a principled decision, a choice of one faith over another. Rather, it was a decision to choose love over religion and the religious community. Sharon's refusal to join her mother in a session, however, precluded an exploration of rebellion against her mother versus a decision to abandon her community of origin.

⁂

Chaim and Naomi, an orthodox Jewish couple, came into therapy frantic about the fact that their only child, Chava, was engaged to a non-Jewish man. Chaim was adamant that this was unacceptable; his wife agreed but was less vocal. Chaim threatened to sit Shiva for Chava if she went through with the marriage.

The clinician felt it was not her place to tell the parents what to do. She also did not feel she could challenge the cultural proscription, why it was forbidden for Jews to marry outside their faith. However, she did feel the couple should explore the consequences of cutting off. If Chava were "dead," what would their lives be like? They would miss out on being grandparents and would not have a daughter to help them as they aged.

The couple did not return, so the clinician does not know if they actually sat Shiva. However, a few years later at the opening of an exhibit at the Jewish Museum of New York, Naomi bumped into the therapist. She volunteered that she regularly visits Chava to spend time with her grandson. Her husband, however, still has nothing to do with Chava or her new family.

In an essay titled "Myth of the Shiksa," the late rabbi and family therapist Edwin H. Friedman (2008) discussed intermarriage. Tracking reactions in families in which children marry out of their faith or culture, Friedman observed that the intensity of rejection does not reflect the history or degree of religious belief or cultural commitment:

> Rather than supplying the determinants of family dynamics, culture and environment supply the medium through which family process works its art . . . only once we see culture as a stain rather than a cause of family relational problems can we devise appropriate strategies" (pp. 60, 61).

Friedman found that while the child's "abandonment" of commitment or loyalty to the religion or culture was the explicit issue, the challenge to the family's delicate balance was really at stake. Families with the most intense negative reactions were ones in which the child who married out was the oldest or only child who had been drawn into parent's conflicts—i.e., "triangulated," just as Bowen hypothesized (Bowen, 1978/1994; Kerr & Bowen, 1988).

The underlying problem—felt but often unrecognized—is the anticipated imbalance that would result when the child breaks away and is no longer involved. Of further interest, Friedman discovered that in these highly charged situations, grandparents were far more accepting of the intermarriage, even when they themselves were more religious than their adult children.

It is critically important for us as clinicians to listen closely to clients' concerns about the religious, racial, or ethnic intermarriage of their children. But it is also essential that we then step back to explore the family dynamics that preceded the child's choice of partner. In many of these cases it is emotional rather than cultural processes that gave rise to the intense negative reaction. We believe, as Friedman found, that when we "switch the focus back to the parents and their marriage, or their families of origin, the cultural issues tend to disappear" (p. 73).

And yet, religious and cultural principles themselves are sometimes the sole basis for cutoffs. Religious affiliation is among the strongest human associations and identifications. It provides the individual and the group with a sense of belonging and cohesion. Such affiliations provide meaning and structure life transitions. They also help explain life and accept death. In fact, studies of immigration reveal that religious affiliation is often the last of what is brought from the "old world" to be recast in the new (Kraut, 1994).

Heresy is often the term used for violation of an important religious principle. The word, in Greek, means a "choice" to disregard an important religious doctrine. The act of denial or disobedience counters the established correct way to live. At stake therefore is not a singular belief, but the community that has been developed by the religion, and the institution itself. The threat is dissolution of the social fabric and is cast as evil and impending chaos. The response to disbelief or disobedience thus tends to be severe.

To maintain the sanctity of the religious community, the individual whose beliefs or actions counter its doctrine is cast out. Excommunication by the Catholic Church, perhaps best exemplifies the cutting off and out of the community of believers. It is social rejection, severing of communication and interaction with the religious institution and often also its members—e.g., "shunning" in the Amish community and "disconnection" by Scientology.

There are many situations in which an individual or a subgroup extracts itself from the larger body, believing that the actions and principles of the body have become, or are contrary, to their own belief system. The creation of alternate or antagonistic beliefs to those in which one has been socialized parallels the developmental process of adolescence especially in Europe and North America. As part of the individuation stage (Erikson, 1959), young people try on different beliefs and actions until they select one or integrate several into an adult identity. The separation is gradual or abrupt, calm or stormy. The individual may reject the faith of his or her childhood, seek out another religion, or join a group that better reflects his or her ideals. The individual may also form his or her own group and recruit others to the new fold. In this case, as the individual "moves away" from his or her roots, he or she inevitably leaves someone behind. Clinicians can support a client's wish to form a new group. They can explain that this is how new sects (and modernization of old ones) are born. In addition, taking a leadership role can be a healthy way to salve and handle the pain of expulsion.

The bidirectional process of community rejection is very important. Institutions don't come knocking on our office door, but families do seek our help to reconnect with someone who has cut off based on a principle. We also see individuals who previously left their family or community of origin, but who now want to find a way to reconnect.

CULTS AND SECTS

And then there are individuals who join a cult or sect that requires complete severance from outside relationships.

༺ ༻

Young-Jae was a freshman at an elite mid-western college when he joined Elixir, a fundamentalist Christian sect. His mother Eun Jung, questioned the legitimacy of the group and what was behind their recruitment of children of wealthy families. Young-Jae defended his decision, insisting that "God called on me to join." Newly indoctrinated Young-Jae saw holiness in the group's leader, Tomas, and accepted the notion that "spiritual parents are more important than worldly ones." In fact, Young-Jae went on, worldly parents can prevent someone from achieving enlightenment. He told his mother he was sorry, but as a member of Elixir, he was required to cut off from his biological family.

Soon after, Young-Jae dropped out of college and ceased biweekly calls to his mother. Initially, Eun Jung thought that at nineteen, Young-Jae was going through a phase. She did not call him for a few weeks but then began to worry and finally called. She told him how worried she was and that he needed to come home, if not go back to college. She had read about cults on the Internet and told Young-Jae that Elixir was probably just after his inheritance from his father. Young-Jae hung up.

Eun Jung continued to call Young-Jae's cell phone, but he never answered. She left multiple messages to the effect that he was messing up his life. She said that his late father, whom Young-Jae deeply respected, would not approve and that he was causing her heartache. Eun Jung then called Young-Jae from other phone numbers, but upon hearing her voice, he hung up. Six months after Young-Jae entered Elixir, Eun Jung, depressed over the loss of her husband and son and furious at the cult for "stealing Young-Jae," sought help.

The clinician who met with Eun Jung empathized with her heartache, common for parents whose children join cults. He learned that Eun Jung was estranged from her own family or origin, but did not focus on that. Instead, after affirming her sense of loss, he explained that young adults often leave home to find themselves, experiment, and rebel against their parents. He advised her not to battle the cult, which would be futile. Rather, he encouraged her to use her energy to reestablish and then maintain some connection with her son—even if he remained in the cult.

In the months that followed, the clinician helped Eun Jung write a series of uncritical letters expressing love for Young-Jae and how much she missed him. She sent these to Elixir's post office box noted on its website. She also left a voice message that she loved him and he was always welcome to come home—no pressure, no questions asked. All she wanted was to know from time to time that he was well. She no longer left angry messages or implored him to leave Elixir, but she told Young-Jae that if he ever needed a ticket home, she would send one.

Outreach and acceptance of the person (not behaviors or beliefs) is the point, a variation of parties "agreeing to disagree." The object is to express love to the individual who cuts off, to send the message that he or she can always come home. Keeping the door open, over many years if necessary, no matter how painful, can be the road to eventual reconnection. Unlike the woman and her daughter in the Preface epigraph, we can report that it worked for Eun Jung and Young-Jae.

NORMS AND ETHICS

Perceived violations of ethics emerge as one of the most frequent reasons for a cutoff. While all religions and cultures have explicit proscriptions about correct behavior, it seems that independent of religion, most people have a built-in sense of right and wrong. Cutting off is often the first knee-jerk reaction to such violations, but not always. For some, the violation has to be extreme. This was apparent in the comments of Milo, a man one of the authors met on an Amtrak train. The affable young man held a rather strict view on cutoffs. They are never justified, because "family comes first, right or wrong." He swore there had never been a cutoff in his family or between him and a friend. The author asked if he could imagine a situation in which a cutoff would be justified. "No," he answered, "Not unless Bin Laden was a member of my family. I suppose I would have cut him off after 9/11!"

The man's answer poses a critical question. Are there actions so heinous that there is no path to forgiveness or reconciliation? Or, should there be, no matter what the behavior, the possibility of some reconnection, a means to keep a door open.

Leah, the second wife of Saul, contacted a therapist. Saul was close to Eli, a son from his first marriage. Saul and Leah have a teenager daughter, Rebecca. At a family event an argument developed between Eli and Rebecca. Eli asked Rebecca to apologize, and she refused. Eli asked his father to intervene and discipline Rebecca. Saul felt both children were to blame. A heated argument then ensued between Eli and Saul. Eli stomped out, saying that if his father didn't intervene on his behalf, he would sit Shiva for him.

For two years there was no contact between father and son. Leah says she will never forgive her stepson for what he said to his father: "to sit Shiva as if he was dead?" She will always resent Eli and the pain he caused Saul.

Recently, Eli invited his father to visit and renew their relationship. However, the invitation included a condition that his father goes into therapy "to work out his issues." Saul rebutted that he had no issues and refused to comply. Eli rescinded the invitation. Leah swore to the therapist she will never go to her stepson's house or forgive him. She can't let go of the image of a son threatening to cut off his father.

Leah came into therapy seeking something, but what it was, was not initially clear. Her devotion to Saul and her daughter was evident. Did she worry about her daughter, whose actions allegedly contributed to the cutoff between father and son, the half-siblings, and the next generation of his family? Was she asking for confirmation that what Eli had said was unforgivable? Or, was she asking for help to heal the family, even though she herself could not let go?

What did Saul think about his son's demands, and his son's statement about sitting Shiva? Saul was invited but did not join his wife in any therapy session.

After hearing Leah's narrative, the therapist felt it was important to reflect on his own reaction. The therapist, a practicing Jew, father, and grandfather, was also remarried and had stepchildren. He recognized his discomfort with Eli's proclamation about sitting Shiva. As he explored with Leah her goals for their work together, he was haunted by this social and religious cutoff and by fears for himself.

A thoughtful and skilled clinician, he was able to analyze and temper his own reaction. He realized that although the threat of Shiva, a permanent cutoff, was incendiary, a single argument rarely results in such finality. So the threat had to be a symbol of other frustrations and conflicts within the family system. This realization facilitated moving the work away from a struggle between right and wrong, living and dying, and led to concentration on the underlying dynamics within and between the generations.

Eli's demand that his father "discipline" Rebecca was really about his feeling that Rebecca was winning an unacknowledged contest for their father's affection. Leah clearly sided with her daughter. Eli's mother, who had died years before, was not there to balance Eli's need for support. So he needed a strong show of approval from his father.

Once principle was set aside, the therapist helped Leah understand Eli's feeling of isolation in the family, his upset that Rebecca had a mother whereas Eli had lost his, and the hurt experienced by everyone. Eventually, Leah "got it" and relented. She took the therapist up on his idea that the whole family convene for a session. After discussing the idea with Saul and Rebecca beforehand, Leah surprised Eli by offering to adopt him. Eli was stunned, but quickly recovered, and accepted.

We now move to the ethics embedded in contracts. What does the marriage vow—"in sickness and in health, 'til death do us part"—truly mean? What is the role of the clinician when a client does not abide by their previously agreed-upon contract? In Chapter 4, Abandonment, we discussed the case of Leo and Sandy. Sandy abandoned Leo after he was diagnosed with what was believed to be a terminal illness. When the diagnosis proved incorrect, Sandy asked to come back; Leo refused. While the precipitant here was in fact abandonment, the stated basis of Leo's refusal was actually a matter of principle, breaking the marriage contract.

This was not a clinical case, but one shared by a therapist with whom we spoke. Listening to the story, we were initially horrified that Sandy had abandoned Leo when he was gravely ill. However, as we mulled it over, we began to consider other aspects of the situation.

After a period of ambivalence, but to satisfy Leo's family, Sandy converted to Greek Orthodoxy, thus surrendering part of her own identity. Prior to Leo's illness, the marriage had been rocky. Was Leo's illness a kind of somatization in response to the failing relationship, an unconscious ploy to keep Sandy in the marriage? Why did Sandy want to come back? Had she experienced the death of someone close as a child and could not bear it a second time? Was her single life too lonely? None of these threads wove a fabric, but we felt each was important to entertain. The point was that Sandy undoubtedly had a story. Since we did not know what it really was, we had to generate the possibilities for her in order to empathize.

Now what happens when an individual crosses ethical boundaries and violates a basic principle of his or her professional community? The following case provides a good example and also resembles a disrupted mentor-disciple relationship.

Diederik Stapel was a well-regarded Dutch social psychologist, dean of the School of Social and Behavioral Sciences at Tilburg University. For more than a decade, suspicions spread that Stapel was inventing data. Given disbelief that someone of his stature would commit such fraud, the suspicions were not investigated. However, in 2010 several graduate students realized that Stapel had in fact manipulated findings. An investigation then determined that much of his research and many publications were fraudulent. Stapel was dismissed and cut off by the academic community. Former students, colleagues, and even his wife reexamined their relationships with him.

His wife said she had "placed Stapel inside an integrity scanner in her mind—scanned his life in terms of being a father, being my hus-

band, being my best friend, being the son of his parents, the friend of his friends, being a human being that is part of society, being a neighbor— and being a scientist and teacher." She went on to say, "I found out for myself that all of these other parts were really okay. I thought, wow, it must be Diederik and science which is a poisoned combination."

A year after his dismissal, Stapel acknowledged his guilt to a former student, telling her, "You came up with these ideas. You designed the studies. I took away one little thing from the process. Don't let people think that you're worthless because you worked with me." The student later stated that she had forgiven the man but not his actions. She further reflected: "There are good people doing bad things; there are bad people doing good things." She put Stapel in the former category. (Bhattacharjee, 2013)

While this was not a clinical case, we believe the manner in which the two women reconceptualized their relationship with Stapel—as husband and mentor—is instructive to clinical practice. Both women were able to place Stapel's professional misconduct in a larger frame. The wife summoned what was real in her relationship with her husband of many years; the mentee took away what was good while not forgetting what was not. However, other mentees who discovered Stapel's fabrications forsook the relationship for principle, for what they believed was the greater good—the "sanctity" of their intellectual community. They never forgave him.

PARENTAL RESPONSIBILITY AND THE ROLE OF FRIENDS

To what extent should one's principles limit one's actions when it comes to children? Is a parent responsible to care for his or her child under all circumstances? These issues were brought to the fore in a case shared by one of our clinician interviewees.

☙❧

My cousin, Hugh, is a devout Catholic. Hugh's son, Patrick, was clearly depressed, and Hugh was concerned. Patrick recently confided in his sister that he might be gay. The sister told the father. Hugh was morti- fied, because homosexuality is an "abomination" according to Church doctrine. Hugh felt his son was struggling with God and that prayer was the answer. Yet he asked me what I thought.

I advised Hugh to set aside his feelings and beliefs and help Patrick locate an impartial therapist. Hugh did not follow through, and within a year Patrick committed suicide. I was so angry that Hugh did not take my professional advice and because of religious principles essentially abandoned his son. So I cut my cousin off.

A decade went by. I was in the midst of a divorce and needed to withdraw some money from a family trust, so I had to call Hugh. He was supportive and facilitated the withdrawal without asking questions or making judgments, surprising me. In fact, Hugh was so supportive that we easily resumed our prior relationship.

The two cousins never discussed the cutoff. In telling us the story many years later, our interviewee realized that Hugh's actions, or lack thereof, reflected how Hugh saw the world and that he had done what he thought was best for his son. For Hugh, Patrick's struggle was in God's hands. While our clinician saw things differently, he realized that he had not fully appreciated Hugh's anguish as a parent, nor had he thought of a dual approach to helping Patrick: religion *and* therapy. Our therapist felt badly that each cousin had rejected the other's alternative strategy. Each had subscribed to his own principle, but neither had sought a bridge. As such, our clinician felt he had not been a helpful cousin, nor had he given his best as a mental health professional.

⌖

The next case also focuses on responsibility and caring, here one friend being protective of another, unable to watch or collude with a friend being abused or taken for granted. This is a case of a friend who cared too much.

Caitlin and Midori had been friends since their sons were little, two or three. Caitlin moved away from Philadelphia and they lost touch for a while, but both landed in New York City in the early 1980s and rekindled their friendship. Midori was a struggling young writer. She left her son with her husband in Philadelphia to pursue a master's degree in creative writing at Columbia. The couple ended up divorcing. When the women reconnected in New York, Caitlin was divorced with two daughters and had a high-paying job in market research. Both women left their marriages by choice. Midori was basically on her own; struggling to move from freelancing to a full-time staff job. Her former husband and son continued to live in Philly.

Caitlin began to date Elliot, a scientist whose behavior was problematic in social situations. On one occasion Elliot nastily refused to give Midori a ride home though it was on his way. Midori became increasingly uncomfortable with Caitlin's relationship with Elliot. She tried speaking to Caitlin, to little effect. Finally, over coffee, Midori told Caitlin she could not continue being friends as long as Elliot was in the picture mistreating her. If or when Caitlin ever decided to end the relationship, Midori would be there. Caitlin was very upset at Midori's decision but felt there was nothing she could do at the time.

In her late fifties, Caitlin entered therapy to deal with the death of her mother. Old issues of abandonment surfaced, and Caitlin began to think about Midori. At the time of their cutoff, Caitlin felt Midori was intrusive, crossing a boundary into her relationship with Elliot, and that Midori had abandoned her. But as Caitlin thought harder, and having broken up with Elliot, she saw that Midori may have tried to protect her.

She found Midori on the Internet and tracked her down in Spain. With some guidance from the therapist who helped her write the first email, Caitlin reached out to Midori. Midori was delighted to hear from her after so many years. The women are now in regular contact and visit back and forth.

As this case illustrates, time and reflection can recast the principles we adopt or the rules we live by, as well as our expectations of others.

Grounded in the cultures in which we were raised and life experiences, we each carry a definition of the good and ethical life. However, we do not usually consciously construct or articulate it until there is a violation. Once there is a breach, the principle surfaces and we have to assess its impact on our life, and on others. Friends come together because of shared values and experiences. It is probably rare that friends abstractly discuss their friendship boundaries or spell out acceptable or unacceptable behavior. These discussions happen after some violation of the implicit "rules of friendship." Can we continue to associate with someone who violates a principle?

Can there be redemption if the violator acknowledges a misstep? And should we, or can we, always inform the violator of our feelings?

The following situation was shared by one of the therapists we interviewed. Again, while it was not a clinical case, we believe it is important to include here as it showcases how behavior that may seem inconsequential may in fact violate someone else's sense of what is ethical. One incident may not by itself lead to a cutoff, but it may be the tipping point that precipitates a cutoff.

Gabrielle, Lilly, and Jeanette had been close friends since high school in Chicago. Jeanette came from a wealthy Lake Forest family, while Lilly and Gabrielle came from more modest backgrounds. After college, Lilly and Jeanette both married. They each remained in Chicago, while Gabrielle moved to New York. In her late thirties, Gabrielle became gravely ill. Over the next year, Lilly and Jeanette each went to New York to keep her company. Knowing she was dying, Gabrielle began to give away her jewelry and clothing, especially to Lilly, who was the same size and had the same taste and coloring. After one visit, Gabrielle gave money to Lilly, and asked her to buy a case of wine for Jeanette. This was one of the ways she wanted to thank Jeanette for her friendship and care.

Lilly bought a case of expensive wine but removed a bottle for herself before delivering the eleven remaining bottles to Jeanette. Jeanette was very upset when she noticed the missing bottle, sensing that Lilly had interfered with Gabrielle's gift. She wrote to Lilly stating she did not want any further contact with her. Lilly was shocked by the reaction and tried to contact Jeanette to no avail. Proper gift-giving etiquette had been violated, and Jeanette found Lilly's actions disrespectful to both Gabrielle and Jeanette. While both Jeanette and Lilly continued to support Gabrielle until she died, the two of them have not spoken since. It has now been twenty-five years.

Lilly's decision to take a wine bottle was the "straw that broke the camel's back." There was actually a long history in which Jeanette felt Lilly overstepped boundaries or been insensitive. Gift giving was never explicitly discussed, but its violation pricked the acute sensitivity to decorum that Jeanette had developed in her home, where significant attention was paid to manners. The rules of friendship were broken; "stealing" from Gabrielle and Jeanette formed the basis for this cutoff.

One certainly wonders if Lilly's theft replayed an existing but unspoken rivalry between Lilly and Jeanette or whether the theft reflected class jealousy. Over the years, Lilly had talked about her parents' distance and lack of affection. Her unresolved need may also have contributed to her behavior. Regardless of the underlying reasons for Lilly's behavior, her friends felt she had crossed one too many lines, unforgivable especially within the context of Gabrielle's terminal illness.

When friends cut off, it is often the tipping point in a series of prior or smaller transgressions. This is important to the therapist who works with one or the other party of a split-up relationship. Too often we get entangled with the *event* that caused the rift. But it is the history of the friendship that matters more. We need to determine the capacity of each individual in the friendship to express feelings when there is an issue or problem as well as to listen and to engage in problem solving—including apologies and restitution when there has been some breach.

Each friend needs to make an assessment. "Do I feel in my gut that I can trust him or her? Does he or she respect my autonomy and feelings? If the client has sufficient trust in the friendship, work toward resolution can take place. The clinician can help the client express his or her dissatisfaction and see whether a common understanding, which may include apology or restitution, is possible. There may be a period of walking on eggshells. But if the friends can identify what the friendship means to each of them and in their lives, they can move forward. In sum, when a cutoff is about rules of behavior between friends or family members, we need to ask how central the behavior is to the ongoing relationship, what other less visible factors are at play, and, whether the history and benefits of friendship outweigh some of its costs.

IDENTITY

In *Hamlet,* Shakespeare, borrowing from Sir Francis Bacon's "Of Wisdom for a Man's Self," gave Polonius the now famous lines:

> This above all: to thine own self be true,
> And it must follow, as the night the day,
> Thou canst not then be false to any man.
>
> *Hamlet,* I.iii.78–81

Individuals' identities are formed through gradual socialization and association. They can also be superimposed by others. Over the life cycle, different aspects of identity emerge, ascend to the forefront, or become dominant in an individual's life and social interactions—e.g., child, parent, spouse, sibling, student, employee, political candidate, and so on. Acceptance of one's many selves, along with acceptance by family and society, may vary over time.

As we've mentioned elsewhere, adolescence is often a time to "try on" new identities and through this process establish more sustained ones. Parents often are unhappy with this experimentation and may despair if chosen identities deviate from family norms. However, the development of identities in each generation must be viewed in a larger context. Social values and beliefs are bound to change over time, as do opportunities. Thus, concurrent with an adolescent's search for identity is a shifting sociopolitical-economic landscape. Given the changing context, cross-generational tensions are to be expected—so much so that anthropologist Margaret Mead (1978) observed that each generation grows up in a different culture. Likewise, family therapists know that each child grows up in a different family.

Parent-child tensions are central to the storylines of film, novels, and news items and are often the focus of the family work we do. The narratives reflect the elasticity of family systems to accept difference and the degree to which the breach deviates from some explicit or implicit notion of normative culture. Further, different breaches result in different responses, both within the family system and within the larger society.

Deeply enmeshed families have lower thresholds as to what deviations they will accept. The teen's choices are influenced by peer culture but may also signal his or her attempt to form a distinct self, apart from the family. Tensions may escalate over this adolescent transition into adulthood and result in temporary or long-lasting cutoffs.

In the last section of this chapter we focus on the experience of individuals who identify as lesbian, gay, bisexual, or transgendered (LGBT). Clients who are LGBT have some of the biggest challenges developing and living their identities, being true to themselves, in the face of familial religious beliefs and social mores.

Historically, homosexuality has been perceived through a lens of morality. Until 1973 it was classified by "science" in the *Diagnostic and Statistical Manual of Mental Disorders* as a form of mental illness, polymorphous perversity. For this reason and others, homosexual individuals have frequently hidden their sexual orientation rather than be stigmatized, unable to find employment or be rejected by their secular or religious communities. In more recent decades, there is increased recognition and acceptance that homosexuality and bisexuality are neither chosen nor a "perverse" form of mental illness. Rather, we are coming to understand that homosexuality is part of a continuum of sexual identities and expression. Despite the increasing recognition of its "normality," including legislation to protect and equalize the rights of the LGBT population, LGBT individuals continue to be challenged with respect to the explicit ownership of who they are. Here the principle is about being able to be oneself.

The following case reflects the limited elasticity of acceptance and the importance of identity for both the individual and his or her family.

James came out to his mother when he was fifteen. Not happy that her son was gay, Judith nevertheless struggled to accept him. She just asked that he not bring his gay friends home. At twenty-two, James informed his mother that he could no longer pretend he was James and that his true identity was Jamie. He had already begun the process of sex reassignment.

Judith was appalled. It was clear that James was insane and needed psychiatric help. He was her son! It was hard enough to accept that he "might" be gay. But to now decide to become a woman—that was going too far! She demanded that James undergo "reparative" therapy. She threatened that if he went through with the surgery, "she" would no longer be accepted in the family; "she" would be cut off permanently.

James rejected his mother's demand to see the "corrective" therapist. Working with the psychiatrist in the reassignment team, James

expressed his wish to be accepted, whatever gender. He could not believe
his mother's ultimatum.

The psychiatrist reached for the pain and frustration underneath Jamie's rage. When the pain dissipated, she slowly encouraged Jamie to "thicken her skin" and understand that parents struggle too. She asked how much Judith knew of Jamie's long struggle to define her sexuality and what it must have been like for her mother already stretched to the limit with her son's gayness to now suddenly be confronted with a sex change. She suggested that while Jamie had every right to be who she was, she might also consider her mother's struggle. Was it worth cutting off or being cut off from her?

Maybe her mother would never be able to accept Jamie's gender transformation and would continue believing Jamie was insane, but was it not important to at least try to reengage? Were there ways Jamie could bring her mother into the process of reassignment, not to dictate the final decision, but to understand the steps already taken and those still to come? Could Jamie share the assessments she had already made, to help Judith understand her deliberations and the fact that she sought competent help to make her decision.

Ultimately, the therapist supported Jamie being true to herself. At the same time, the clinician recognized the incipient cutoff and the possible damage it would do to both Jamie and Judith. She therefore worked hard to find ways Jamie could reach out to Judith and have her join in what was a difficult journey. Unfortunately, the therapist did not think to suggest inviting Judith into sessions with Jamie, which might have hastened the rapprochement. Luckily, Jamie saw an ad on the transgender bulletin board at the clinic for a parents' support group. Judith attended and gradually came around to accepting Jamie's identity as a woman.

⌘

Clarity and honesty about one's own identity allow a person to be forthright and true in dealing with others. However, some parents are simply unable to accept their LGBT children and cut them off. At the same time, children may preemptively cut themselves off from their parents. Others choose to disguise themselves and live double lives.

Akilah sought the help of a therapist during a period of severe depression. Initially she spoke about her unemployment and seeming inability to succeed as an actor, but over the course of a few weeks she revealed her deep, ongoing dilemma.

Born in the United States, Akilah was the only child of conservative Iranian parents. Her parents, successful in business, generously helped to support her and their extended family in Washington, DC. Akilah has never told her parents she is a lesbian; she leads a double life.

In Boston, she shared an apartment with Amanda, her partner of 5 years. However, she referred to Amanda as her roommate. Formerly very close to her family, Akilah now stayed away from family occasions and rarely spoke to her parents. Phone conversations were short, and she shared little about her life.

Akilah's secret exacted a toll and was no doubt the source of much of her depression. She wished she could resolve her double identity, but "knew" she could not. The therapist was not sure if Akilah's assessment was accurate, but did not challenge it. Instead, she reflected back how denial of her true self was causing great pain. Akilah agreed but was adamant. In her community, being gay was still severely stigmatized. It went against the principles of their faith. If her parents knew, they would abandon her completely, and she would lose them as well as the larger Iranian community.

After fully exploring the situation, the therapist agreed with Akilah's assessment. The risk of being open about sexual orientation was just too great, given the world in which Akilah's family lived. The best Akilah could hope for was to continue her superficial contact. This strategy prevented her from being victimized by her parents and extended family. It also prevented a complete cutoff and her parents losing face if their community knew the truth about their daughter.

The therapeutic work focused on helping Akilah become more comfortable with her lesbianism as well as her decision to live two separate lives. Over time Akilah's depression lessened, she obtained a new coveted job, and she left therapy. We do not know if she ever told her parents the truth.

One of the clinicians we interviewed works primarily with the LGBT community. Many of her patients were cut off or cut themselves off from their families of origin. For them, their sexual identity and ability to express it trumped the loss of their biological families. Many of these individuals, especially the lesbians with whom she worked, established lifelong bonds with other lesbian, gay and straight friends, gaining open acceptance, support, and love in these new "second family" constellations.

The same therapist, however, also observed that for many LGBT clients, the pain engendered from their cutoffs from family contributed to a host of emotional problems as well as substance abuse and dangerous risk-taking behavior. For many, choosing which identity to embrace had been costly. In this context, Akilah's partial cutoff and difficult balance—while not pain-free—has to be appreciated as an important strategy to prevent a complete cutoff. It therefore needs to be offered and accepted as we work with LGBT individuals and other clients who are torn between the "truths" of two conflicting principles.

At the same time, the complexity of experience and culture, expectation and reality, and the uniqueness of each individual and family always need to be front and center when we work with LGBT and other clients who are torn between their identities and the principles that guide their families.

⟨🙵⟩

To end this chapter we share a story about a client, Sahar, also Iranian, and her family. This woman, born in a small mountain town to schoolteacher parents, was married at eighteen to an older man, a celebrated agronomist. After the shah was disposed, she and her husband fled to the United States. Years later, she sought therapy on her own to discuss some marital problems. In one particular session, Sahar announced that her daughter, now twenty, had just come out to her parents the day before.

Both parents were astounded, but Sahar had quickly recovered and decided in the session that "I won't do anything to spoil my relationship with my daughter." While the father took a while to come around, Sahar was clearly with her daughter almost overnight. Over time both parents welcomed their daughter's partner into the family. Anything is possible.

Chapter 7

MENTAL HEALTH

How could we explain that we had changed our names so she could never find us? That we had been so scared of her all these years? She was the cry of madness in the dark, the howling of wind outside our doors.

Bartok (2011, p. 16)

As we discussed in Chapter 1 and elsewhere, a common factor underlying many diagnoses and most "normal" cutoffs is emotional hijacking, the tendency to rush to judgment of others or oneself, and impulsively act or react based on those hasty judgments. At least one party to a cutoff is likely to be a victim of hotheadedness. We also briefly mentioned Goleman's book *Emotional Intelligence* (2005), which brought the concept of hijacking to light, and briefly described Gottman's videotaped studies of couple interaction at his Institute's "Love Lab," along with key findings.

When someone involved in a cutoff is mentally ill, the cutoff is usually more brutal and harder to reconcile. The difference, however, is a matter of degree rather than kind. The following characteristics distinguish those cutoffs in which people with a diagnosable mental illness are likely involved:

- Repetitive behavior resulting in cutting off or being cut off, a history of cutoffs

- Inflexibility or rigidity—seeing only one right way
- Inability to empathize
- Intense anger or destructive impulses toward others
- Tendency to misinterpret others' communication, motives, or actions, to cast situations and see people in a negative light
- Serious lack or loss of communication skills necessary to resolve conflict
- "Thin skinned" or easily wounded
- A tendency to under-communicate; fear of expressing or inability to express one's needs

Most, though not all, of the case examples in this chapter are plucked from previous ones, revisited in the light of mental illness. We took only those cases for which we knew enough to say a diagnosis was probably in order or for which we knew a diagnosis was already established. At any rate, clinicians tackling a cutoff need to develop a working diagnosis while simultaneously thinking systemically about the interpersonal dynamics. It is simply the case that some strategies will be more effective with one diagnosis than another.

Here we turn our attention away from wondering *why* people cut off, from their reasons, to considering *who* is likely to cut off. But first there is a caveat. As discussed in Chapter 1, as systemic thinkers, we usually view psychopathology as interactional, as mostly a problem between people and in their relationships, not just lodged in individuals. And it is comforting to know that neuropsychology research supports this position. However, we also know it can be helpful to shift paradigms, to understand a phenomenon from more than one perspective.

Approaching our topic from the vantage point of individual mental illness is also, at least to some extent, consistent with our view that it is useful to sort out the particular contribution of each party in a cutoff dyad. At the end of the day, perhaps both interactional and individual perspectives give the fullest understanding of what is happening and what goes wrong in a relationship. Perhaps it is not either/or, but both/and.

Now, what about the argument that emotionally healthy people cut off too? Of course healthy people become involved in dysfunctional relationships, and also precipitously terminate them. But looking back at the plethora of cases we amassed for the book, it is clear that many of the parties, sometimes both, could be said to have a diagnosable condition. We also want to bear in mind that mental illness is rarely static, and in cases where one—let us say "sick"— person in a relationship improves, the relationship will inevitably change, and there will be an end to the cutoff or a permanent end of the relationship.

DIAGNOSES AND CUTOFF

When one family member is or becomes mentally ill, other family members often experience guilt: "Was it my fault?" The ill person's behavior may also be frightening: "What does this mean for me, for the family? If this person is mentally ill and he can do *this*, what's to stop him from doing something worse?" Perhaps physical danger is involved: "Could someone, could I, get hurt?" Realistically, especially when someone is out of control, there can be good reasons that family members distance or cut off, at least temporarily. Mira Bartok, quoted at the beginning of this chapter, had many reasons in relation to her very ill mother.

At the same time, it is the very lack of emotional closeness and family support, on top of biological vulnerability, that so often contributes to the manifestation of illness. If the clinician listens closely and probes enough, there are usually reasons—a family story—that help explain the illness. It stands to reason, then, that while we do not say the family is at fault (because no one intends it to happen), the family is nevertheless part of the problem. And, on a more positive note, family is one of the surest routes to solution. A cutoff may be necessary for some period of time, but if healing is the goal, a cutoff is rarely healthy forever.

GENERALIZED ANXIETY DISORDER

Remember Ruby and Heather, the enmeshed mother-daughter pair in the Betrayal chapter? Miraculously, with credit to Ruby and Ruby's strengths as a parent, Heather survived and has done well. We looked at Ruby through the systemic lens of enmeshment, but an individual diagnosis casts further light. Ruby suffered from extreme anxiety. It is well known that high anxiety masquerades as many other things, such as phobia, somatization, mania, even schizophrenia; Ruby's therapist and other professionals mistakenly assigned them all.

Finally, her most recent therapist saw through to what was underneath her "all over the place" craziness. Ruby lacked only one thing—a solid sense of herself—and was blown like a feather in the wind by whatever came along. Or, perhaps better images: she lived every day like a deer caught in the headlights or as if she were clinging to a floating log in a tsunami. All of these images came to her therapist's mind as they worked together. Everything terrified Ruby. She could not concentrate, think clearly about anything; she could not make a single realistic decision. At the start of therapy, she not only distrusted herself, she trusted no one else and had no experience or concept of a good respectful relationship.

She was financially supported by elderly parents whose demands on her time were incessant. They ran her life and were running out of money. Ruby pursued and clung to her daughter, Heather, who resisted her mother at every turn. Ruby lived in the past and refused to let the therapist help her plan for the future. Heather needed her own future and grabbed it by cutting off. She would see her mother and grandparents, but share nothing, inquire about nothing, show no mercy. She would be physically present, but emotionally absent.

For generalized anxiety disorder, especially one with the severity of Ruby's, establishing basic trust in someone who could be a true friend is essential, the first order of business. Ruby's parents, in their eighties and utterly stuck in their ways, were not about to change. Heather was unwilling, and appropriately so. Ruby had no friends and no community support. So it was up to the therapist, who stepped in once a week for 5 years. The clinician explained enmeshment and Ruby gradually understood how she was submerged and entangled in her family of origin, how it hurt her, and why her daughter had to escape.

Ruby learned that extreme anxiety explained most of her symptoms. She feared her father's temper and terrible demands, she experienced anxiety over her own unrecognized hostility toward him and toward her mother, who loved her but who was completely under the thumb of her husband, subjugated and anxious herself. She saw how her mother never defended her, how she could not trust the parents who held her so close, who loved her almost to death. To an outsider, and even to the therapist at times, Ruby did not seem to be changing, but standing up to her father or walking away when he barraged her with questions was monumental for Ruby.

Once Ruby saw that her daughter had to break away, that it was developmentally necessary—no, critical—in an enmeshed family, Ruby took Heather's rejection less personally. It hurt, but she could tolerate it. And the therapist reframed Ruby's loss by telling Ruby to consider that she had actually raised Heather to be strong enough to do it. Predictably, Heather began to contact her mother, first for material things—something she had left in her room, something she forgot about another relative that her mother would know. Little by little, she reconnected.

MAJOR DEPRESSIVE DISORDER

Major depressive disorder can be looked at in at least two ways in relation to cutoffs. Focusing on couples for the moment, when one partner is debilitated by depression, the other one is scared, confused, guilty, frustrated, and left with all of the responsibility. Given these awful feelings, the partner reacts by catering to the depressed one, by getting professional help, but eventually by distancing or cutting off if nothing improves. According to this conceptualization, depression is a condition independent of the relationship but that affects the relationship, with the power to destroy it.

Another way of viewing it, and more likely the truer way, especially if psychotherapy or medication do not help, is that the depression is an (unconscious) statement by the depressed person of his or her unhappiness in a primary relationship. It can be a way of distancing, leaving, ending a marriage, without having to actually make the decision, face breaking up, divorcing, or being alone. In this view, depression is a silent, slow, insidious cutoff by the depressed member of the couple.

Simultaneously, it is a cutoff from oneself, a way of saying, "I am not ready or I lack the ability or courage to make this decision." Rather than punish myself for not making it, or force myself to do it when I can't, I'll run away from myself mentally, withdraw, paralyze myself so I don't have to think about it anymore."

Remember Cynthia, who stopped speaking to her brother Ron in the Jealousy chapter? She is a good case in point regarding depression and marital woe. While discussing her relationship with her second husband, Sanjay, a few months before she descended into an unremitting depression, she asked her longtime therapist, "Is this all there is? If I stay with Sanjay, I'll have nothing more to look forward to. The real reason he's with me is to get his green card, and we really have nothing in common. Yet, I can't bear the thought of being alone again." Three years later, depression now firmly ensconced despite the best treatment available (psychotherapy, medication, hospitalization, ECT) Cynthia stepped off a curb, was hit by a truck, and was instantly killed. The driver was not found liable; friends speculated it was suicide.

In mulling over Cynthia's death, the therapist concluded that his client had found the ultimate way to end a relationship that was not working. The therapist regretted not having more strongly encouraged Cynthia to focus on her misgivings about the relationship, finally linking the depression to her relationship dilemma. Had she been able to help Cynthia gather strength to leave, the therapist recriminated in hindsight, Cynthia's depression might have resolved. She would have faced her feelings and either fixed the relationship or ended it in a healthy way.

∞∞

But major depression is not only an expression of marital unhappiness. Here is the start of an unfinished memoir by Mark Madoff, son of Bernie Madoff:

> After forty-four years of life, I found out that my father was
> not the person . . . I knew . . . the man who . . . taught me the
> importance of integrity had just told me that he was a thief . . .
> I lived in awe of my father from a very young age. He was the
> man that everyone wanted to be . . . I wanted so badly to be
> the person . . . my father was . . . and now I can't get far

enough away . . . my own father has stolen my life from me. It's a pain that is beyond description . . . The business that I spent twenty-three years building gone, I am unemployed, my livelihood destroyed, and my family will forever live with the shame of what my father has done. There were so many victims of my father's fraud, so many horrible stories. How do I explain to my children what I do not understand myself? (Quoted in Madoff-Mack, 2012, pp. 207–210)

Depression, as we know, is often about loss. And Mark Madoff had enough of it. Mark apparently adored and idealized his father, worked for him, and could not accept the public insinuation that he and his brother had been complicit in his father's crimes. Mark felt he had no other choice but to cut his father off, and then his mother and brother who would not follow his lead. For Mark, the betrayal and losses were simply too much, and he eventually committed suicide. We do not know if Mark had a therapist, but it should be no surprise when primary relationship ruptures of epic and highly publicized proportions result in depression and suicide.

In cases like this, and other multiple primary family cutoff situations such as we saw with Carrie and Nora, suicide or homicide prevention is the first order of business. A temporary cutoff from the offending person and from others who stick with them may be necessary. But beforehand, ideally, a mutual understanding of each family member's predicament should be reached, coupled with an agreement to reconvene—with a therapist, perhaps more than one—at a specified time in the near future.

From the moment of Bernard Madoff's confession, someone, some clinician, would need to have been engaged. He or she could have explained that each family member was in crisis trying to deal with the catastrophe and that it would take time for each to work it through and regroup as a family. Someone could have explained that this crisis presented an opportunity to know the truth and base the rest of their lives on it. A clinician could have raised the possibility of future dialogue with Bernie, not necessarily to reconcile but at least to understand how the situation all came about. A clinician could have advised that while a short-term cutoff might be in order, a permanent one may not be in anyone's interest in the long run.

In situations like Mark Madoff's, the family he needed in the crisis was the very family that had betrayed him. He needed to express his pain and rage toward his father rather than go silent. At some point he needed to give voice, perhaps first in writing, but ultimately in person. He certainly knew where to find his dad! He began to write a memoir, from which the above quotation is an excerpt. Writing and other forms of creative outlet are excellent ways to release feelings, which Mark began to use shortly before his suicide. They might have helped, but it was apparently too late.

There were many red flags, beginning with Mark's overdose of prescription medication soon after the revelation. Mark and his wife Stephanie made a pact never to mention it, or the ensuing hospitalization. This denial could not have helped the situation. To the extent that depression is withdrawal from a problem, the clinician's job would be to help Mark reengage, first with the therapist, then with his family. As Bowen would have said, he would need to individuate from his father and see that despite the public outrage, insinuations, and accusations, Mark could still be his own person. Most important, by surviving in spite of it all, he would become the hero in his children's eyes that his father never really was.

Here is where a cognitive behavioral therapy approach comes in handy, by which we mean identifying and catching repetitive negative trains of thought, interrupting them, questioning them, and replacing them with realistic, self-affirming appraisals. Yes, Bernard Madoff behaved monstrously, but did he literally *steal* his son's *life*? Would Mark, Stephanie, and their children have to live with the shame *forever*? Countering these self-destructive thoughts is the essence of the individual work required of clients such as Mark Madoff before any type of family reconciliation can take place.

In preparation for family contact after a temporary cutoff, the goal has to be crystal clear. For example, it is usually impossible to have the same relationship(s) as before. The first new goal could simply to be in each other's presence, able to breathe. There needs to be an understanding that contact does not mean acceptance or approval. The goal is probably to gain a sincere apology, or have it understood that "I don't approve of what you did, never will, but I will do my best to put what you did into perspective since in some other ways you were a good father. I will do it for the family as a whole."

BIPOLAR DISORDER

Remember Chelsea from the Betrayal chapter whose parents were frantic because she was going to leave school to live with a much older man in Europe? She initially received a diagnosis of bipolar from a psychiatrist, though he later retracted it. In Carrie's case (Abandonment chapter), the diagnosis was textbook clear and bears revisiting here. On her way from debilitating depression to a series of manic episodes, Carrie lost everything in her life. Whereas in her depressed state she could not leave the house, in one manic episode she was "on her way to Nashville to collect three country music awards." This seemingly sudden shift was incomprehensible and alarming to everyone who knew her, but not to Carrie herself. Her energy was off the charts and she couldn't sleep. During this time, she saw a psychiatrist for "meds" but did not take them. Instead, she secretly self-medicated with alcohol, stayed up nights feverishly working on songs, and flew off the handle if challenged or thwarted. Though ostensibly back at work, she was unreliable.

By the time she was floridly psychotic a month later, no one in the family, none of her friends, was speaking to her. Worse, the ex-husband who had promised to stay friends was also not there. There were few visitors over the course of her six hospitalizations. At some point, the family was informed of her bipolar diagnosis.

Family therapists and others with a systemic orientation will say that Carrie is not the only one responsible for all the cutoffs. Many would insist that the family is actually the cauldron that produced the illness. Further, they would declare that the same family members who cut her off are themselves implicated in the family drama and that to treat Carrie alone without the family would never work or would take forever. The mother, herself hospitalized for years, and the father, undiagnosed but clearly narcissistic, had essentially abandoned her.

Carrie protested by acting out, and the more she did, the more the family rejected her. The more they rejected her, the more alone she felt and the wilder, more bizarre her thought patterns and behavior became, until she spiraled completely out of control. However it came about, though, at the end of the day, she was a diagnosed a mentally ill family member in a very dysfunctional family system.

Even disregarding the systemic interpretation, bipolar illness like

Carrie's often causes family members to distance themselves, if not cut off entirely. They cannot take the swings, vicissitudes, demands, insults, and unpredictability. In Carrie's case, the family, though geographically close enough, chose not participate in family sessions or treatment planning. They did step in, but then quickly stepped out. They had reasons, their own problems to be sure, but the effect was devastating, and the repeated cutoffs and abandonments became the problem.

As we wrote in the Abandonment chapter, by the time Carrie found her way to her current therapist she was essentially alone. Her therapist stretched the 50-minute session rule and accepted calls at night and on weekends. She became a virtual surrogate parent to fill the void until Carrie could engage in her own recovery and until the family would reengage.

But as we indicated, it soon became clear that psychotherapy was not enough. Fountain House in New York City was a godsend, and through a physician the therapist referred her to, Carrie found a smart, caring community psychiatrist who also saw Carrie's strengths beneath the illness.

Carrie was there for her father in his final illness and impressed her siblings by acquiring a country music agent and selling two songs to a popular performer. She expresses her feelings about abandonment through her lyrics, without alienating family as they drew closer again. It took a village, but she is finally doing well.

In contrast to the manic state, a client with bipolar illness in the depressed state may be extremely needy, pressuring the family for help. More often than not, it is the family that cuts off. With borderline personality disorder, however, a cutoff comes about either way. Just as often, maybe more often, the borderline person cuts off.

BORDERLINE PERSONALITY DISORDER

Someone with borderline personality disorder (BPD) will turn on a dime, in a sudden, dramatic overreaction to a small perceived slight. Another aspect of the condition is "a pattern of unstable and intense interpersonal relationships characterized by alternating between extremes of idealization and devaluation" (American Psychiatric Association, 2013, p. 663). He or she will place the other person on a pedestal and then, after a minor misstep, instantly remove the person. Those with borderline personalities are expert at expecting rejection and masters of angry preemptive cutoffs. They will switch off the current relationship in a rush to find someone else who is "more available." No wonder so many examples of borderline behavior are in the Abandonment chapter! Sadly, a temper fit over a seemingly minor disappointment only drives others away. Who can take being yelled at for being 5 minutes late? (For more detailed diagnostic criteria see *DSM*-5.)

As we saw with Kenny in the Abandonment Chapter, sometimes clinicians learn about borderline behavior the hardest way, when a client cuts them off. Suddenly and without warning, Kenny's therapist received the following "Dear John" by email:

I will not be coming to see you again. My experience has been extremely disturbing and harmful. Although you know I had severe childhood trauma, you purposely withheld helpful ideas about what to do. Your one suggestion that someone with severe depression take yoga is insulting. You selfishly ignored my needs as a patient, when I could have been receiving help from someone else, a better therapist who would take my illness seriously. I can't understand it, but when I told you how terrible I felt, you did not even want to know why. You obviously don't care, and all of your actions show it. I regret wasting the past year trying to get you to listen, which you clearly can't be bothered to do.

Kenny's repeated references to his therapist's inattention signal the borderline person's fear of abandonment and preemptive rush to cutoff. The thought process is: "If my therapist is inattentive, she will ultimately cut me off. I better protect myself by bailing first." In this case, the therapeutic relationship was over before it ever formed. And while the therapist needed to soul search and perhaps better attune herself to his needs, she was never really given a chance.

As upsetting as this cutoff was, if the therapist had realized Kenny's behavior was indicative of borderline personality disorder, she would have been less distraught and might have tried to reengage him, not just let him go. Certainly, she would have been prepared.

She would have understood that though he initially begged for help, she would eventually be suspect and subject to a cutoff herself.

With the tendency to cut off a constant concern with borderline clients, the clinician might include, in an initial therapy contract, an agreement that any dissatisfaction with therapy or the therapist be discussed first, that any wish to unilaterally terminate be discussed in person. Some therapists ask at the outset of therapy for prepayment for a last session. This practice does not guarantee prevention of cutoffs from therapy, but it does increase the likelihood that clients will raise problems in the therapeutic relationship that can be promptly addressed to avoid premature termination.

In another circumstance, a New York supervisor failed to read the warning signs. Working with a student therapist named Wendell, who was from California, several months post-9/11, the therapist made an offhand remark about the collapse of the World Trade Center. "It is ironic how many New Yorkers," he explained, "voiced strong objections to the Twin Towers architectural design in the 1970s when the towers went up, and now—*leaving aside the fact that lives were lost*—find they are oddly consoled that at least the buildings came down."

Shortly after, the student complained that the supervisor was callous and did not care about the lost lives, and he refused to work with the supervisor again. With no discussion, the relationship was abruptly severed. It didn't matter that the student knew the supervisor had spent countless hours volunteering at Ground Zero, the Trade Center site, and saw families who lost members pro bono. Wendell displayed borderline behavior in its purist form.

Clinicians are right to worry about clients with BPD cutting off from them or from other people in their lives. When such cutoffs occur, someone with BPD may blame the other person or themselves. They may experience it as "the end of the world," to quote one client. They then either lash out at the other person or engage in self-punishing behavior. They sometimes decide life is not worth living.

Remember Nora, the teenager in the Abandonment chapter who was rejected by her father, stepmother, siblings, and stepsiblings after her mother died? At the time, Nora did everything she could to draw attention to her pain and her need for someone to recognize her loneliness and to love her. But her acting out just escalated the tensions within the newly constituted family, and Nora made a suicide attempt.

Years later, Nora returned to her old therapist and was helped to mourn her mother and reconnect with her older brother. We return to Nora now because from the beginning her therapist recognized within all the drama of Nora's childhood that she exhibited some borderline characteristics. The therapist contracted that she would continue to be a reliable ally if *and only if* Nora would agree not to hurt herself. The strategy worked so well that despite other impulsive behavior and Nora's tendency to see others as either with her or against her, she has not attempted suicide again.

Further, by remaining a presence in her life—even if just a phone call away—the therapist provided a stable context from which Nora could discover her own talents and establish more positive ways with which to interact with others. Recently, Nora married, and her father, stepmother, and brother attended the wedding.

Remember Raphael and Lucy in the Betrayal chapter? The basic story was that Raphael, after a painful breakup he initiated with a prior girlfriend, went into therapy. A few months later, he found "adorable" Lucy and shortly moved in with her. But things quickly deteriorated. Lucy's younger sister got engaged, stoking Lucy's jealousy. At thirty she *had* to get married, and Raphael by this time was ambivalent. He left because the pressure on him was too great.

What we did not reveal in the first iteration of this case is that Raphael discovered Lucy pulling her hair out strand by strand when she was upset, such as when Raphael did not come home precisely when promised. Moreover, when he finally decided to leave, she would not let go. She pursued him with phone calls and texts, begging him to come back. She also made a suicide attempt. Although she did have her own therapist, she did not always keep appointments. Despite his reservations, Raphael was still tempted to go back.

Raphael's therapist, who had met Lucy, decided to share her perceptions with Raphael. Absorbing the seriousness of Lucy's problems, Raphael decided not to move back. A job offer in Houston supplied an external reason. Here is another example of a cutoff that needed to happen. Lucy had to work on herself and would not have been a healthy partner without it. The therapist urged Raphael to explain his reasons to Lucy, which he did, and it seemed to him that they parted amicably, leaving the door open.

SCHIZOTYPAL PERSONALITY DISORDER

Carl's therapist in the Jealousy chapter shared his impression of Max to help Carl accept the twenty-year cut off from his brother. Learning that Max was schizotypal helped Carl understand his brother's vulnerability, lifelong behavior problems, talking to himself, and unwillingness or inability to discuss what had happened between them.

According to the *DSM-5*, "The essential feature of schizotypal personality disorder is a pervasive pattern of social and interpersonal deficits marked by acute discomfort with, and reduced capacity for, close relationships as well as by cognitive and perceptual distortions and eccentricities of behavior. This pattern begins by early adulthood and is present in a variety of contexts" (American Psychiatric Association, 2013, p. 656). The hallmark of schizotypal disorder is precisely that the affected person cannot sustain a relationship with much intensity or conflict. Such individuals often simply withdraw. And that is what Max did, quitting jobs, leaving town, moving to a remote area in the mountains, cutting off his brother who, despite his gruffness, did care.

With respect to the family's role in the cutoff, the therapist also told Carl about the negative effects of high *expressed emotion* (Hooley, 2007). Carl understood it immediately. "This is exactly the way it played out for Max in my family," he responded. "My parents provided the criticism, I provided the hostility, and my sister overprotected him. I guess we combined to produce the perfect storm."

But the therapist reminded Carl that it was not only the family. Piled on top of Max's probable vulnerability and the family problems, Max had experienced significant stress in the military. He joined the Air Force in his early twenties, was deployed to Thailand, and was assigned to load bombs onto planes destined for Vietnam. A number of studies suggest that having to kill—even in war, even once removed—is as traumatic as or more traumatic than even the fear of being killed (Dau, 2013; Grossman, 2009). This perspective on Max's life also helped ease Carl's pervasive guilt.

As happened with Max and Carl, when one party to a cutoff has a schizotypal diagnosis, the cutoff can be resolved *if* the other party can accept a modified relationship in which conflict is minimized or avoided entirely. That is the simple strategy. Reconnecting is agreeing to avoid tension and enjoy what is possible without expecting depth or working out differences. Carl was more than happy to do that to have Max back in his life.

In sum, a cutoff with someone with a schizotypal disorder may be avoided if the other party understands and accepts these limitations. Decreasing expressed emotion can be reframed as respect.

SCHIZOPHRENIA

Today, the medical/scientific consensus about schizophrenia is that it is a genetically based neurological disorder. Its effect is to essentially cut off the afflicted person from reality. Acknowledging the obvious strength of the genetic component, it is still only a biological *predisposition*. There are still environmental influences, such as viruses to malnutrition, and family factors that may explain, or play a role in, whether the predisposition is expressed, whether the person becomes overtly symptomatic:

> it probably takes more than genes to cause the disorder. Scientists think interactions between genes and the environment are necessary for schizophrenia to develop. Many environmental factors may be involved, such as exposure to viruses, malnutrition before birth, problems during birth, and other not yet known psychosocial factors. (National Institute of Mental Health, n.d.)

So while family therapy pioneers believed that family problems are a major causal factor in schizophrenia and gained prominence with a treatment for the disorder, that is not now considered the best explanation or the treatment of choice. Once medication was shown to partially controlled symptoms and became more cost effective, family as an explanation for the development of schizophrenia and family therapy as a modality for treatment of schizophrenia lost ground.

Given, however, that the family does still play a role in whether the illness is expressed and its course, we must consider how a schizophrenic person and his or her family interact. In addition, we have to consider how a schizophrenic family member may come to be involved in a cutoff. To begin with, if the affected person cuts off from reality, family systems logic says that reality, and specifically the reality of, the affected person's particular family situation, is just too hard to bear. Add to this the family's fear, the amount of care and attention required, and the stigma that still accompanies this dreaded diagnosis, we can understand the high likelihood of cutoff. Better the schizophrenic family member is institutionalized or forgotten than for the family to be perennially embarrassed, dragged down, compromised, or terrified. Sometimes it is a matter of "us or them."

Another quotation from Mira Bartok in her moving account of life with and life-saving cutoff from her schizophrenic mother says it all:

I imagine my life if nothing is done to change things—I see a pale green hospital waiting room at midnight, a television blaring soap opera reruns, and a vending machine dispensing endless cups of burnt coffee . . . I see myself eternally waiting, unemployed and alone. This will be my purgatory: the knock at the door at midnight, my mother, hair wild as snakes, the sound of sirens and doors slamming shut, the violent rush of arms and hands, my mother placed in restraints and handed over to strangers.

And me, sitting in a green room beneath cold fluorescent lights, tapping my foot to a song I played long ago. A quote by the Italian philosopher Antonio Gramsci that I write down in my journal a month after my mother returns home: "The old world is dying away, and the new world struggles to come forth: now is the time of monsters." If I don't do something different, who will become the monster, my mother or me? (Bartok, 2011, pp.138–139)

The most incredible thing about Bartok's story is that in spite of her mother's raging insanity, including threats on Mira's life, Mira knew she was loved, and she loved her mother. This was a painful cutoff to enact, but a necessary break if we ever saw one. Fortunately for both mother and daughter, there was a good death-bed reunion.

❧❧

Remember MaryAnn, who made peace with her mother-in-law upon her husband Julio's death in the Jealousy chapter? The story of

MaryAnn's brother, Mitchell, shows how much family support matters when it comes to alleviation and treatment of symptoms. As MaryAnn told her therapist:

> *My brother Mitchell is schizophrenic, but I prefer to think of him as just paranoid because it isn't as definitive. There is less negative connotation. All eight of us kids were taught to stick together. We were each responsible for the next youngest when we were out and about. We fought, but there was a lot of love. Mitchell was responsible for me, and before he got sick, he was a good brother.*
>
> *It was late-onset schizophrenia, in his thirties. Before that he was a very capable guy. He's still capable in many ways. But he began hearing voices saying a SWAT team was after him, to run away, and he would listen. Mitchell disappeared often in the beginning. But wherever he was, one of us would go get him. He was hospitalized many times, but we always wanted him home. For most of his life after he was diagnosed, he lived with my mother. His therapist told my mother that without our family, Mitchell would no doubt be homeless.*

When the therapist expressed admiration for the family's decision to keep Mitchell at home and their role in helping him, MaryAnn replied, "He was never violent, so that made keeping him home possible." The therapist thought the reverse: "Maybe he isn't violent because the family figured out how to live with him." MaryAnn and her siblings learned through reading, observation, and experience that "Mitchell's illness is biological. So he's very fragile. He can't help it. He can't take anyone talking at him for too long, and he certainly can't handle criticism or yelling. You have to wait, sometimes a long time, for him to respond in a conversation. But he always does."

What MaryAnn's family discovered is the benefit of "low expressed emotion," i.e.: the reduction of hostility, over-involvement, pity, or criticism. According to proponents who have amassed considerable supportive evidence, people with schizophrenia whose families manage to keep the emotional climate calm tend to relapse less. A high expressed emotion level within family has become of sufficient concern to warrant a "v" code in *DSM-5*. A number of psychoeducational approaches (including individual family and family groups) are used to help families with a schizophrenic member lower their expressed emotion and thereby avoid hospitalization and family cutoffs (Falloon, Boyd, & McGill, 1984; Hooley, 2007; Miklowitz, 2004). The approaches have also been applied to other mental health problems such as bipolar disorder.

NARCISSISTIC PERSONALITY DISORDER

Remember Mark Sichel, whose family cutoff we discussed in the Abandonment chapter? He is the psychotherapist whose parents stopped speaking to him a second and apparently last time because he had failed to adhere to what he termed "the happy family myth." He failed by not congratulating his sister on her son's engagement in a timely fashion. Mark came to terms with this devastating, apparently irreparable cutoff by accepting that people like his father cannot tolerate dissent in the ranks.

People with narcissistic personality disorder (NPD) are especially prone to interpersonal difficulties and ultimately to relationship cutoffs. The salient features of NPD include "grandiosity, sense of entitlement, lack of empathy, arrogance, exploitation, requiring excessive admiration" (American Psychiatric Association, 2013, pp. 669–670—see *DSM*-5 for more specific criteria). It is not surprising that other people cower or cut off from the person, and since social status is paramount to someone with NPD, he or she may cut off in a flash if a friend or lover is not seen as important enough. No wonder so many of our cases—fictional, public, personal, clinical—involve narcissistic personality disorder.

The clinical case of Maddy and Martin from the Jealousy chapter provides an example of narcissistic personality disorder as well:

He could be charming, but also opinionated, critical, dismissive, self-aggrandizing, inconsistent, unpredictable, unreliable, calculating, and seemingly bent on making others around him unhappy. He established rules for Maddy to keep, and would then break them himself, change them at whim, or claim he never made them in the first place. Martin once proudly announced he had scored zero on a test of empathy. He had taken it at work as part of a corporate assessment process. When asked how he felt about it, he was not upset; he was amused.

Maddy and Martin tried couple therapy, which didn't help, and they stopped on the advice of the therapist, who told Maddy she honestly saw nothing changing. It still took Maddy many years to detach. She kept trying and hoping, to no avail. She was kept waiting on windy cold street corners because Martin never knew his schedule until the last minute or would change plans and not show up at all. It was his way or the highway, no compromise, no discussion. Yes, he was the classic "male chauvinist," but it was more than that, because his behavior was not mindless. Rather, it seemed premeditated, designed to frustrate, mean spirited, and hurtful on purpose. Maddy was so low after many years of this that she barely had the strength to divorce. But she finally did and has been much better since.

One of the clinicians we interviewed pointed out that a cutoff may be necessary if the aggrieved party will simply be reinjured by staying in, or returning to, the relationship. Sadly, this is most likely the case if one party clearly has a pernicious narcissistic personality disorder; if so, it may be the therapist's responsibility to help the other party extricate.

Unfortunately, diagnostic labels do stigmatize and objectify the carrier, locking the person into a marginalized "other" category. With respect to cutoffs, the labels also have a rigidifying effect on relationships, decreasing the supposedly well person's willingness to reengage or attempt reconciliation. But the opposite can also happen. After Max was labeled by Carl's therapist as having a schizotypal personality disorder, Carl was more empathic, understanding of Max's strange behavior, and relieved of some fraternal guilt. In Sichel's case, since the father has been unrelenting, the narcissistic label helped his therapist son accept the cutoff's finality. In sum, there are instances in which providing a diagnosis can help a client through a cutoff.

PARANOID PERSONALITY DISORDER

People with paranoid personality disorder are perennially suspicious and rarely forms close ties. In the rare instances in which they do allow themselves to get close, they constantly question the other person and the relationship. They demand complete loyalty and are often jealous for no apparent reason. They cannot trust anyone or any situation. (For greater specificity regarding paranoid personality disorder, see the *DSM*-5.)

Dylan, in the Jealousy chapter, was very likely paranoid. He thought the neighbor and his family "had it in for me," and were "purposely making life difficult." The cutoff was the only way Dylan could deal with feeling rejected and with his paranoid ideation. Even at that, he obtained little relief. He could not see his role in the family and friendship drama, could not accept an iota of responsibility for his actions. If one party in a cutoff cannot begin to believe in the other's goodwill, reconciliation is impossible. Theoretically, a good individual therapy experience will enable someone with paranoid tendencies to begin to trust, but it takes years—more time than most therapists and clients have the patience or stamina to devote. Sadly, because of the inability to trust, we have found that couple or family therapy with a paranoid member is generally contraindicated. Individual therapy is challenging enough.

ANTISOCIAL PERSONALITY DISORDER

Though few of our clinical and personal cases have involved blatant antisocial behavior, we feel it is important for clinicians to consider this possibility when a cutoff surfaces. The essence of antisocial personality disorder (ADP) is "a pervasive pattern of disregard for, and violation of, the rights of others that begins in childhood or early adolescence and continues into adulthood" (American Psychiatric Association, 2013, p. 659). Other criteria include failure to conform to social norms, repeatedly performing acts that are grounds for arrest, deceitfulness, impulsivity, irritability and aggressiveness, reckless disregard for the safety of self or others, consistent irresponsibility, and lack of remorse, making them extraordinarily difficult clients. These characteristics easily explain why those in relationship with someone with APD may not only want to cut off, but may also refuse to reconnect. People with APD make extraordinarily difficult clients and this condition certainly makes Nathaniel's refusal to reconnect with Sam (see the Jealousy chapter) easy to understand.

For those with antisocial personality disorder, relationships are only a means to an end. The other person has no value except as a vehicle to better their circumstance. Templeton the rat in E. B. White's children's classic *Charlotte's Web* personifies this disorder by his dead giveaway refrain, "What's in it for me?" If saving Wilbur the pig from being slaughtered does nothing for the rat, if a friend has no current value, he or she is discarded, kicked to the side of the road, at the drop of a hat—no regret, no remorse, no recognition of the hurt inflicted, no apology, no making amends.

Contrary to the wry humor of TV's mafia king Tony Soprano see-ing a therapist, those with antisocial personality disorder rarely seek therapy on their own. They do, however, occasionally get dragged in by a spouse or other relative, or ordered in by the court. And though they rarely see themselves needing psychological help, they almost always wreak havoc on other people, who then need therapy them-selves. One way or another, either directly or through other clients, therapists cannot avoid antisocial personality disorder.

As with narcissistic and paranoid personality disorders, with this diagnosis we also depart from our general stance. A cutoff from someone with antisocial personality disorder may be not only war-ranted but necessary, for the other party's self-respect, emotional survival, or physical safety. We often have to support a client's wish or decision to cut off from someone with consistent, obvious behav-ior characteristic of APD.

SUBSTANCE ABUSE

Many of our cases have involved substance abuse, either primary or secondary to other diagnoses or issues (dual diagnoses)—so much so that it is beyond our scope to delve into all of them. But we will dis-cuss several cases from the following list, and the reader can look back at other cases presented in earlier chapters with a substance abuse lens in place. This is a cursory list, and as so often occurs with drugs and alcohol, it is probably just the tip of the iceberg:

- Carrie
- Nora
- Lucy
- Nathaniel
- Ruby

- Ron
- Clem
- Nick
- Natasha
- Tom

- Chelsea
- Stephen
- Max

- Alec
- Harold
- Mike & Kathy

The important point connecting addiction and cutoffs is that the addicted person, simply by virtue of being addicted, has already begun to cut off. Another way of saying it is that addiction, somewhat like schizophrenia, is an indirect cutoff. We already think of addiction as escape, a way to be physically present while mentally gone. When one's work, one's relationship—one's life—reaches an intolerable threshold, there is an "out."

Though rarely on purpose, the addicted person "chooses" the substance(s) over other relationships and is, therefore, not as accessible as he or she might otherwise be. The person is driven by the substance and, under the influence, has no choice but to care more about the substance than anything or anyone else. The substance is the lover, and those who love the person usually feel ignored or abandoned.

The non-addicted person's behavior may be placating, enabling, vengeful or self-protective. In self-protection mode, the other person may cut off. That is what happened to Harold and Stephen.

✒︎✒︎

Harold was a commercial real estate broker and a confirmed alcoholic for the majority of his adult life. He plowed through three marriages and at times could barely function at work. His unmarried son moved across country right after college and rarely speaks to him. His daughter, Amy, cut him off 25 years ago, and he has not seen or spoken to her since. He has never seen Amy's children. After years of psychotherapy and three AA meetings a week, Harold stopped drinking and has been sober for 20 years. But Amy has not relented. His therapist reported that the courage and strength Harold musters to cope with these losses is incredibly moving; she only hopes Amy will agree to some form of reconnection with her father before he dies. "God knows I keep trying," Harold said, apologizing over and over in letters to Amy.

✒︎✒︎

If possible, Stephen's story is sadder still:

Stephen was left at a very young age by his mother and was raised by a father who did his best but who was uneasy with children, couldn't offer much affection, and was a closet alcoholic. A very bright fellow, Stephen excelled in school and held himself together with recognition for his many talents. A successful undergraduate, he went to graduate school and became an aerospace engineer working for an offshoot of NASA. He met and married Amber at twenty-five. They had two children, a son and daughter, and although he occasionally drank to excess, he managed his life reasonably well in spite of it. A sudden tragedy, the death of his daughter in a skating accident on a semi-frozen lake near their house, plunged him into despair, and he withdrew into an alcoholic haze. Then, although his remaining family gave him many chances, he ultimately lost everything, his wife, his son, his livelihood and his life.

As is the case with so many people where drugs or alcohol are involved, Harold's and Stephen's relationships were not reparable. However, we end the chapter with the story of Mike, whose relationship was repaired with the help of many caring people in his life.

Mike was a topnotch ski instructor who hired Kathy, twenty-two, just out of college. Her job was to assist with beginners, mostly children. They fell in love and got married on a whim. He was forty-one, eager to start a family. The only problem was that he drank too much, but he offered on his own initiative to quit when she got pregnant. She soon did, but he didn't stop drinking and "kicked the can down the road." He said he would stop when the baby arrived. She didn't believe him. They went for couple therapy. The therapist knew the importance of motivation in someone's decision to get sober, so she probed the pros and cons.

It appeared that Mike needed alcohol to cope with certain work-related social situations. His desire to stop was, therefore, not strong. He might do it for Kathy, but he was annoyed that she had begun pressuring him. One day after a binge, he blacked out and couldn't remember a thing leading up to it. Kathy told the therapist that she wanted a divorce, pregnant or not. Mike believed she was overreacting— "hormonal," he said, and that she would calm down. Kathy threat-

ened to move out unless he took it seriously. He claimed no one else thought he had a problem and that everyone in the ski world at his level drank the way he did.

She challenged him to ask his parents and siblings for their opinion. In an extended family intervention, Mike got an earful about his drinking behavior. The entire family affirmed Kathy, even encouraging her to move out "until he gets a grip." The real prospect of losing Kathy and their baby hit home, and Mike finally took the problem seriously.

He supported Kathy's decision to move out, including her proviso that they not reconcile until she was sure he was sober and could maintain it. After a thirty-day in-patient rehabilitation program, daily AA meetings afterward, and three months with no contact, Mike and Kathy resumed couple therapy, and Kathy came home. At that point the therapist confronted Mike with her hypothesis that social anxiety disorder was at the root of his alcoholism. He not only accepted it, but agreed to a medication consultation and individual therapy.

This case contains just about every strategy known to be successful in overcoming an addiction: motivational inquiry, couple therapy, family intervention, individual therapy, rehabilitation, Alcoholics Anonymous, medication, strict limit setting, conditional family cutoff, and threat of permanent loss of family. Time intensive and costly in the short run, it saved a life and a family in the end.

CLINICIANS' EDUCATIONAL ROLE

If one party in a relationship suffers from a mental illness, the chances are that the necessary interpersonal skills were never developed, are buried, are inaccessible, or were lost in the course of the illness. It is therefore incumbent on the other party in the relationship to maintain composure, to avoid escalation at all cost. The communication burden is uneven when one person is mentally ill, just as it is when someone is physically ill. The well person has to stretch beyond his or her ordinary relationship responsibility. As we saw with schizophrenia, the other person's challenge is to decrease the amount of hostility, criticism, judgment. But because the relationship is at least temporarily one-sided, the risk is that the person putting more into it will find it too much and cut off. Respites also help, as they do when someone is physically ill.

When one family member is sick, the entire family may become rigid in its patterns and be unable to adapt to the requirements of the situation. In these instances, third-party professional assistance will be necessary to avoid or repair a cutoff.

Clinicians need to share their understanding that when one person in a relationship becomes mentally ill, it is a major status and relationship change and that many of the factors that build to a cutoff may be present. The ill person may be jealous ("Why am I sick and unable to function when my partner/husband/wife/friend is well?"), feel abandoned ("If I can't keep up my end of the marital bargain or get better, he or she will leave me"), or feel betrayed ("My family is carrying on without me"), and so on. The well person usually experiences something akin to survivor guilt ("Do I deserve to be well and carry on when my mate is ill?) or fear for the future and loss of the relationship that was. The first therapeutic step to avoiding a cutoff is to support the healthier one by empathizing with him or her, since he or she now has the greater relationship burden. This goes without saying, but will he or she accept it? Here is where the therapist becomes a teacher who explains that:

- The ill person's behavior is not purposeful.
- The ill person either never had a chance to develop good communication skills or has temporarily lost them because of the illness.
- Stigmatizing the person prevents others from seeing what may still be healthy in him or her.
- If the ill person's behavior is odd, he or she may be bullied or become a scapegoat.

It is important for partners or families struggling with mental illness to have time to regroup. Dealing with mental illness can be a long haul. No one can be an ever-present caregiver without it negatively affecting the relationship. Time apart has to be scheduled and agreed on to avoid a cutoff. It is critical for the healthier one not to pull away in moments of conflict or anger. The ill one, to the extent possible, must learn his or her own triggers, accept therapy and other forms of assistance, make and accept apologies, and help keep the waters calm.

Family members need education about the particular mental illness and what the ill person needs. Again, generally, these needs include lowering emotional excitability, calming down the family system, and lowering the reactivity level. Interestingly, this older approach meshes well with newer ones. Even cognitive behavior therapists are now promoting "acceptance" (Arch et al., 2012; National Association of Cognitive-Behavioral Therapists, n.d.). All assure the family members that they are not necessarily or solely accountable for the problem but that they must be part of the solution. And by the way, when the clinician helps the family adopt salutary behavior for the "sick one," the family simultaneously changes and heals itself!

Medication has a role, and the need to refer for psychiatric evaluation is clear when the situation has solidified to the point where one person is carrying an excess of symptomatology. Medication may jolt, soften, or regulate his or her psychic pain and problematic behavior. Certainly, no one in a psychotic state can function properly, and he or she is almost always in either a weakened or overly powerful family position. A positive change in family dynamics at this point may not be sufficient to relieve internal pressure or reactivity.

The need for medication can be explained as leveling the family playing field, to help the ill one regain strength and status. Whether it works as a psychological placebo or on a direct physiological level, some clients improve, and we have witnessed a few transformed. Sometimes, medication seems to work because of the physician who prescribes it. If it works, it works, and we are grateful.

In the final chapter, we cover other ways to prevent relationship cutoffs. We also address our own major conclusions and concerns. We offer them as food for thought and as action items for our colleagues and ourselves.

Chapter 8

CONCLUSION

Tout comprendre c'est tout pardonner.
(To understand everything is to forgive everything.)
Madam de Stael

Though as yet undocumented, the consequences to society of cutoffs in terms of individual and family dysfunction are likely tremendous. Future studies will be needed to measure the cost of psychic pain and somatization in terms of absenteeism from work and school, doctor visits, medication, psychotherapy, and the like.

While we do not know the actual prevalence of cutoffs, we do know they are ubiquitous. Nevertheless, cutoffs remain stigmatized, causing embarrassment and shame, a sign of being unable to keep one's house in order. For these reasons, cutoffs usually fly under the radar, a hidden epidemic. One hope for this book is that it will help people—therapists and clients—begin to talk more openly and freely about their experiences.

We believe that something on an educational policy level is needed to prevent cutoffs, or at least reduce their incidence. Thus, our first concern as we draw the book to a close is primary prevention. How, on a macro level, can we help people avoid cutoffs in the first place?

PRIMARY PREVENTION

Primary prevention is about what it takes to have a good relationship, before one becomes "involved." To prevent a cutoff, clearly one has to know how to relate to others in problematic situations, how to behave! Trite, but true. And in addition to basic mental health, basic communication and problem-solving skills are what it takes. They make relationships hum along day to day, help them last. Without these skill sets, even otherwise healthy people and healthy relationships wither or explode, and a painful cutoff will be the result.

Our strong conviction is that self-awareness (mindfulness), communication, and problem-solving skills must be instilled and reinforced in the society at large beginning in nursery school and should be a prerequisite for parenthood or a marriage license—in other words, *before* couples proceed to have children (Lesser Bruun & Ziff, 2010). We are ultimately talking about education for civility and well-being at every level of society, so that the wherewithal to solve problems and resolve conflict without cutting-off is in place before trouble starts. Lest the reader think we are dreaming, there is substantive hope in this regard.

Some schools have already embraced the idea, teaching these skills and giving children the chance to practice them whenever there is an interpersonal problem in the classroom. These skills and the time devoted to them are not ancillary. They have a legitimate place in the curriculum, and practicing them on the spot as problems erupt is prioritized along with reading, math, social studies, and science. Two schools we know of with programs like these in place are Nueva School in California (Nuevaschool.org) and Packer Collegiate in New York (Packer.edu) where children have an opportunity to "talk it out" as needed.

At a conference in New York City as we were putting finishing touches on the book, Jack Kornfield, psychologist and renowned Buddhist therapist and teacher, declared that 5,000 schools across the country are using mindfulness techniques combining Eastern and Western ways to teach children self-awareness, empathy, and gentle ways to handle conflict both in the classroom and out. We refer the reader to the George Lucas Foundation website Edutopia

(Taran, 2013) to obtain a feel for this evolution in school curricula. Or, the reader can simply Google *social-emotional learning (SEL)* and go from there.

From personal relationships, to couples, to corporations, there is a well-established industry devoted to social or communication skills training for adults in a variety of formats—books, online courses, in-person classes. We especially encourage utilization of these programs and materials to prevent problems, recognizing that they are also useful in ameliorating cutoffs, and helpful in repairing a definitive cutoff. An Internet search yields a host of programs and possibilities. Among the most effective is David Olson's "PREP," originally designed for premarital couples but we think adaptable for other relationships as well (Olson & Olson, 2002; www.prepare-enrich.com).

Arguably the most important skill for everyone, therapists included, is the ability to avoid getting hijacked, a point that cannot be stressed enough. In this regard, Goleman's *The Meditative Mind* (1977/1988) and Siegel's *Mindsight* (2010a) or *The Mindful Therapist* (2010b) are good places to start for those who have not yet explored this domain. The content can be helpful within our own lives as well as providing helpful recommendations for our clients.

All of the above is "pre-therapy," preparation everyone needs in order to establish good relationships. In some cases, individuals absorb these skills at home from parents and other caregivers throughout childhood. In other cases, they are learned later, in school or in the community. If successfully ingrained, they may obviate the need for third-party assistance, including therapy! Until that day, the need will continue for secondary prevention, whose aim is to prevent further erosion or an entrenched pattern of cutoffs.

SECONDARY PREVENTION

Secondary prevention is about remediation, in which an important already existing relationship is in trouble, has gone sour, or has been cut off. Here the idea is to prevent further erosion and an entrenched pattern of difficulty. This is where therapy comes in.

Anger management courses are also helpful in some cases, but they are most often urged by therapists, mandated by courts, or demanded by a spouse (usually the wife) as a condition of staying, rather than sought by clients themselves. And then there all of the therapeutic strategies discussed in Chapter 3, which is essentially devoted to secondary prevention.

As we've discussed in the book, clients often fixate on the incident (what the other person last said or did) that caused the cutoff. The proverbial last straw provides the initial hook for clinical work, a window into the relationship and a key to possible reconciliation. However, as we have discussed, cutoffs rarely emerge out of the blue. In most cases, some pre-cutoff stress or tension existed in the relationship, and some deeper cause or theme explains it. Did jealousy cause the rift, or some type of betrayal or sense of abandonment? Was it a matter of principle, such as a clash over religion or politics? Or was it mental illness or drug abuse?

We used these underlying themes, or "causes," to structure the chapters of the book to stress their importance and to help therapists bear them in mind to reduce the potential for cutoffs in their clients' lives. We believe that when clients become aware of these underlying issues, cutoffs can be avoided or resolved, and when the cutoff is beyond repair, they can move forward.

BACK TO US

Because the work on cutoffs is so challenging, we therapists have to want to—be motivated to—do therapy with cutoff parties. And to be successful at it, we have to work on ourselves, starting with the self-reflection exercises outlined in the Strategies chapter. As the reader will recall, this tactic is to combat our own transference and countertransference regarding cutoff experiences in our own lives. That is a given. But there is more.

The therapists we interviewed often had trouble summoning up their own cases involving cutoffs. Because there are so many cases of cutoffs in the news media, fiction, and film, and personal stories flowed so easily from the laypeople we queried, we cannot help wondering why therapists were not easily accessing their clients' stories, why cutoffs seemed to be below their radar. Cutoffs are scary; there is no predicting what will happen, and the therapist starts off with the disadvantage of a relationship that is already severed or close to it. The chance of failure is great, and no one likes to fail. The therapist's ego cannot help but be involved.

Perhaps the most striking and lasting impression of our interviews is that most therapists we interviewed stayed with individual work on cutoffs and did not tend to bring cutoff parties into the room. We found that even clinicians trained in family and systems therapy reverted to individual work when faced with high conflict, especially with cutoff couples or families.

Working on a cutoff relationship is not only more difficult than working with couples, families, or friends who are still in the room, still talking; it is also different. In addition to the general fear of failure, there are a host of specific, practical reasons clinicians may be avoiding work with cutoff parties:

- They are afraid to antagonize a client by suggesting the other party be invited into the room, afraid to lose the client, and yes, afraid to lose the income.
- Having formed an alliance with the client, the therapist worries it won't be possible to even things out if the other party enters therapy midway or late in the process.
- The therapist fears or believes the other party will feel at a disadvantage, not trusting the therapist to see their point of view.
- The clinician may have already taken sides with the client against the cutoff party and not know how to shift to a more neutral stance about the other party in order to help the original client accept the other party in the room.
- The client may be uneasy or not see a benefit in sharing the therapist with the cutoff party.
- There may be logistical difficulty (such as geographic distance) in getting parties together.
- The client or the other party is or seems unmotivated.
- Issues of confidentiality are always in the background. A relationship has existed between the original client and the therapist wherein secrets were revealed. The cutoff party might want to know them, but the original client may not want to divulge. This leaves the therapist holding secrets.
- The client denies or minimizes the pain of a cutoff or convinces the therapist it is irreparable.
- Both client and therapist are afraid and thus conspire to avoid

the whole issue. The client does not raise the issue of a cutoff and the therapist does not ask. The cutoff stays hidden.

• The therapist does not believe the client is strong enough to handle the stress of attempting reconciliation or even to reach a decision to try. One clinician interviewee said, "I find that clients are afraid to reconnect, so I don't push them. They have to find their own way to forgive and reestablish a new relationship."

Is this true, that clients are too afraid, or is it the therapist's projection? Is the therapist's fear preventing him or her from taking a more positive, "can-do" approach, reassuring the client with words like "Don't worry, I'll have your back"?

These apprehensions are understandable, especially since few of us had an opportunity to work with cutoff problems in our training days. Seeing cutoffs in training would have alleviated many of these concerns through role play, with supervision and later on in continuing education courses. In any case, none of these concerns should stop us from trying. We know of many instances in which the other party entered late and reconciliation was accomplished in spite of initial roadblocks or hurdles. In the future, we hope clinicians will probe for cutoffs early in the assessment process and not wait for a client to bring them up.

If a therapist is hesitant to bring in the other party midway or late, as a last resort, he or she might consider referring both parties to another therapist. Again, part of the reluctance to such referral could be giving up the client—and the income.

The following exchange took place between family therapy pioneer Carl Whitaker and a clinician in the audience during a question-and-answer period following Whitaker's talk at a conference. It is a poignant illustration of how out of touch some clinicians are about the significance of cutoffs in their own lives and how a firm commitment on the part of the therapist to bringing parties together truly matters. Whitaker had just expressed his opinion that the only good therapy was family therapy and that it was necessary to have all family members in the room.

Q: What happens when there are no family members? What do you do?

A: What do you *mean,* no family members?

Q: Well, I have no family members.

A: None at all?

Q: Well, I have a son who lives in the midwest, but we haven't spoken for years.

A: If you were my client, I'd insist you call him.

Contrast that questioner's naiveté with a reasonable facsimile of another therapist's remarks, and let this one below be a model for the thoughtfulness we all need to strive for:

I'm an eternal optimist, though I come from a family where my parents divorced and never spoke again. I can't help wanting people back together, or at least trying. As a therapist, my childhood experience informs my approach. My motto is, whatever you do, don't give up. I've said to clients "If the door is slammed in your face, go through a window or down the chimney." I know. I still have to keep in mind that some situations cannot or should not be fixed. And I'm often afraid to make matters worse by bringing cutoff parties into the room, but I push past the fear and often get a positive outcome.

In those cases where reconciliation does not seem possible, I try to help clients gain perspective. The cutoff is not their whole life and cannot now be their only focus. I aim to help them make life as fulfilling as possible in other ways. The work switches to becoming the best person you can be in the meantime. Something will change, and you'll hopefully get another chance to work it out.

We end with a new case of ours that both beginners and more experienced colleagues who have not yet tackled cutoffs on a regular basis can "cut" their teeth on. It needs a strategic plan and a happy ending:

Sisters Vicki and Phoebe are married to brothers Ethan and Sebastian. Sebastian was unhappy with Phoebe for several years and treated her badly. He then asked for a divorce, which she reluctantly granted. One of their three children, Danielle, is depressed and dropped out of school last month. The other two are faring better than Danielle, but not as well as before. Sebastian sees the children infrequently and is behind in child support. Phoebe is miserable.

Vicki and Phoebe's parents are angry at Sebastian and unhappy about the divorce, especially since there has never been a divorce in their entire extended family. They do everything possible to help Phoebe and her children, to no avail. As a last resort out of loyalty to Phoebe and to pressure Sebastian, they asked Vicki and Ethan to cut Sebastian out of their lives. But Ethan and Sebastian are close, and Vicki and Ethan are firm that they will not cut Sebastian off. Vicki and Phoebe's parents are no longer on speaking terms with Vicki or Ethan, and have cut off from Vicki and Ethan's children as well.

Vicki's Dilemma

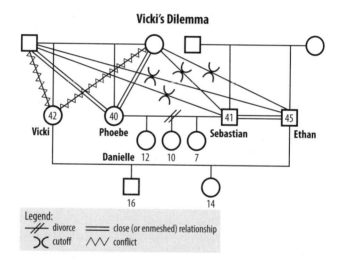

Legend:
—*//*— divorce   ═══ close (or enmeshed) relationship
)(cutoff   /\/\/ conflict

Vicki is the client and this is the story she recounts in the first session. What are your thoughts about Vicki and her family, and what thoughts do you have about her predicament? What questions would you ask; where might you start? And what would be a reasonable tentative plan and goal?

We are just beginning to understand relationship cutoffs and how to work with family members and friends experiencing them. We hope you, our colleagues, contemporaries, and clinicians in training, having read *Not on Speaking Terms*, are stimulated and eager to develop new insights and strategies going forward. Meanwhile, if we, by this book, spare just a few people the pain of a valued relationship cutoff, we have accomplished our purpose.

REFERENCES

Ahrons, C. (2005). *We're still family: What grown children have to say about their parents' divorce.* New York, NY: Harper Perennial.

Ainsworth, M. D. S., & Bell, S. M. (1970). Attachment, exploration, and separation: Illustrated by the behavior of one-year-olds in a strange situation. *Child Development, 41,* 49–67.

Ainsworth, M. D. S., Blehar, M. C., Waters, E., & Wall, S. (1978). *Patterns of attachment: A psychological study of the strange situation.* Hillsdale, NJ: Erlbaum.

American Psychiatric Association. (2013). *Diagnostic and statistical manual of mental disorders* (5th ed.). Washington, DC: American Psychiatric Association.

Arch, J. J., Eifert, G. E., Plumb, J., Rose, R., Davies, C., & Craske, M. G. (2012). Randomized clinical trial of cognitive behavioral therapy (CBT) versus acceptance and commitment therapy (ACT) in the treatment of mixed anxiety disorders. *Journal of Consulting and Clinical Psychology, 80*(5), 750–765.

Avnett, J. (Producer). & Aronofsky, D. (Director). (2010). *Black swan.* [Motion picture]. United States: Fox Searchlight Pictures

Bacon, F. (1612/ n.d.). Of wisdom for a man's self. Retrieved July 2013 from www.authorama.com/essays-of-francis-bacon-24.html.

Baez, J., & Golenbock, P. (2012). *Presumed guilty: Casey Anthony: The inside story.* Dallas, TX: BenBella Books.

Bardin, L. (2000). *Coping with cult involvement: A handbook for families and friends* (2nd ed.). Bonita Springs, FL American Family Foundation (International Cultic Studies Association).

Bartok, M. (2011). *The memory palace.* New York, NY: Free Press.

Belkin, L. (2010, July 2). Why is it so hard to apologize well? *New York Times Magazine.* MM9

Bernheimer, K. (2005). Other women. In J. Offill & E. Schappell (Eds.), *The friend who got away.* New York, NY: Doubleday.

Bhattacharjee,Y. (2013, April 26). The mind of a con man. *New York Times Magazine.* MM44

Bonanno, G. (2009). *The other side of sadness: What the new science of bereavement tells us about life after a loss.* New York, NY: Basic Books-Perseus Books.

Böszörményi-Nagy, I., & Spark, G. S. (1973/1984). *Invisible loyalties.* New York, NY: Brunner/Mazel.

Bowen, M. (1976). Theory in the practice of psychotherapy. In P. J. Guerin (Ed.), *Family therapy.* New York, NY: Gardner Press.

Bowen, M. (1978/1994). *Family therapy in clinical practice.* Lanham, MD: Jason Aronson.

Bowlby J. (1969/1999). *Attachment and loss* (2nd ed., Vol. 1). New York, NY: Basic Books.

Bowlby J. (1973). *Separation: Anxiety & anger. Attachment and loss* (Vol. 2). London: Hogarth Press.

Bowman-Kruhm, M. (2010). *The Leakeys: A biography.* Amherst, NY: Prometheus Books.

Brandon, D. (1978). *Zen in the art of helping.* New York, NY: Dell.

Buber, M. (1923/1958). *I and thou* (R. G. Smith, Trans.). New York, NY: Scribner.

Cacciatore, J., Schnebly, S., & Froen, F. (2009). The effects of social support on maternal anxiety and depression after stillborn. *Health and Social Care in the Community, 17*(2), 167–176.

Cain, J. M. (1941/2003). *Mildred Pierce.* In *The Postman always rings twice, double indemnity, Mildred Pierce, and selected stories.* New York: Everyman's Library – Random House.

Carstensen, L., Gottman, J., & Levenson, R. (1995). Emotional behavior in long-term marriage. *Psychology and Aging, 10*(1), 140–149.

Carter, E. A., & McGoldrick, M. (1999). *The expanded family life cycle: Individual, family, and social perspectives* (3rd ed.). New York, NY: Allyn & Bacon/Pearson.

Chapman, G., & Thomas, J. (2006). *The five languages of apology: How to experience healing in all relationships.* Chicago: Northfield.

Child Welfare Information Gateway. (2013). Working with birth and adoptive families to support open adoption. Washington, DC: U.S. Department of Health and Human Services, Children's Bureau.

Dattilio, F. M., & Nichols, M. P. (2011). Reuniting estranged family members: A cognitive-behavioral-systemic perspective. *The American Journal of Family Therapy, 39,* 88–99.

Dau, J. (2013, February 22). Drone pilots are found to get stress disorders much as those in combat do. *New York Times.* A9

Davis, D. A. (1997). Oedipus redivivus: Freud, Jung, and psychoanalysis.

Retrieved from http://www.haverford.edu/psych/ddavis/jungfreu
.html

Davis, L. (2002). *I thought we would never speak again: The road from estrangement to reconciliation*. New York, NY: Quill-HarperCollins.

Dunham, L. (2012, August 13). First love: memories of an elusive boyfriend. *The New Yorker*, pp. 48–50.

Engle, B. (2001). *Power of apology: A healing strategy to transform all your relationships*. Hoboken, NJ: Wiley.

Erikson, E. (1959). *Identity and the life cycle*. New York, NY: International Universities Press.

Falloon, I. R. G., Boyd, J. L, & McGill, C. W. (1984). *Family care of schizophrenia: A problem-solving approach to the treatment of mental illness*. New York: Guilford.

Freud, A. (1936). *The ego and the mechanisms of defense: The writings of Anna Freud*. Madison, CT: International Universities Press.

Friedman, E. H. (2008). The myth of the shiksa. In *The myth of the shiksa and other essays* (pp. 57–89). New York, NY: Seabury Books.

Fromm, E. (1941/1994). *Escape from freedom*. New York, NY: Holt.

Galanes, P. (2012, May 10). Social Qs: A Playmate for Benji? *New York Times*.

Gardner, R. A. (1985). Recent trends in divorce and custody litigation. *Academy Forum, 29*(2).

Gardner, R. A. (1998). *The parental alienation syndrome* (2nd ed.). Cresskill, NJ: Creative Therapeutics

Gilbert, R. (2006).*The eight concepts of Bowen theory*. Falls Church, VA: Leading Systems Press.

Goleman, D. P. (1977/1988). *The meditative mind: The varieties of the meditative experience*. New York, NY: Tarcher/Putnam.

Goleman, D. P. (2005). *Emotional intelligence: Why it can matter more than IQ*. New York, NY: Bantam.

Gottman, J. M., Coan, J., Carrere, S., & Swenson, C. (1998). Predicting marital happiness and stability from newlywed interactions. *Journal of Marriage and the Family, 60*, 5–22.

Gottman, J. M., & Krokott, L. J. (1989). Marital interaction and satis—faction: A longitudinal view. *Journal of Consulting Psychology, 57*(1), 47–52.

Gottman, J. M., & Levenson, R. W. (1992). Marital processes predictive of later dissolution: Behavior, physiology and health. *Journal of Personality and Social Psychology, 63*, 221–233.

Gottman, J. M., & Silver, N. (2009). *The seven principles for making marriage work: A practical guide from the country's foremost relationship expert*. New York, NY: Crown.

Grossman, D. (2009). *On killing: The psychological cost of learning to kill in war and society*. Boston, MA: Back Bay Books.

REFERENCES

Hart, S. L., & Carrington, H. A. (2002). Jealousy in 6-month-old infants. *Infancy, 3*(3), 395–402.

Hart, S. L., Carrington, H. A., Troznick, E. Z., & Carroll, S. R. (2004). When infants lose exclusive maternal attention: Is it jealousy? *Infancy, 6*(1), 57–78.

Harvard Health Publications. (2012). *The sensitive gut.* Retrieved from http://www.health.harvard.edu/special_health_reports/the_sensitive_gut

Heitler, S. M. (1993). *From conflict to resolution: Skills and strategies for individuals, couples, and family therapy.* New York, NY: Norton.

Hooley, J. M. (2007). Expressed emotion and relapse of psychopathology. *Annual Review of Clinical Psychology, 3,* 329–352.

Johnson, S. M., & Whiffen, V. E. (Eds.). (2003). *Attachment processes in couple and family therapy.* New York, NY: Guilford.

Jones, D. (2000, May 23). The return of Jim Pierce. Retrieved from http://observer.theguardian.com/osm/story/0,,255396,00.html

Kado, J. (2009). *Effective apology: Mending fences, building bridges, and restoring trust.* San Francisco, CA: Berrett-Koehler.

Karren, K. J., Smith, L., Hafen, B. Q., & Gordon, K. J. (2010). *Mind, body health: The effects of attitudes emotions and relationships* (4th ed.). New York, NY: Pearson.

Kerr, M., & Bowen, M. (1988). *Family evaluation: An approach based on Bowen theory.* New York, NY: Norton.

Kraut, A. M. (1994). *Silent travelers: Germs, genes and the "immigrant" menace.* Baltimore: MD: Johns Hopkins University Press.

Kübler-Ross, E. (1969). *On death and dying.* New York, NY: Scribner.

Larsen, J. T., Berntson, G. C., Poehlmann, K. M., Ito, T. A., & Cacioppo, J. T. (2010). The physiology of emotions. In M. Lewis, J. M. Haviland-Jones, & L. F. Barrett (Eds.), *Handbook of Emotions* (3rd ed., pp.180–195). New York, NY: Guilford.

Lazare, M. (2004). *On apology.* New York, NY: Oxford University Press.

LeBey, B. (2001). *Family estrangements: How they begin, how to mend them, how to cope with them.* New York, NY: Bantam Books.

Lenzenweger, M. F. (2008). Epidemiology of personality disorders. *Psychiatric Clinics of North America, 31*(3), 395–403.

Lesser Bruun, E., & Ziff, A. (2010). *Marrying well: The clinician's guide to premarital counseling.* New York, NY: Norton.

Levinson, D. (1986). *Seasons of a man's life.* New York, NY: Ballantine.

Lewin, R. (1997). *Bones of contention.* Chicago, IL: University of Chicago Press.

Madanes, C., with Keim, J. P. & Smesler, D. (1995). *The Violence of men: New techniques for working with abusive families: A therapist for social action.* San Francisco, CA: Jossey-Bass.

Madoff Mack, S. (2012). *The end of normal: A wife's anguish, a widow's new life.* New York, NY: Plume/Penguin.

Mahon, E. K. (2008, August 12). Uncivil wars: Lillian Hellman vs. Mary McCarthy and the question of Julia. Retrieved from http://scandal ouswoman.blogspot.com/2008/08/uncivil-wars-lillian-hellman-vs -mary.html

Margulies, D. (1998). *Collected stories*. New York. NY: Dramatists Play Service, Inc.

Mayo Clinic (n.d.). Anger management. Retrieved from http://www.mayo clinic.com/health/anger- management/MH00102/NSECTIONGROUP=2

McGoldrick, M., Gerson, R., & Petry, S. (2008). *Genograms: Assessment and intervention* (3rd ed.). New York, NY: Norton.

McGuire, W. (Ed.) (1974/1994). *The Freud/Jung letters: The correspondence between Sigmund Freud and C. G. Jung* (R. Manheim & R. F. C. Hull, Trans.). Princeton, NJ: Princeton University Press.

Mead, M. (1978). Preface to the revised edition. In *Culture and commitment: A study of the generation gap*. Garden City, New York, NY: Natural History Press.

Miklowitz, D. J. (2004). The role of family systems in severe and recurrent psychiatric disorders: a developmental psychopathology view. *Development and Psychopathology, 16,* 667–688.

Miller, A. (2006).*The body never lies: The lingering effects of hurtful parenting* (A. Jenkins, Trans.). New York, NY: Norton.

Minuchin, S. (1974). *Families & family therapy,* Cambridge, MA: Harvard University Press.

Mock, D. W. (2004). *More than kin and less than kind: The evolution of family conflict*. Cambridge, MA: Harvard University Press.

Nadler, S. (2013). Baruch Spinoza. In E. N. Zalta (Ed.), *The Stanford encyclopedia of philosophy*. Retrieved from http://plato.stanford.edu /archives/fall2013/entries/spinoza/

National Association of Cognitive-Behavioral Therapists. (n.d.). Cognitive-behavioral therapy. Retrieved from http://www.nacbt.org /whatiscbt.htm

National Institute of Mental Health. (n.d.). What is schizophrenia? Retrieved from http://www.nimh.nih.gov/health/publications/ schizophrenia/index.shtml

Neisser, P., & Hess, J. (2012). *You're not as crazy as I thought (but you're still wrong): Conversations between a die-hard liberal and a devoted conservative.* Dulles, VA: Potomac Books.

Netzer, C. (1995). *Cutoffs: How family members who sever relationships can reconnect.* Far Hills, NJ: New Horizon Press.

Noggle C., & Dean, R. (Eds). (2012). T*he neuropsychology of psychopathology.* New York, NY: Springer.

Olson, D. H., & Olson, A. K. (2002). Prepare/Enrich program version 2000. In R. Berger & M. T. Hannah (Eds.), *Preventive approaches in couple therapy.* Philadelphia, PA: Brunner Mazel.

REFERENCES

Orwell, G. (1949/1984). New York, NY: Signet.

Rabinowitz, P. (n.d.). Core principles, assumptions, and values to guide the work. Retrieved from http://ctb.ku.edu/en/tablecontents/sub _section_main_1005.aspx

Rawls, J. (1971/1999). *A theory of justice.* Cambridge, MA: Belknap Press of Harvard University Press.

Rensberger, B. (1981, February 22). About to be human. *New York Times.*

Saint-Louis, C. (2012, June 14). In the Facebook era, Reminders of loss after families fracture. *New York Times.* A1

Sher, L., & Braswell, K. (2010, May 11). Most infamous alleged mommy murderers in history. ABC News. Retrieved from http://abcnews.go .com/2020/infamous-cases-moms-allegedly-murder-kids/story?id =10588541

Sichel, M. (2004). *Healing from family rifts.* New York, NY: McGraw-Hill.

Siegel, D. (2010a). *Mindsight.* New York, NY: Bantam Books.

Siegel, D. (2010b). *The mindful therapist.* New York, NY: Norton.

Siegel, D. H., & Smith, S. L. (2012). *Openness in adoption: From secrecy and stigma to knowledge and connections.* New York, NY: Evan B. Donaldson Adoption Institute.

Soares, A. (2013). Olivia de Havilland on Joan Fontaine. Retrieved from http://www.altfg.com/blog/movies-431/olivia-de-havilland-joan -fontaine/

Steinbeck, J. (1952/1984). *East of Eden.* New York, NY: Penguin.

Suarez, E.C. (2004). C-reactive protein is associated with psychological risk factors of cardiovascular disease in apparently healthy adults. *Psychosomatic Medicine, 66*(5), 684–691.

Taran, R. (2013). Building social and emotional skills in elementary students: Share your gifts. Retrieved from www.edutopia.org/blog /elementary-social-emotional-curriculum-2-appreciation-randy- taran

Taylor, A. (2002). *The handbook of family dispute resolution: Mediation and theory.* Hoboken, NJ: Jossey-Bass.

Titelman, P. (Ed.). (2003). *Emotional cutoffs: Bowen family systems theory perspectives.* New York, NY: Haworth Clinical Practice Press.

Weir, K. (2011). The exercise effect. *APA Monitor on Psychology, 42*(11). Retrieved from http://www.apa.org/monitor/2011/12/exercise.aspx

Williams, T. (1944/1998). *The glass menagerie.* New York, NY: Dramatist- Play Service, Inc.

White, E. B. (1952/2004). *Charlotte's web.* New York, NY: Harper Collins.

White, R. W. (1959). Motivation reconsidered: The concept of competence. *Psychological Review, 66*(5), 297–333.

Yager, J. (2002). *When friendship hurts: How to deal with friends who betray, abandon, or wound you.* New York, NY: Riverside/Fireside.

INDEX

INDEX

INDEX

group principles, 161–62
growth
    from cutoff, 49–50
guilt
    familial mental illness and, 185

Hamlet, 177–78
Hart, S., 85
Healing from Family Rifts, xii, 59
health
    jealousy and envy related to, 108–9
    mental, 183–208. *see also specific disorders related to and* mental illness
Hellman, L., 146
heresy, 167
Hess, J., 159–60
homosexuality
    DSM on, 179–80
    identity and, 179–82
honor killings
    principle and, 154, 156
hotheadedness
    cutoff related to, 183
humanitas, 88
humiliation
    public, 146–48

I Thought We Would Never Speak Again, xii
identity(ies)
    homosexuals, 179–82
    individual's, 177–82
    LGBT persons, 179–82
    principles related to, 177–82
ideological cutoffs, 158–60
ill will, 116–17
illness(es)
    abandonment related to, 77–80
incest, 137–43
    defined, 137
    mother-daughter, 141–43
    sibling, 139–41
incipient cutoff, 11
indirect cutoff, 12
individuation stage, 167
Inferno, 116
infidelity
    extra-familial, 125–26, 143–45
initiating contact
    in reconciliation attempt, 30–33
insecurity
    jealousy and envy related to, 86
instigated cutoff, 13–14
intermarriage
    cutoffs related to, 163–66
intermediaries
    in reconciliation, 33–34

invidia, 86, 88
invisible loyalty, 64
irony
    cutoff-related, xxi

jealousy, 84–115
    accomplishment-related, 106–8
    balance in relationships and, 87
    beauty-related, 96–97
    causes of, 86
    defined, 84
    family-related, 97–101
    Freud and Jung, 156–57
    friendship-related, 105–6
    health-related, 108–9
    insecurity and, 86
    major depressive disorder and, 188
    meaning-related, 109–10
    mentor-protégé relationship–related, 103
    money-related, 92–93
    NPD and, 200–1
    object-related, 93–96
    paranoid personality disorder and, 202
    parental favoritism and, 91–92
    power-related, 110–12
    property/land–related, 93–96
    public recognition–related, 113–15
    reactions to, 88
    romantic, 88–91
    satisfaction-related, 112–13
    schizophrenia and, 198–99
    sibling-like, 127–28
    universality of, 85
    violence related to, 86–87
    youth-related, 101–4
Jobs, S., 14
Johanson, D., 114
Johnson, S., xxvii, xxxiii–xxxv, 7
Jolie, A., 14, 146
Jung, C., 102–3, 156–57

Kado, J., 44
King Lear, 56
Kornfield, J., 210
Kübler-Ross, E., 5

land
    jealousy and envy related to, 93–96
Lazare, A., 43, 44
Leakey, L., 114
Leakey, M., 114
Leakey, R., 114
leave-taking(s)
    developmentally appropriate, xxvi
LeBey, B., xii

228

INDEX

INDEX